WEAK
LINK

WEAK LINK: The Feminization of the American Military

Brian Mitchell

REGNERY GATEWAY
Washington, D.C.

Library of Congress Cataloging-in-Publication Data

Mitchell, Brian, (Brian P.), 1958–
  Weak link.

  Includes index.
  1. United States—Armed Forces—Women.   I. Title.
UB418.W65M57   1989   355′.0088042   88-32539
ISBN 0-89526-555-9

Published in the United States
by Regnery Gateway, Inc.
1130 17th Street, NW
Washington, D.C. 20036

Distributed to the trade by
Kampmann & Company, Inc.
226 W. 26th Street
New York, NY 10001

798365

Contents

To my wife Cindy

Preface

I HAVE BEEN ADVISED by wise men to declare my true colors up front, lest the reader misunderstand my motives and beliefs. I will do so here.

First, I do not hate women. No man who has had a loving mother, wife, or daughter can hate women, and I have all three. Secondly, I do not believe that men are, overall, superior to women, as is often assumed about critics of feminism.

I also do not believe feminist claims that women are oppressed by men, that traditional sex roles are solely the result of sexist socialization, and that men and women can be somehow un-sexed with the proper upbringing. Even if men and women could be manufactured in the feminist mold, I would reject the product. Feminists themselves are not sure what the product would look like, but the image that appears most often in their literature bears more resemblance to the drearily androgynous drones of science fiction than to my friends in the real world. In the words of George Gilder, "Feminists refer often in their books to 'human beings,' but I do not care to meet one. I am interested only in men and women."

It is not necessary for the reader to share my objections to feminism to agree with the conclusions drawn in this book. I did not intend to make a greater sociological, physiological, or metaphysical case for traditional sex roles. I did intend to tell how sexual integration of the military has not worked the way our military leaders say it has.

I regret that I cannot name the many military men to whom I owe thanks without placing their careers or reputations in jeopardy. Among the men and women I can name are Don Starck, Darrell

Davis, Steve Horton, Ted Fichtl, Avery Foster, James Binder, Michael Levin, Phyllis Schlafly, Stan Evans, Jim Doyle, Tom Philpott, Bob and Wren Ennis, my parents J.T. and Jean Mitchell, and the faithful crew at Regnery Gateway—Al Regnery, Jennifer Reist, Debbie Stone, and my editor Harry Crocker.

My daughter Alma Jean and my son John provided charming diversion when I needed it. Without my wife Cindy, I fear I would never have written anything. For them all, I thank God.

Alexandria, Virginia
May 4, 1989

WEAK
LINK

CHAPTER I
Military Secrets

The greatest change that has come about in the United States forces in the time that I've been in the military service has been the extensive use of women. . . . That's even greater than nuclear weapons, I feel, as far as our own forces are concerned.

GEN. JOHN A. VESSEY, AS CHAIRMAN OF THE
JOINT CHIEFS OF STAFF[1]

AT FORT MCCLELLAN, Alabama, Military Police recruits are treated with "the LaBarge Touch," a celebrated method for handling female trainees devised by a drill sergeant named LaBarge. The cardinal tenet of the LaBarge touch is "Be Nice"—no loud shouting or angry snarls for which drill sergeants are famous, but smiles and soft words and lots of encouragement.

Drill Sergeant LaBarge, who describes himself as a "female chauvinist pig," teaches his young female recruits that they are not equal to men but better than men because they have "no macho mentality" and have better communicative skills. LaBarge promotes "snobbery" among his women to make them feel psychologically superior to men. His "attitude check" (a motto shouted on cue by a formation of troops) for the women in his charge is: "When God created man, She was only joking." LaBarge encourages his female MPs to use feminine charm "when it's to their advantage" and advises them to try

breaking up a barroom brawl by "being sweet." He avoids unpleas-
antness in his training and refrains from telling his women that the
M-16 rifle will actually kill if used properly, telling them instead that
the rifle was "made to wound people."[2]

There can be no doubt that the American military has undergone
radical change in the last two decades. Twenty years ago, the role of
women in the military was still following a long downward trend.
After a failed attempt to involve large numbers of women in the
military during the Korean War, military planners were convinced
that American women would not play a significant role in any peacetime force. The number of women in service and the number of jobs
open to them shrank steadily for fifteen years following the war. In
1967, the participation of women in the American military reached
its lowest point since World War II, with barely 20,000 women in
service, not including nurses. Women made up less than 2 percent of
the total force.

Then the trend was abruptly reversed. The shift to the All-
Volunteer Force and the political success of the American feminist
movement combined to bring about a re-direction of military manpower thinking and a rapid expansion of the military use of women.
In a very short time, the number of women increased fivefold. Today,
the American military has more than 221,000 women in active
service—10.3 percent of its total force. Fifteen percent of first-year
students at the nation's service academies are female, and one out of
every seven enlisted recruits is a woman. Only a handful of specialties and assignments are still closed to women, and each year sees
more and more positions opened, thanks to the elastic quality of the
so-called combat exclusion laws, which always seem to permit today
what they were understood to forbid yesterday.

No other military in the world depends so heavily upon women.
The U.S. employs more women as a percentage of its total force than
any country on earth. Canada is second, with women representing
9.2 percent of its total force, followed by the United Kingdom with
5.1 percent. The Soviet Union's 4.4 million-member armed force
includes only 10,000 women, performing largely clerical and medical work. Israel drafts women, but the jobs open to them are more
limited than the jobs open to American military women during World

War II. A handful of small, secure NATO nations have opened combat units to women, but the numbers of women involved are very small, and expectations that they will ever actually see combat are even smaller.[3]

The official position of the U.S. Department of Defense is that integration has proceeded without the slightest decline in the combat capabilities of the armed forces. The modern All-Volunteer Force is far superior to any earlier force of volunteers or conscripts, say defense officials. Today's recruits are the finest the services have ever seen: the best educated, the best motivated, the best behaved. As for women, official phraseology makes them "an integral part" of the armed forces. "We can't go to war without them," say the admirals and the generals; women are "here to stay." They perform "as well or better than" the men. They are promoted faster. They add an air of civility to military service. Their effect on morale and readiness is positive.

For all the flattery that military women receive, one might expect the Defense Department to be eager to repeal the combat exclusions. After all, the department's official position is that the exclusion of women from combat is based solely on the cultural preference of the American people and not on any military consideration. Because repeal would expand greatly the pool of possible recruits and simplify the services' personnel management systems, enabling them to make more efficient use of all personnel, the only responsible action on the Pentagon's part should be to request that the laws be repealed.

A recent report on the All-Volunteer Force by the General Accounting Office, however, provides a clue as to why neither the Defense Department nor any of the services are inclined to request repeal:

> While women have enabled the services to meet recruiting goals in the volunteer environment, this contribution has come at a cost of (1) driving military planners toward assignment decisions that they might not ordinarily make and (2) possibly adversely affecting military morale and readiness. Women are, on the average, smaller and not as strong as men; they have a higher rate of first-term turnover; and they take more time off

from duty for medical reasons (though less than men for sub-
stance abuse and disciplinary reasons).[4]

It would seem, then, that there are military reasons for excluding
women not only from combat but from military service, despite the
Pentagon's pro-integration propaganda.

Until recently, the services themselves admitted that the presence
of women causes many unresolved problems. Indeed, most of our
knowledge of those problems comes from the services' own studies.
Thanks to the services, we know that, by most measures, women are
a bad buy for the military. They suffer higher rates of attrition and
lower rates of retention. They are three times more likely to be
discharged for homosexuality. They miss more than twice as much
duty time for medical reasons. They are four times more likely to
complain of spurious physical ailments. When men and women are
subjected to equally demanding physical regimens, the injury rates of
women can be as high as fourteen times that of men.

In the course of a year, 10 to 17 percent of all servicewomen will be
pregnant. At any one time, 5 to 10 percent of all servicewomen are
pregnant, though small units have at times reported pregnancy rates
as high as 50 percent. Servicewomen are eight times more likely to be
single-parents than men. Though at one time, single-parents were
routinely discharged for the good of the service, the services must
now expend extraordinary efforts to accommodate their presence, the
"protected" status of military women having been extended to all
single-parents.

Servicewomen have led repeated assaults against traditional bans
on fraternization between persons of different ranks. They also have
forced the services to accommodate a growing number of "dual
service" marriages, which complicate assignment systems and force
the services to sacrifice the efficient use of individual service members to the domestic needs of the more than 56,000 such couples
already in service.

Physical limitations make it impossible for most women to live up
to the boast that they are performing as well as or better than men.
Contrary to popular belief, technology has not relieved service members of the need for above-average physical strength. A 1982 Army

study found that barely one tenth of Army women possessed the strength to meet minimum physical requirements for 75 percent of the jobs for Army enlisted personnel, yet half of the Army's enlisted women were assigned to those jobs. In 1985, the Navy found that a predominantly female fire-fighting unit at a naval station in Alaska required a 25 percent increase in personnel to make up for the lack of physical strength among female fire-fighters.

The services have also documented psychological differences that make women less effective members of the military. Military women are less aggressive, less daring, less likely to suppress minor personal hurts, less aware of world affairs, less interested in military history, less respectful of military tradition, and less inclined to make the military a career. They are more likely to suffer emotional distress as a result of changes in their lives and are better suited for routine, sedentary duties. They score lower than men on entrance exams in those subjects most relevant to the majority of modern military jobs. They overwhelmingly prefer traditionally female jobs and pleasant working environments. Women steered by recruiters into traditionally male jobs suffer higher rates of attrition and tend to migrate into traditionally female jobs.

Women offer the services one single advantage over men: they are better behaved. They lose less time for disciplinary reasons and are less proned to drug and alcohol abuse. They are also more likely to have completed high school before entry, but high school completion is only significant as an indication that a recruit will complete an enlistment contract. Because women are less likely to stay in the military, the fact that women are more likely to have completed high school hardly matters.

None of these problems are unknown to the nation's top military leaders, who, despite their public support for sexual equality in the military, are not clamoring for more women. The fears of military women that the services are insincere in their support for integration are well-founded. In truth, the services would rather have men if they could get them. They put up with women for two reasons: first, most of them believe that the success of the All-Volunteer Force depends upon the use of women, and second, politics gives them little say in the matter.

The merit of the first reason is debatable. The AVF was never allowed to work without women. At the start, its architects resorted to greater use of women without considering the possibility that an all-male military, with its distinctly masculine appeal, might attract more young men than a more feminine force.

The merit of the second reason is undeniable. Pressure from feminists in and out of the federal government has made resisting the march toward full sexual equality in the military suicidal for defense officials. Twice each year, the Defense Advisory Committee on Women in the Services, or DACOWITS, meets to oversee the progress of the march. High-ranking service representatives appear before the mostly female committee like pop-up targets absorbing the committee's fire on behalf of their service. Their primary concern is to avoid angering the committee. They praise military women effusively and dare not confront the committee with the any of the problems just mentioned. Their mission is to keep the committee and its Praetorian guard of active and retired military women from appealing directly to the Secretary of Defense or elevating the dispute to the House Armed Services Committee.

Under present conditions, it is impossible to trust what defense officials tell us about women in the military because they testify under duress.

Even so, we know that much of what they tell us about women in the military is not true. It is not true, for instance, that military women are meeting the same standards as men. In fact, women enjoy preference and protection in a variety of forms. Nowhere are women required to meet the same physical standards as men, and nowhere are women subjected to the military's sternest trials of mind and body that many men face. Pregnancy remains the only "temporary disability" that gives a service member the option of breaking a service contract without penalty. It is also the only disability for which service members cannot be punished for deliberately inflicting upon themselves.

It is not true that the presence of women has had only a positive effect on morale and readiness. Instead, the effect of their presence has been a general softening of military service. Conditions and performance requirements that aggravate attrition among women and expose their limited abilities have been systematically eliminated. The LaBarge touch, with its myopic focus on getting recruits through training instead of preparing them for wartime service, has cheated the field and fleet of the manpower needed to fight and win. The modern military's emphasis on "positive motivation," inspired by the need to protect women from the harshness of military life, has led the military to an excessive reliance upon "leadership" and a potentially fatal neglect of discipline.

The integration of women has also threatened the very values upon which all militaries depend. Civilized militaries are necessarily hierarchical, anti-egalitarian, and altruistic (in that they exist to serve not themselves but the state). The campaign to win approval of women in the military has argued against the institutional values behind all of these qualities. Proponents of women in the military have founded their arguments on the absolute equality of all persons, they have pitted the rights of individuals against the authority of the hierarchy, and they have encouraged military women to think of themselves and their careers before thinking of the good of the organization and of national defense. Forced to adopt those arguments to defend the task of integration, the services now excuse and even condone among women what they would reprove as selfish careerism among men.

In recent years, the Defense Department has moved to squelch dissent on the issue and labored to ensure that only the approved view of women in the military is presented to the American people. In so doing, it has fostered cynicism and resentment among military men whose intelligence, integrity, and trust is too often abused by the deceitfulness of those charged with making integration work. At times, the integrators resort to sophistry and newspeak. Cadets at West Point are told that separate standards for women are "dual standards," not double standards. Eliminating tasks too difficult for women is described as "normalizing requirements" to avoid the embarrassing admission that standards have been lowered. At other times, the integrators simply hide the facts. The Defense Department frequently insists that single-parenthood is not a "female problem," pointing to its own statistics which show that three quarters of all military single-parents are men. It does not explain that most men counted as single-parents are actually divorced parents without custody of their children.

The feminization of the American military is perhaps the greatest peacetime military deception ever perpetrated. It continues today to mask the drive toward full sexual equality in the military, which will only be achieved when women are no longer barred from combat and when the numbers of women in the military match the numbers of men.

We are closer than most anyone imagines to both events. Today, the combat exclusions have been sliced so thin that they no longer keep women out of combat but only arbitrarily out of some combat jobs. The very arbitrariness of the exclusions makes them not likely to withstand the next challenge in the courts. The danger to all American women is that their exemption from the military draft depends upon the combat exclusions. When the Supreme Court upheld draft exemptions for women in 1981, it cited the combat exclusions as the only legal grounds for doing so. If the exclusions fall, the draft exemption will find no support in the courts. In the coming battle over the combat exclusions, the American people are on their own. The Defense Department's official non-position on women in combat means that the military will take no part in the battle, except to bear witness to the official view of the record of women in the military so far.

This book is not a history of the involvement of women in the military, nor a complete appraisal of their military performance, nor even simply an argument against their military use. It is, rather, an account of the creation of a lie, written on behalf of the many thousands of military men who know the truth but are under orders to think and say the right things and not to notice that the Emperor has no clothes.

NOTES ON CHAPTER I

1. Statement to the House Armed Services Committee, reported by *The Washington Post*, 3 February 1984, p. 12.

2. Sandra L. Beckwith, "Teaching Women to Soldier: The LaBarge Touch," *Army*, March 1982, p. 44.

3. Women constitute more than 1 percent of the total armed forces of six NATO countries (other than the U.S., Canada, and the UK), but less than one tenth of 1 percent of the total forces of four NATO countries: Luxembourg, Portugal, Turkey, and the Federal Republic of Germany. Three NATO countries (Spain, Italy, and Iceland, which has no military) have no women in military service at all. For more on Israel, see Chapter X. An analysis of the historical use of women by the militaries of countries other than the United States is beyond the scope of this book.

4. The General Accounting Office, *Military Draft: Potential Impacts and Other Issues* (Washington, D.C.: GPO, 1988), p. 15.

CHAPTER II
Myths in the Making

War hath no fury like a noncombatant.

C. E. MONTAGUE

THE FIRST AMERICAN WOMAN to serve in combat was Molly Pitcher. Few American school children escape the lower grades without hearing the story of Molly's heroism. They will not have heard of Alvin York or Audie Murphy, but the image of the petticoated heroine fetching water and swabbing gun-barrels for the hard-pressed continental artillery stands clearly in their minds. In the minds of modern historians, however, Molly's image is much less clear. Was she Mary Hays or Margaret Corbin? Was she any one woman at all, or a legendary composite of hundreds of camp followers who lent a hand in the heat of battle? While the latter seems more likely, one thing is certain: Molly Pitcher made a good story.

Lately, good stories about women in combat are receiving greater attention. Feminist historians, eager to provide today's military women with a heritage of their own, are revising the history of every American military conflict to include women as soldiers, sailors, and secret agents. Male historians have heretofore neglected the role of women in war and habitually minimized the contributions of individual women, say the revisionists. The revised history will correct this deficiency by including all that has been left out, while at the same time magnifying the record of the few who did participate. It is

12

history with a purpose. Every odd and improbable precedent is meant to prove that women can indeed be warriors. Every legendary wonder-woman who defied convention and credibility by masquerading as a man among men is supposed to bolster the argument for mustering regiments of riflewomen.

Sometimes, however, the revisionists' enthusiasm for a good story overcomes their natural skepticism. Fancy is often mistaken for fact when titillating tales of soft breasts beneath coarse uniform tunics are accepted at face value. Most such tales escape close scrutiny, but one that did not involved a prostitute by the name of Lucy Brewer. Lucy's tale has come down to us in a number of recent "histories" of fighting women, few of which show the slightest inclination to doubt her incredible claim of having passed herself off as a male Marine aboard the USS *Constitution* during the War of 1812. The revisionists seem to accept Lucy's claim on faith alone, without explaining how Lucy managed to conceal her sex for three years aboard the cramped frigate. Conditions on the ship alone would have made her masquerade impossible. The ship had no toilet facilities and no private quarters for enlisted Marines. Fortunately for persons inclined toward greater skepticism, Marine Corps historians have discovered that Lucy was a fraud. Her published accounts of her wartime exploits were lifted "almost verbatim" from official after-action reports filed by the *Constitution's* commanding officer. Officially, the legend of Lucy Brewer is a "mockery of the bona fide traditions" of the Corps.[1]

The history of American servicewomen truly begins with the establishment of the Army and Navy Nurse Corps in 1901 and 1908. By the turn of the century, nursing had become an exclusively female occupation, so the need for nurses who could be sent wherever and whenever there were troops made necessary the admission of women to the services as auxiliaries. Nursing, however, has little to do with soldiering. The first military nurses held no rank and wore uniforms bearing no resemblance to the men's uniforms, and no one seriously referred to them as soldiers or sailors.

The same was true of the first non-nursing servicewomen inducted during World War I. In need of clerks, typists, and telephone operators, all of which were recently feminized occupations, the services avoided the chore of training men for such work by employing women for the task. The Navy enlisted some 12,500 "yeomanettes" in the Naval Reserve, circumventing a law requiring all sailors to be assigned to vessels by assigning the women, on paper only, to river-boats on the Potomac. The Army and Marine Corps also recruited women for work as secretaries and telephone operators, but the status of the Army's women has been a matter of debate. Some authorities say the women were never formally inducted as enlisted members. Others say they were. Either way, the participation of women in the American armed forces during the war is but a footnote in history. All of the 49,000 women to serve in uniform during World War I were returned to civilian life when the war was over, except a handful of nurses.

World War II brought more women to arms and into uniform than any event in human history before or since. Some 500,000 Soviet women are estimated to have served among the 7 million Soviet combatants in the war. Great Britain employed more than 450,000 women in uniform. The United States ranked third in the world in the military use of women: 350,000 American women donned uniforms of khaki or blue from 1942 to 1945.

No doubt many women did serve well during the war and do not deserve to have their personal reputations deflated, but lately the wartime record of the women's corps has received such purposeful praise that a critical appraisal of their contribution to the war effort is in order. The emerging myth about the use of women in World War II includes a dire shortage of American men and a stirring response from patriotic American women who supposedly turned out by brigades to "free a man to fight." Indeed, had the Army been able to recruit a million women as it had hoped in 1942, the creation of a women's corps might have made a dent in the demand for men. As it turned out, neither the manpower shortage nor the mass mobilization of American women materialized. At no time did women amount to more than 2.3 percent of all U.S. forces. Though 350,000 women donned uniforms, the combined strength of the women's components and both nurse corps never exceeded 266,000 at any one time.[2] The difference between the two figures reveals an astounding rate of personnel turnover for a force whose battlefield casualty rate was insignificant.

The truth about women in World War II is that, as soldiers, sailors, or Marines, they simply were not needed. Twenty-two million American men registered for the draft during the war; only ten million were drafted. The duties military women performed for the War and Navy Departments in Washington, D.C., where the lion's share of WACs and most WAVES were stationed, could easily have been performed by the men who were not drafted or by civilian men and women.[3] Their other uses hardly justified the trouble of establishing and maintaining separate women's components of the Army, Navy, Coast Guard, and Marines. In the end, the women's components served only to satisfy the ambitions of a handful of influential women and sympathetic men in Washington, among them, First Lady Eleanor Roosevelt, Congresswoman Edith Nourse Rogers of Massachusetts, and Army Chief of Staff General George C. Marshall.

The establishment of separate women's components of the armed services was perhaps the most difficult legislative battle of the early war years. Marshall was an exception among the nation's military leaders, most of whom were not convinced they needed women's components. Most members of Congress were also reluctant to resort to the military use of women even after Pearl Harbor. Not until May 1942 did the Congress, its arm twisted by Marshall's projected manpower shortage, authorize creation of the Women's Army Auxiliary Corps (WAAC). Two months later, pestered by Congresswoman Rogers and prodded by the First Lady, Congress authorized a women's component for the Navy, for which the Navy contrived a name to fit the acronym WAVES: Women Accepted for Voluntary Emergency Service. An unnamed component of female Marines was established shortly thereafter, followed by the Coast Guard's SPARS (short for *Semper Paratus,* the Coast Guard's motto). Last came the Women's Air Service Pilots (WASP). Much mentioned today in any brief history of military women, the WASPs were technically not servicewomen but civilians contracted to perform routine flying duties until the services could train enough male pilots.

Once established, the women's components fulfilled no one's expectations. Female recruits were slow in coming, as the nation's women proved much less progressive than the activists in Washington. Many Americans could only believe that the kind of women who would join the Army were not the kind to take home to mother. As the first few women wandered in, rumors arose impugning the honor of the recruits. Tales of rampant promiscuity and lesbianism were met with indignant denials from the services. Official investigations found little to substantiate the rumors, but the damage was done nonetheless.

The Army had both the highest hopes and the least success in attracting women. WAAC recruits, as members of an auxiliary, were not given full military status. Their simplified rank structure meant nothing to Army men, and their training and facilities were regarded as inferior to the other services. Worst of all, their uniforms were ugly and unfeminine. The Army's experience had taught it that soldiers complained about their uniforms only when they were too hot or too cold. It was surprised to learn that female recruits were much more concerned with their appearance and much more likely to join the WAVES whose uniforms were more glamorous. Some of the WAAC's problems were solved when the auxiliary was reorganized as the Women's Army Corps (WAC) in 1943, but the search for more attractive, more feminine uniforms continued well into the war.

Just as the women's components were overcoming the public's initial disgust and enjoying some success in recruiting, their reason for being began to wane. By late 1943, the Army Air Corps had trained more male pilots than it needed, so the civilian WASP was disbanded. The manpower shortage had always been a matter of having enough trained men in the right place at the right time, not a matter of there being too few men in America. In the summer of 1944, the Allies could not get enough infantrymen into France fast enough. Non-infantry regiments in the States were deactivated so the men could be retrained as infantry replacements. Boatloads of support personnel disembarking at French ports were instantly reclassified as riflemen with the stroke of an adjutant's pen, an expedient not available to the modern integrated Army. Then, as the Allies tightened their grip on the European continent, the flow of troops through the manpower pipeline suddenly slowed. New recruits in the States marked time by repeating training cycles over and over again, being shipped overseas only after the war's end to replace combat veterans in the army of occupation. The supply of men had caught up with the demand.[4]

As the war reached its climax, the enthusiasm of the first women recruits began to waiver. The morale of the WAVES sank as the glamor of Navy uniforms wore off and the dreary tedium of military service made itself felt. WAVES began to complain about bad assignments, unrewarding duty, poor living conditions, and the lack of recreational opportunities. Some complained about not having enough to do. Others buckled under the strain of too much work.[5]

The WAC war effort also faltered. As early as 1943, WAC leaders noticed a surprising increase in the number of company-grade officers requesting transfer because they had "gone stale" and felt they had nothing left to offer their units. The WAC director, Colonel Oveta Culp Hobby, was able to persuade Marshall to order the establishment of "refresher training" for WAC officers, over the objection of the Army's chief of training, who argued that no such training was necessary or available for male officers, but there was little else Hobby could due to boost morale. Some WAC leaders blamed low morale on a lack of gainful employment and respect for the corps, but the women in the ranks filed different complaints in letters to the director. Wrote one, "We don't want appreciation; we just want to go home."[6]

As morale crumbled, discharges for medical and other reasons soared. In January 1945, the rate of WAC medical discharges was twice that of January 1944. The rate of discharge under other than honorable conditions was many times that of the previous year. From January to December 1945, the WACs discharged 44,315 officers and enlisted women for reasons other than demobilization—almost twice the number demobilized that year. Other services experienced similar problems. Attrition among the elite WASP had ranged between 36 to 40 percent, most of whom chose the alternative of getting married and going home over the opportunity for continued service. The experience of WASP leader Jacqueline Cochran led her to testify against admitting women to the Air Force Academy thirty years later.

At the war's end, all was forgiven if not forgotten. In the glow of victory, only good things were said about the women who had served. No one had expected them to be anything other than ladies in uniform, anyway. No one noticed the high rates of attrition or estimated the cost-effectiveness of the women's components. No objective evaluation of the performance of the women's corps was ever done. Instead, the women got their share of exaggerated accolades along with everyone else. In a post-war interview with a senior WAC commander, Douglas MacArthur even dubbed the WACs "my best soldiers."[7] Today, some proponents of women in the military are quite willing to pretend that he meant what he said.

After the war, the heads of the women's components and their staffs expected and sought demobilization of all women and deactivation of the women's corps. But once their foot was in the door, they found it difficult to remove. First, the services decided to keep many women in service to speed the demobilization of combat veterans. Then, as the leadership of the women's corps passed into the hands of the minority of women who did not choose to return to civilian life, the services decided to retain the women's corps indefinitely. High-level staffs had come to depend on women in administrative and clerical roles, and no one wanted to give up their faithful and charming wartime secretaries for male draftees fresh out of clerk school.

Demobilization of women proceeded much slower than most women would have preferred, while the services did what they could to encourage women to stay on voluntarily and the War and Navy Departments petitioned Congress to establish the women's corps as permanent features of the new Department of Defense. In 1947, Congress authorized the integration of the nurse and medical specialist corps into the regular and reserve Army and Navy. In 1948, Public Law 625-80 allowed women veterans to rejoin the reserves, thus establishing a permanent place for women of other specialties. In the next two years, only 4,000 women with prior military service signed up for reserve duty, so in 1950 the law was amended to allow women without prior service to join. At the start of the Korean War, there were still less than 22,000 women on active duty, one third of whom were nurses or medical specialists. The 15,000 women in the "line" components made up less than 1 percent of the total U.S. armed forces.

Though small to the point of insignificance, the women's components had friends in high places. General Marshall was then Secretary of Defense, with Anna Rosenberg as his Assistant Secretary of Defense for Manpower. Rosenberg quickly revived fears of another manpower shortage and began pushing for greater utilization of women by the services. At her urging, Marshall created the Defense Advisory Committee on Women in the Services, a blue-ribbon committee of prominent civilian women, known since as DACOWITS. With DACOWITS's assistance, the Defense Department mounted a massive publicity campaign to call American women to arms, shelling out large sums of advertizing dollars. Slogans such as "America's Finest Women Stand Beside Her Finest Men" were trumpeted across the country by radio, television, magazines, newspapers, and billboards.

Aside from insulting the majority of American womanhood, the slogans did little else. Rosenberg and DACOWITS had completely misread the national mood and the ambitions of the nation's women. The campaign fell well short of its objectives, adding only 6,000 women in the time allotted to recruit 72,000. Many of the women it did attract were of the lowest category of recruits, as America's finest women apparently had other ideas about where to stand. Female strength peaked in October 1952 at 47,800, still less than 1 percent of the total force and well below the desired 112,000.

America's female population remained stubbornly unresponsive to recruiting through the end of the war. By 1955, female strength was down to 35,000. In 1956, Dr. Eli Ginzberg, a manpower expert with the National Manpower Council, told DACOWITS, "One cannot turn the country on its head in order to get a few more women into the services of the United States."[8] For many in the Defense Department and in Congress, the nation's second failure to mobilize significant numbers of women on a voluntary basis reinforced the experience of World War II and spoiled enthusiasm for women in the military for the next decade.

Bureaucratic inertia and the firm support of a small group of women in and out of uniform kept the women's components alive in the years following the Korean conflict, but the Defense Department no longer considered them a manpower advantage. The peacetime draft gave the services all the men they needed, and abysmal rates of attrition among women made the components more trouble than they were worth. Seventy to 80 percent of first-term female enlistees in the late 1950s did not complete their initial term of enlistment. Most left voluntarily to get married. Many others were separated involuntarily for unsuitability, an avenue of exit always more accessible to women than to men. Pregnancy in or out of wedlock was another cause for involuntary separation. The component directors still believed that motherhood took precedence over military service and were extremely sensitive to charges of immorality within the corps. Most staunchly defended the policy of discharging pregnant women as a means of protecting the corps' honor.

Year after year the components atrophied, as women veterans hung on to serve out their time before retirement. To their services, they were little more than window dressing. As such, it was most important for the token force to look good. The services began requiring full-length photographs of potential female recruits, taking only the best-looking among them. Recruits were not instructed in marksmanship or combat survival, but they did learn how to properly apply make-up and to conduct themselves as ladies. Their physical training was intended to maintain trim figures, not to increase strength, endurance, or coordination.

Appearance was always important, even in Vietnam. Jeanne Holm quotes the WAC director writing to a senior WAC officer in Vietnam in 1967:

> I am aware that conditions are bad and its must be difficult to maintain a neat and feminine appearance. . . . I do not want anything to spoil their image or standing as women. The matter of proper dress is very important to me.[9]

The Director of the WAVES echoed the same sentiment, reminding her charges that "WAVES are ladies first and always."

While the civilian world was becoming increasingly feminized, the nation's armed forces were actually moving in the opposite direction. Military jobs open to women shrank. In 1965, 70 percent of enlisted females were in administrative and clerical work, as opposed to 50 percent in World War II. Another 23 percent were in medical professions. Seventy-five percent of women officers were in administrative fields. Opportunities for promotion and assignment dwindled. The strength of the line components, not including medical women, dropped to 30,600 in 1965 and then to 20,000 in 1967.

The limited role of women in the services necessitated limitations on promotions and assignments for women officers. Until 1967, the highest pay grade or rank a woman could hold in any of the services was O-6.[10] Sometimes the only woman in a service to hold that rank was the director of the women's component. All other female officers held lesser rank, depending as much upon their assignment as anything else. As the directorship rotated among the most senior female officers, an outgoing director would sometimes accept a reduction in grade to remain on active duty in lieu of retirement.[11]

Though today such limitations on the careers of women are considered grossly unfair, twenty years ago it was assumed that the needs of the service came first, and the services simply did not need more high-ranking female officers. None of the services at that time promised equal opportunity for women; combat restrictions and the segregation of the ranks meant that opportunities were inherently unequal. Furthermore, the prevailing philosophy was that military service was both a privilege and an obligation but not a right or entitlement. Women, like men, served at the pleasure of the Commander-in-Chief and therefore had no grounds for grievance.

This philosophy of service was lost upon the civilian members of the once ineffectual Defense Advisory Committee on Women in the Services. Since the Korean War, DACOWITS had concerned itself with recommending improvements in the "quality of life" of military women, which led in time to increasing opportunities for advancement. As early as 1960, when the size and the role of the women's components were shrinking, DACOWITS began arguing that the components had reached "a maturity which calls for re-examination of the structure with respect to the maximum career potential afforded new recruits." The committee focused its efforts on removing restrictions that prevented women from becoming admirals and generals and on promoting the women's component directors to O-7 (one star). DACOWITS felt that with a flag officer of their own the women's components would receive the professional recognition they deserved and junior officers would have more toward which to aspire.

The services unanimously opposed the promotion of the component directors to star rank for a variety of reasons. First, they felt the responsibilities of the directors were too limited in scope to warrant stars. Second, the promotion of a director to star rank would automatically mean one less admiral or general somewhere else, since the total number of flag officers was limited by Congress. Third, promotion policies as applied to men meant that women would never truly qualify for star rank. Selection of officers for promotion to O-7 was based upon a variety of things, not the least of which was the assignment history and professional experience of the candidate for promotion. Combat service was naturally a big plus for an organization which existed for the purpose of doing battle. Candidates who had not served in combat but were especially qualified in non-combat fields were still expected to have a firm professional foundation in the business of war, as practiced by their branch of service.

Female officers lacked these primary qualifications. Not only had they never served in combat, they had never even been trained for combat. In the early 1960s, few had ever supervised—much less commanded—men in any capacity, since most of them spent their entire careers within the women's corps. They were, in fact, the least "general" of officers, for their experience was limited to a small, vestigial appendage of the services. None of the women then on active duty had even enough years in service to warrant consideration for promotion beyond O-6, and many men felt that if the ceiling on female promotions were removed, the promotion of a few unqualified women as tokens would be inevitable.

But the services were on the wrong side of time. Political pressure was mounting against all governmental distinctions between men and women. Congress passed the Equal Pay Act in 1963 and the Civil Rights Act, with Title VII concerning women, in 1964. In March 1965, President Johnson ordered equal treatment, respect, service, and support regardless of sex for all employees of the executive branch of the federal government. Though the executive order was not aimed specifically at the military services, the civilian heads of the Defense Department could tell the way the wind was blowing.

The same year, the Defense Department gave in to DACOWITS's demand and submitted legislation to Congress to remove the ceiling on promotions for women.

The battle was not over. The proposed bill died in the 89th Congress and was revived in the 90th only after DACOWITS stepped outside its charter to assume a more active role. Until this time, DACOWITS's participation in the legislative process had been limited to recommending and endorsing legislation to the Department of Defense. Under the leadership of Chairman Agnes O'Brien Smith, the committee began to deal directly with Congress. According to Holm:

> From the time the DOD proposal was finally drafted until its enactment on 27 October 1967, committee members pulled out all the stops—soliciting support from women's groups, encouraging letter-writing campaigns, focusing media interest, and individually lobbying Congress. . . . Smith held regular strategy planning sessions with military women; after each DACOWITS meeting, the members fanned out over Capitol Hill, paying court to whomever they knew, gaining support for the legislation. Many had political connections in the White House and on the Hill, others direct access to the media, which they used.[12]

Two former DACOWITS members testified before the House Armed Services Committee in September 1966, urging support of the bill, both mentioning their membership in DACOWITS. Active members, however, were told that they "are not lobbyists for DOD and are *not even to mention* DACOWITS when they urge a congressman to support legislation."[13] (Original emphasis.)

Considering what they were up against, it should hardly have taken so much effort. Lawmakers may have lacked enthusiasm for the bills, but there was no organized opposition. At the time, Congress, the White House, and the Defense Department had other things to worry about, and it was easier to give the women what they wanted than to defend the silent services, which were muzzled by the Defense Department.

Among those who contributed to the consideration of the bills, only DACOWITS and its supporters understood the bills' significance. If anyone else on Capitol Hill had any idea how the bills would affect the military in the future, they were careful not to show it. Defense Department representatives naively, if not deceitfully, minimized the bills' impact. The Assistant Secretary of Defense for Manpower, Thomas D. Morris, testifying in support of the bill before the House Armed Services Committee, said, "We believe that the Nation still adheres to the concept that combat, combat support, and the direction of our operating forces are responsibilities of male officers."[14] The House report showed the same lack of foresight:

> there cannot be complete equality between men and women in the matter of military careers. . . . The Defense Department assured the Committee that there would be no attempt to remove restrictions on the kind of military duties women will be expected to perform.
>
> Within the framework of this understanding, the Committee believes that women officers should be given equality of promotion opportunity consistent with the needs of the service.[15]

No one imagined that five years later both the House and Senate would demand absolute equality for women in all military matters.

DACOWITS's seven year campaign to improve the lot of the most privileged military women culminated with the signing of Public Law 90-130. "Had it not been for DACOWITS," wrote Holm, "the struggle might have taken another seven."[16] The somber service chiefs who were assembled for the signing heard President Johnson remark, "There is no reason why we should not someday have a female Chief of Staff or even a female Commander-in-Chief."[17]

Two and a half years after the passage of PL 90-130, the Army promoted Anna Mae Hays and Elizabeth P. Hoisington to the rank of brigadier general. The Air Force followed suit in 1971 by promoting Jeanne Holm. The Navy waited until 1975 to promote Fran McKee to flag rank, and the Marine Corps did not promote Margaret Brewer (no relation to Lucy) to flag rank until 1977.

PL 90-130 did more for military women than open the way to the stars, however, and other effects were more immediate. The law also opened up promotions for women to other officer ranks and repealed the 2 percent ceiling on the strength of the women's components. At the time, female strength was at its lowest level since the Korean War, again less than 1 percent of the total force. But the Johnson Administration was looking for ways to lighten the burden of the draft on the nation's men and so planned to increase female strength from 20,000 to 35,000 in two years, to reach the 2 percent mark in four or five years.

The first increase in female strength in fifteen years came in 1968, when 6,500 women were added to the rolls. This hefty boost for the women's components was nevertheless an imperceptible addition to the mammoth wartime armed forces. The participation of American military women in the war in Vietnam was miniscule. The 7,500 women, mostly nurses, to be honored with the addition of a feminine form to the National Vietnam War Memorial, account for less than one tenth of one percent of all U.S. Vietnam veterans. The tribute, now backed by many feminist supporters of women in the military, is late in coming. During the war, the needs of women veterans were ignored completely by the strongly pacifistic American feminist movement. After the war, the fight to further expand roles for military women proceeded on other grounds, for other reasons.

NOTES ON CHAPTER II

1. U.S. Marine Corps, History and Museums Division, "The Legend of Lucy Brewer," 1957. This report lists a number of objections to Lucy's claim, the only basis for which is a series of pamphlets Lucy wrote and published after the war. Among the report's objections: the similarity between some of Lucy's accounts of the *Constitution*'s naval engagements and contemporary newspaper reports; the unlikelihood that Lucy, as an inexperienced marksman, would have been assigned as a sharpshooter in "the fighting tops," as she claimed she was; her accounts' overabundance of technical detail, of which a Marine at his post in the topsails would have had no knowledge; and the fact that Marine Corps regulations at the time required all Marine recruits to strip, bathe, and don a Marine uniform in the presence of their commander, who would have been derelict in his duties not to ascertain the physical condition of the men in his charge. Among those who have perpetuated the myth of "the first girl Marine" are Martin Binkin and Shirley Bach in *Women and the Military* (Washington, D.C.: Brookings Institution, 1977), p. 5,

and Jeanne Holm in *Women in the Military: An Unfinished Revolution* (Novato, Calif.: Presidio Press, 1982), p. 3.

2. WAC strength peaked at 99,000 in April 1945. The WAVES, SPARS, and Women Marines peaked in September 1945 with 83,000. The remainder of the 266,000 were Army and Navy nurses.

3. Robert R. Palmer et al., *The Procurement and Training of Ground Combat Troops* (Washington, D.C.: Historical Division, Department of the Army, 1948), p. 41. Between August and November 1943, the Army alone discharged 55,000 men as ineligible for overseas assignment because of such things as missing teeth, hernia, perforated eardrums, and excessive nervousness.

4. Palmer, p. 212.

5. U.S. Navy, Bureau of Naval Personnel, "History of the Women's Reserve," an unpublished draft manuscript produced in 1946, p. 153. Navy units, particularly medical units, reported that men bore up much better under the strain of being over-worked, while women suffered inordinate rates of stress-related breakdown working the same hours as the men.

6. Mattie E. Treadwell, *The Women's Army Corps* (Washington, D.C.: Office of the Chief of Military History, Department of the Army, 1954), p. 711–712. Treadwell, herself a WAC veteran, produced this thorough history of both the successes and failures of the Women's Army Corps nine years after the war's end. The Navy's unpublished history of the WAVES was written within the first year after V-J day and is entirely too self-congratulatory to give an adequate appraisal of the WAVES's record.

7. Treadwell, p. 460.

8. Quoted by Holm, p. 159.

9. Quoted by Holm, p. 182.

10. Officers of all services hold pay grades numbered 1 to 10 in increasing seniority. Each grade has a corresponding rank, though ranks vary depending upon the service. An O-3 in the Army is a captain, but a captain in the Navy is an O-6. An O-6 in the Army, Air Force, and Marines is a colonel. Admirals and generals are O-7s, 8s, 9s, or 10s and are often called flag officers.

11. Flag officers are still sometimes asked to take reductions in rank to accept certain positions. When General Andrew J. Goodpaster took over as superintendent of the U.S. Military Academy at West Point, he accepted a reduction to lieutenant general, the highest rank authorized for the superintendency. Prior to 1967, the women's components were, in a sense, miniature armies. The system for managing women's promotions and assignments therefore resembled the way promotions and assignments are managed by smaller foreign armies, in which an officer must resign, retire, or die before another can move up.

12. Holm, p. 199.

13. Margaret Eastman, "DACOWITS: A Nice Little Group That Doesn't Do Very Much," *Army Times,* Family Supplement, 15 March 1972, p. 11.

14. Thomas D. Morris, Assistant Secretary of Defense for Manpower, Statement before the House Armed Services Committee on a proposal to remove restrictions on female officer promotions.

15. The same House report admitted: "It is recognized that a male officer in arriving at the point where he may be considered for general and flag rank passes through a crucible to which the woman officer is not subjected—such as combat, long tours at sea, and other dangers and isolations."

16. Holm, p. 197.

17. Quoted by Holm, p. 192.

CHAPTER III

The All-Volunteer Surprise

The conscription calls out a share of every class—no matter whether your son or my son—all must march; but our friends—I may say it in this room—are the very scum of the earth.

THE DUKE OF WELLINGTON[1]

THE EQUALIZATION OF PROMOTION policies for male and female officers and the removal of ceilings on enlisted women achieved by PL 90-130 may have been the opening shots in the assault on the all-male services, but in themselves they were little more than stones thrown in the enemy camp. What was needed was a Trojan horse that would slip large numbers of warrior women into the citadel before the defenders knew what was happening. That horse appeared in the form of the All-Volunteer Armed Force.

By 1968, the draft had been an accepted part of American life for twenty years. Since passage of the Selective Service Act of 1948, the draft had provided the necessary manpower to back up the nation's global commitments and fostered patriotism, discipline, and civic responsibility among the nation's restless young men. Most American men who had served their time in war or in peace saw nothing wrong with conscription per se and were quite willing to allow younger men the privilege of serving, whether they wanted to or not. Proud veterans still outnumbered libertarians who saw conscription as inconsistent with civil liberty. Civil liberty, in the minds of many Americans, still entailed civic responsibility.

As a result of the Vietnam War, however, organized opposition to the draft grew rapidly. Anti-war activists portrayed the draft as an immoral means of supporting an immoral war. Hotheads like the Berrigan brothers responded violently by raiding, burning, or bombing draft board offices. Celebrity clerics like Bishop James Pike and the Rev. William Sloan Coffin Jr. joined Dr. Benjamin Spock in publicly supporting civil disobedience to draft calls. A handful of draft-age men left the country. Many more marked time in college or evoided the draft by other legal means. The Supreme Court obligingly broadened defensible grounds for conscientious objection, and the number of conscientious objectors doubled between 1967 and 1970.

Those who obeyed the draft summons were disproportionately poor and poorly educated, and among the many good men drafted were many rotten apples—disgruntled, disillusioned, disobedient fellows who lacked the intelligence or the foresight to avoid military service before it was too late. They were the source of many of the problems that plagued the services during Vietnam: desertion (up 300 percent from 1966 to 1970), drug addiction, racial conflicts, disrespect toward superiors, and a general breakdown of discipline. Because the draft brought them in, the draft was sometimes blamed for the trouble they made. If we only took those who volunteered, thought some officers and NCOs, we'd only have happy campers.

Of course, with a war on, ending the draft was out of the question. The best that President Johnson could hope to do was to make the draft more equitable. In July 1966, he created the National Advisory Commission on Selective Service, headed by Burke Marshall, former assistant attorney general in charge of the Civil Rights Division under President John F. Kennedy and author of the original version of the 1964 Civil Right Act. The commission submitted its report seven months later, recommending that draft policy be "uniformly developed and centrally administered" through 500 area centers instead of the much more numerous local draft boards. The report also recommended random, impartial call-ups and the elimination of student and occupational deferments. A single sentence in the report recommended that the services "broaden the opportunities" of women and civilians to reduce the number of men drafted, though no discussion of this option was presented.[2] The Burke Marshall report served as the basis for Johnson's 1967 draft reform proposals, but little became of the proposals in Congress and the report was soon shelved.

Flawed though the system was, selective service itself was strongly supported in Washington. In 1967, only two votes were cast in Congress against a draft extension. Still, the temptation to please vocal segments of the electorate was too great for many in Washington to withstand a serious suggestion to end the draft from a well-respected leader. The man to make that suggestion was Richard M. Nixon.

Running for president as the end-the-war-with-honor candidate in 1968, Nixon departed from the Republican Party platform by calling for an end to the draft to coincide with the end of the war. In a radio broadcast on 17 October 1968, Nixon told the American people that it was time to take a "new look" at selective service. He said that the draft was a relatively recent invention, that Americans were wrong to think of it as a natural part of life, and that the dignity of the individual should not be subject to the supremacy of the state. He promised that, if elected, he would find a way to end the draft as soon as our involvement in Vietnam was ended.[3]

Once elected, Nixon created the President's Commission on an All-Volunteer Armed Force. Headed by former Secretary of Defense Thomas S. Gates Jr., the commission included noted economists Milton Friedman and Alan Greenspan, two former supreme allied commanders, the director of the National Association for the Advancement of Colored People, various academicians and businessmen, a student from Georgetown University, and one woman, Jeanne Noble, New York University professor and vice-president of the National Council of Negro Women.

The Gates Commission initiated a number of studies on the relevant issues, then drew its conclusions to be included in the final report. To maintain an all-volunteer force of 2.5 million men, the commission estimated that the services would need to attract 325,000 men per year. 500,000 men had volunteered for military service in each year of the Vietnam War, and surveys of volunteers indicated that as many as 250,000 were "true volunteers" who would have enlisted anyway had there been no draft. It seemed, then, that the services would need to attract only 75,000 more men each year to man an all-volunteer force. The commission was confident that higher pay and other improvements in service life would easily bring forth the extra 75,000 men.[4]

Eight objections to an all-volunteer force were summarily dismissed. The commission's report admitted that while the "budgetary expense" of a volunteer force would be greater, the "actual cost" to the nation would be lower because the nation's young men would no longer be taxed in time and effort to subsidize the national defense. The report also argued that the savings from the low pay for first-term servicemen represented "discrimination" which needed correcting for reasons of equity alone.

Years later, the Government Accounting Office submitted a report to Congress on the additional costs of the All-Volunteer Force, or AVF, as actually instituted. According to the GAO, the Gates Commission had based its conclusions on several invalid assumptions and inaccurate estimations. The Gates Commission erroneously assumed that an AVF would have a lower personnel turnover rate that would reduce both the number of men needed each year and the cost of training them. The commission failed to appreciate the differences between the Army and the other services and wrongly assumed that an all-volunteer Army would enjoy the same success in recruiting that the others enjoyed. The commission overestimated the number of "true volunteers" by failing to consider the declining popularity of the military. It underestimated the cost of extra inducements for reservists and critical specialists. It also underestimated the cost of the more attractive benefit package offered to all new recruits and the total additional cost of the AVF. Its report claimed that an AVF of 2.5 million men would cost an additional $2.1 billion per year, but the GAO estimated that the AVF had actually cost an additional $3 billion annually since its creation, though its total strength never exceeded 2.1 million.[5]

Two of the Gates Commission's errors were not mentioned by the GAO. One was that the commission had noted that the population of enlistment-age men would increase in the 1970s but had failed to warn that the increase would be short-lived and that the same population would begin to decrease by the end of the decade. The other was that the commission had failed to consider the impact of large numbers of women drawn into the AVF as substitutes for men. In fact, the commission's report and supporting research barely mentioned women. Not only did the commission fail to consider that an all-volunteer force might become too dependent upon women, it failed even to recommend recruiting women to reduce the need for men. Members of the commission say the subject of using women as substitutes simply never came up in any commission meetings. Ironically, the oversight probably helped the commission make its case for an all-volunteer force. A recommendation to greatly expand the role of women would only have strengthened the military's opposition to the AVF.

The Gates Commission delivered its report to the President in early 1970, having agreed unanimously that an all-volunteer force should replace the current mixed force of conscripts and volunteers as soon as the war in Vietnam was over. On 23 April 1970, in an address to Congress, President Nixon used the report to justify his decision to institute the All-Volunteer Force as soon as possible. For the rest of his first term, Nixon spoke often of draft reform to goad Congress into approving the necessary legislation and to remind the electorate, which for the first time included everyone over the age of eighteen, to thank the Nixon Administration for the eventual end of the draft.

Nixon's decision to shift to the AVF in the early 1970s showed the worst possible timing. Never was patriotism in shorter supply throughout the fifty states, and never was public confidence in the American military at a lower ebb. After an inglorious retreat from Indochina, the military came home to Watergate, women's rights, and a "zero draft" future. It was still shaking the mud off its boots when it was ordered to pretty itself up for a recruiting drive.

Implementation of the AVF began with the appointment of the Central All-Volunteer Task Force within the Department of Defense. The task force quickly developed a two-fold strategy to ensure success. First, it planned to increase enlistments by offering recruits higher pay, shorter tours, better living conditions, bonuses for special skills, veteran's benefits, allowances for dependents, and a host of other inducements. Second, it sought to decrease the need for men by making greater use of civilians and women, never considering that an all-male military might attract more men than a thoroughly feminized force.

The reason the task force did not consider the possibility of an all-male volunteer military was the coincidence of the AVF and the ERA. In March 1972, while the task force was still at work, Congress cleared the Equal Rights Amendment for ratification by the states. Debate in both houses was light, considering the hard road ahead for the amendment. Most of the argument was not over the wisdom of the amendment itself, but over the need for special exemptions in the amendment to protect women from combat and compulsory military service. All such exemptions were rejected. Feminists feared that any exceptions to the amendment would weaken it. Senator Birch Bayh of Illinois argued, "If a woman wants to volunteer [for combat], should she be treated differently from a man?"[6] Senator Sam Ervin of North Carolina led the fight in the Senate against the amendment and for the combat and draft exemptions, but fifteen senators who had favored such exemptions when the amendment was first proposed in 1970 had changed their minds in two years. The final version of the amendment, approved by overwhelming majorities in both houses, called for nothing less than absolute equality between the sexes.[7]

Also in March, the House Armed Services Committee established the Special Subcommittee on the Utilization of Manpower in the Military, which published its report in June, flaunting the latest fashion of thought about the place of women in the military:

> We are concerned that the Department of Defense and each of the military services are guilty of 'tokenism' in the recruitment and utilization of women in the Armed Forces. We are convinced that in the atmosphere of a zero draft environment or an all-volunteer military force, women could and should play a more important role. We strongly urge the Secretary of Defense and the service secretaries to develop a program which will permit women to take their rightful place in serving in our Armed Forces.[8]

In December 1972, with the ERA rapidly approaching ratification (so it seemed), the Central All-Volunteer Task Force published its own report, marrying the weakness of the all-volunteer military to the strength of the equal rights movement:

> The pursuit of these two goals, equal opportunity and greater utilization, may well bring about the most revolutionary policy changes experienced in the history of military women.[9]

The AVF's future dependence on the ever-expanding utilization of women was assured. The task force instructed the services to double the number of women in their ranks by 1977. Only the Marine Corps, with its high ratio of combat troops to support troops, escaped with a modest, mandated 40 percent increase in its tiny female contingent.

At the start of 1972, the women's components composed 1.5 percent of the total force, with 12,600 women officers and 32,400 enlisted women. That year, before the end of the draft, the services enlisted 13,000 additional women making them 3.3 percent of total recruitments. It was only the beginning.

On 1 July 1973, following the signing of the Paris peace accords and the expiration of the selective service authorization, Defense Secretary Melvin Laird announced the birth of the All-Volunteer Armed Force, a final step after hundreds of preparatory changes. The base pay of a first-term enlisted man had more than doubled, and life in the services had softened considerably. Open-bay barracks with rows of bunks were being divided into dormitories with two or three-man rooms, which the occupants were allowed to decorate as they pleased. Mess halls became "dining facilities," with carpeting and drapes and smaller tables with chairs instead of benches. Saturday morning fatigue duty and inspections were becoming less frequent. Sailors in port were allowed to live ashore. Soldiers were allowed to wander on and off post anytime they were not on duty. Many more officers and enlisted men resided off-post, and many more privates had wives and children.

By the same summer, however, it had already become apparent that the services were not attracting enough of the kind of men they needed. Entrance exam scores plummeted, and the percentage of high school graduates among "true volunteers" fell from 60 percent in 1972 to less than 50 percent in 1973. The induction of college-educated enlisted men, fairly common during the draft, all but dried up. Personnel turnover, instead of decreasing as predicted by the Gates Commission, actually increased because of two-year enlistments and a doubling of the rate of early discharge for indiscipline and unsuitability. Medical and technical fields requiring special skills and extensive training were the hardest hit by low enlistments and high attrition, but the services also found it difficult to enlist men for the dirty jobs in the combat arms. The supply of men for reserve components slowed to a trickle, once the incentive of evoiding the draft by enlisting in the reserves disappeared.

To solve the problem, the Defense Department set aside $225 million in 1973 for various bonuses to attract doctors, nurses, technicians, and infantrymen. It then requested from Congress another $400 million over the next three years for the same purpose. The Defense Department also raised its requirement for recruits to 356,000 per annum to maintain a force of only 2.1 million, rather than the Gates Commission's 325,000 for a force of 2.5 million. Three years later, the department estimated it needed 365,000 to maintain 2.1 million Americans in uniform.

Proponents of women in the services seized upon recruiting shortfalls and the "low quality" of enlisted men as an argument for enlisting more women. A report prepared for the Senate Armed Forces Committee in 1973 recommended raising the number of women as a percentage of the total force possibly as high as 20 percent to make up for the lack of quality men. Historically, the women's components had maintained their integrity by carefully selecting their recruits, who were, on average, better educated, more articulate, and more intelligent (according to scores on entrance exams) than men. The Senate report stated in passing that its recommendation was based upon the assumption that the quality of female recruits would remain constant as their numbers increased, an assumption that later proved invalid. [10]

Yet the services hardly needed to be told by Congress to recruit more women. Charged with making the AVF work one way or another, the manpower managers in the Pentagon saw that the only way, or at least the easiest way, to meet their quotas for enlistments was to recruit more women. With their very careers on the block if the AVF faltered, they wasted little debate on the matter. Contingency plans providing for an increase of 170 percent in the strength of the women's components were executed on order. The female share of total enlistments increased from 5 percent in 1973 to 9 percent in 1975. The Navy and Air Force women's components tripled in size.

By 1975, the armed forces were recruiting more women each year than the total strength of the women's components just three years earlier. In the fourth year of the All-Volunteer Armed Force, there were 109,133 women in uniform, making up more than 5 percent of the total force. A contemporary report by the Brookings Institution estimated that the United States had 44 percent more women in uniform than twenty other major nations combined, including the Soviet Union.[11] The trend of expanding the number of women in the military would continue through the decade, to the alarm of the nation's warrior chiefs who were taken by surprise by the unexpected impact of the AVF.

While the women's components swelled with recruits and the Equal Rights Amendment gathered state ratifications, proponents of military women obtained another victory in the case of *Frontiero v. Richardson*. Lieutenant Sharron Frontiero was an Air Force physical therapist married to a veteran who had been denied status as an Air Force dependent under a federal law requiring female service members to prove that they provided more than half of their husband's support before they received dependent privileges and allowances. The Frontieros sued the government and won. In May 1973, the Supreme Court ruled that the federal law in question was unconstitutional and that military women must receive the same dependent benefits as military men. Four justices sided with Justice William J. Brennan's opinion that sex, like race, was "inherently suspect" as a category of discrimination, requiring "strict judicial scrutiny." Three other justices agreed with the ruling of unconstitutionality but rejected the characterization of sex as "inherently suspect." Only Justice William H. Rehnquist dissented.[12]

Feminists were jubilant. Ruth Ginsburg of the American Civil Liberties Union, who had argued for the plaintiff as an *amicus curiae,* was quoted by *US News & World Report* as saying, "It is the most far-reaching and important ruling on sex discrimination to come out of the Supreme Court yet. It will spell the beginning of reforms in hundreds of statutes which do not give equal benefits to men and women."[13] She had every reason for such confidence. Justice Brennan had made perfectly clear in his written opinion where he stood on the subject: "There can be no doubt that our nation has had a long and unfortunate history of sex discrimination."

His opinion, however, did not stop the Court from turning around two years later and ruling in *Schlesinger v. Ballard* that the Navy could use sex as a discriminator for promotion policy—apparently as long as the offended party is male. Robert C. Ballard, a former Navy lieutenant, had sued the Department of Defense for discharging him after he failed to be promoted twice in nine years, arguing that female Navy lieutenants were allowed 13 years in which to be promoted. Ballard's counsel argued that the Navy's nine year limit on the time in which Ballard could try for promotion violated his right to due process under the 5th Amendment of the Constitution. Writing for a five-justice majority, Justice Potter Stewart argued that Ballard had not been deprived of due process because the Navy's different promotion policies for men and women served a legitimate government purpose by providing for the needs of the service and compensating female officers for their limited military role with longer tenure before promotion. Justice Brennan's dissent argued that the Navy's promotion policy did not serve a legitimate government purpose because Congress had not intended the Navy's promotion system to compensate women with longer tenure and because limits on tenure before promotion were set administratively.[14]

Frontiero v. Richardson also did not stop Judge Oliver C. Gasch of the U.S. District Court in Washington from upholding in 1974 the exclusion of women from the U.S. Naval and Air Force Academies, in a suit brought against the Defense Department by Congressmen Don Edwards and Jerome Waldie of California, on behalf of two women they had nominated for admission. The plaintiffs had argued that excluding women from the service academies violated constitutional guarantees of equal protection and due process under the Fourteenth and Fifth Amendments. The Defense Department had argued that excluding women served a legitimate government purpose because the academies existed to train combat leaders for the Navy and the Air Force, and women were excluded by federal law from engaging in combat. An appellate court denied an appeal.

Congressmen Edwards and Waldie were not the only members of Congress trying to get women into the service academies. In 1972, Senator Jacob Javits of New York nominated a woman to the Naval Academy. One week after Congress passed the Equal Rights Amendment, Senator Javits and Congressman Jack H. McDonald of Michigan introduced concurrent resolutions to prohibit denial of admission to the service academies on the basis of sex. Javits argued that the services all had women officers, some of whom were on the academies' faculties, and that admission to the academies would improve the women's chances of promotion. He also argued that the ERA when ratified would accomplish the same thing, but not in time for his nominee to enter Annapolis with the next class. The Senate passed the resolution easily. The House referred it to the House Armed Services Committee, chaired by Congressman F. Edward Hébert of Louisiana, a strong ally of the Pentagon who had supported the war in Vietnam and opposed the AVF. In his hands, the resolution died.[15]

But confidence was high among feminist organizations in the early 1970s. As the ERA gained momentum, several women's groups began the push toward integration of the academies as an intermediate objective. Representatives of the National Organization for Women and the Center for Women's Policy Studies boldly challenged the Defense Advisory Committee for Women in the Service, silent through the worst of the Vietnam war, to endorse integration. DACOWITS, which had recently opened its meetings to the public, was unable to resist pressure to endorse both the ERA and integration. It called for the services to yield to the inevitability of integration before the courts or the Congress forced it upon them.[16]

With pressure mounting outside Congress, sympathetic members inside persisted in their attempts to integrate the academies. In two years, no less than six bills to admit women were submitted in the House, four of them by Congressman Pierre "Pete" du Pont of Delaware. In 1973, Senator William D. Hathaway of Maine sponsored an amendment to a military appropriations bill to open the academies to women, but the amendment was stricken from the bill by the conference committee. By the next year, however, Hébert could no longer put off hearings on the issue. Du Pont's bills were referred to the subcommittee on military personnel, which began hearing testimony in May 1974.

Just before the hearings began, Undersecretary of Defense William P. Clements sent Congressman Hébert a letter outlining the Defense Department's objections to the bills. The letter argued that the academies trained men for combat service and sea duty, from which women were barred by law. If not all graduates served at sea or in combat units immediately upon graduation, most did. Furthermore, limitations of funding and facilities would mean fewer men admitted if women were, and the services were receiving all the women officers they needed through the Reserve Officers Training Corps (opened to women in 1972), officer candidate schools, and direct commissions.[17]

At the hearings, fourteen representatives of the Department of Defense, including the three superintendents, a recent graduate of West Point, and a West Point senior, testified against admitting women, each one echoing the arguments of Clement's letter. Secretary of the Army Howard H. Callaway testified that 94 percent of West Point graduates entered combat arms upon graduation, the rest being physically disqualified from doing so. To dramatize the point, he submitted into the record General MacArthur's famous "Duty, Honor, Country" speech, which emphasized combat leadership as the reason for West Point's existence. Lieutenant General Albert P. Clark, superintendent of the Air Force Academy, testified that more than 70 percent of Air Force Academy graduates entered fields closed to women and cited higher attrition among female Air Force officers as a reason why integration was not cost effective.

Several Defense witnesses seemed most concerned about the disruptive effect the presence of women would have on the academies. Said Secretary Callaway:

> Admitting women to West Point will irrevocably change the
> Academy. And all the evidence seems to say that the change

could only be for the worse. The Spartan atmosphere—which is
so important to producing the final product—would surely be
diluted. . . . [18]

Lieutenant General Clark concurred: "It is my considered judgment
that the introduction of female cadets will inevitably erode this vital
atmosphere." He predicted that the academies would

inevitably find it necessary to create a modified program to
accommodate the female cadet, or, God forbid, be required to
water down the entire program. . . . [19]

The Defense spokesmen were seconded by a single private citizen,
Miss Jacqueline Cochran, famed aviatrix, test pilot, and veteran
leader of the Womens Air Service Pilots in World War II. Miss
Cochran strongly opposed the admission of women to the academies
on the grounds that the academies trained men for combat and
putting women in combat was "ridiculous." Her experiences in
World War II convinced her that women "have no business" in
combat. Members of the subcommittee pointed out that she herself
was just the kind of woman to be admitted to the academies, but
Cochran took a different view of her own example:

when I was a child I went to work 12 hours a night in the cotton
mill before I was 8 years old without shoes, and I became pretty
hardened to the facts of life. I don't think that is the way women
should be brought up. I certainly don't think I was properly
brought up.[20]

Two representatives of the Maritime Administration testified that
the Merchant Marine Academy, recently integrated, was experiencing no significant problems. Eight concerned citizens, most representing the Center for Women Policy Studies and the Women's Lobby,
testified in support of integration. Nineteen members of Congress
expressed their support. Among them were Congressmen Pete Du
Pont, Don Edwards, and Patricia Schroeder of Colorado. Schroeder
argued that "imminent ratification" of the two-year-old ERA made
integration inevitable. Edwards accused the Defense Department of
opposing integration for "essentially frivolous reasons and outmoded

patterns of thinking." All of them reduced the argument for integration to a simple matter of equity. Most dismissed the largest stumbling block to integration—the issue of combat—by observing that not all academy graduates served in combat. One representative who did not thus dismiss combat was Congressman Charles B. Rangel of New York, who went so far as to call for the integration of the battlefield also. Rangel pointed to Israel and the Soviet Union, saying, "If fighting must be done, women should join men in doing it."[21]

The hearings concluded in August with the Defense Department thinking it had won, comforted by Hébert's private assurances that the committee would not report a bill for integration out to the full House. But other portents were not encouraging. Not a single member of Congress had dared to speak openly against integration in the hearings, and in June, the Senate again passed a resolution proposed by Senator Hathaway in favor of integration.

The House committee had still taken no action by January 1975, when the Democratic Caucus, dissatisfied with Hébert's pro-Pentagon views, forced him from the chairmanship of the HASC and replaced him with Congressman Melvin Price of Illinois. The push then began again to put a bill before the House. Early that spring, the new military personnel subcommittee chairman argued successfully to allow the Defense Department another opportunity to testify against integration, but the department declined, perhaps under the woefully mistaken impression that integration of the academies was a dead issue.

Time was running out for those who hoped to see women admitted to the academies in the bicentennial year, so in April 1975, Congressman Samuel Stratton of New York, a strong proponent of integration on the military personnel subcommittee, bypassed both committees and introduced an amendment to a military appropriations bill then before the full House for consideration. Again, debate centered on the issue of combat. Despite their enthusiasm for equal rights and the ERA, neither the House nor the Senate was ready to repeal their own laws restricting women from combat service, which the ERA would surely have done. The matter was finally resolved by drawing a line between the academies' responsibility to prepare officers for combat and their responsibility to prepare officers for careers in the armed forces. In the words of Judith Stiehm: "By making this distinction between combat and career training, Congress sidestepped having to decide whether women should enter combat; that, it reasoned, was not the central issue."[22]

Last minute suggestions that Congress establish separate academies for women went nowhere. Thus, left to themselves without the annoying arguments of military men, 303 congressmen voted on May 20, 1975, to admit women to the service academies in the next calendar year. Ninety-six voted against the admission of women. The Senate endorsed the amendment by voice vote on June 6. In an afterthought, Congress realized that it had overlooked the Coast Guard in the legislation. A bill hastily introduced to integrate the Coast Guard Academy proved unnecessary; the Coast Guard announced in August that it would admit women the following year.

On October 7, 1975, President Gerald Ford signed a massive appropriations bill into law, a small segment of which would radically alter the nature of the American military's most sacred institutions. Public Law 94-106 required the service secretaries to ensure that:

> (1) female individuals shall be eligible for appointment and admission to the service academy concerned, beginning the appointments to such academy for the class beginning in calendar year 1976, and (2) the academic and other relevant standards required for appointment, admission, training, graduation, and commissioning of female individuals shall be the same as those required for male individuals, except for those minimum essential adjustments in such standards required because of physiological differences between male and female individuals.

For feminists, the law's stipulation that admission would be "consistent with the needs of the services" left too much for the services to decide. For opponents of integration, the requirement that the authority of the service "must be exercised within a program providing for the orderly and expeditious admission of women" meant that there would be no "survival of the fittest" in the admissions process: the services were compelled to admit some women one way or another.

The passage of PL 94-106 was the highwater mark of the American feminist movement, the crest of a fifteen-year wave of legislative action. Along the way, feminists won for their flag a daunting array of campaign streamers: the Equal Pay Act of 1963, Title VII of the Civil Rights Act, Title IX of the Education Amendment of 1972, the Equal Employment Opportunity Act of 1972, congressional approval of the Equal Rights Amendment, and numerous other laws to protect and extend the rights and prerogatives of women in all areas of public and private life. They celebrated 24 August 1974 as National Women's Equality Day and all of 1975 as International Women's Year. In that year, the ERA was just three states short of the three-fourths needed to make it the 27th Amendment to the Constitution of the United States. Few expected anything but ratification.

Meanwhile, the All-Volunteer Force limped along, spiritless and barely able to man itself for all of its efforts. Wrestling with the problem of making military service attractive when the honor of serving was gone, it inevitably fell back on the venal and illusory lures of money and easy living. The Volunteer Army wanted to join you, and to persuade you to let it, it offered short tours, fast cars, college educations, and off-post housing. An early "VOLAR" commercial featured actor John Travolta as a new recruit behind the wheel of a Pontiac Trans Am. Later ads were equally ignoble, as the Army sold its soul to low-minded advertizing experts who may have understood the salivating solipsism of seventeen-year-olds, but doubtlessly did not understand the concept of the citizen-soldier. The focus was all on self-interest.

Self-interest was the focus that served military women best. They had come a long way since the 2 percent ceiling on women was lifted in 1967. The faltering volunteer force had opened a gap in the ranks which they rushed to fill. Their battle-cries vaunted a new-found "right to serve." No longer were they merely support troops, freeing a man to fight. Now they had equal status, equal advancement, and equal benefits, and they were moving in large numbers into previously all-male units and specialties. Only the laws excluding women from combat remained, and they seemed doomed by the ERA.

But it was not to be. American women did not want to be *that* equal, as the state legislatures were finding out. The United States

Congress had rushed to radical extremes in the name of sexual equality as long as they angered only military men, a thoroughly subjugated, politically docile constituency. It would not confront the whole of American womanhood directly, however, and the ERA's indirect approach had run into trouble. The very year that saw the first perfumed plebes enter West Point also saw the ERA sitting dead in the water, the victim of Phyllis Schlafly's STOP ERA counter-offensive.

The turning point came too late for the nation's service academies. Had they held out against integration a year or two longer, they might not be integrated today.

NOTES ON CHAPTER III

1. Quoted by Max Hastings, ed., *The Oxford Book of Military Anecdotes* (New York: Oxford University Press, 1985), pp. 223–224.

2. National Advisory Commission on Selective Service, *In Pursuit of Equity: Who Serves When Not All Serve?* (Washington, D.C.: GPO, 1967).

3. Richard M. Nixon, "The All-Volunteer Armed Force," address given over the CBS Radio Network on Thursday, 17 October 1968.

4. President's Commission on an All-Volunteer Armed Force, *The Report of the President's Commission on an All-Volunteer Armed Force* (New York: The Mac-Millan Company, 1970).

5. U.S. Comptroller General, *Additional Cost of the All-Volunteer Force* (Washington, D.C.: GPO, 1978), p. ii.

6. *Congress and the Nation* (Washington, D.C.: Congressional Quarterly, Inc., 1973), III, p. 510. In arguing against exemptions from combat, Bayh minimized the likelihood of just what he was arguing for, a common tactic among radical reformers. He said, "There is an extremely small likelihood that any [women] will really reach combat service."

7. Among them were Senators Howard Baker of Tennessee and Robert Dole of Kansas. The effect of the defeat of the military service exemptions, and perhaps the

intention of some of those who opposed the exemptions, was to make the ERA unacceptable to a larger segment of the American public.

8. Report 92-51 of the Special Subcommittee on the Utilization of Manpower in the Military.

9. Central All-Volunteer Task Force, *Utilization of Military Women* (Washington, D.C.: Department of Defense, 1972).

10. Martin Binkin and John D. Johnston, *All-Volunteer Armed Forces: Progress, Problems, and Prospects* (Washington, D.C.: GPO, 1973), p. 3.

11. Martin Binkin and Shirley Bach, *Women and the Military* (Washington, D.C.: Brookings Institution, 1977).

12. Frontiero v. Richardson, 36 L.Ed. 2d 583 (US Supreme Ct. 1973). Noting that the Equal Rights Amendment, then before the states, would have accomplished the same effect as Brennan's characterization of sex as "inherently suspect," Powell argued that "the Court has assumed a decisional responsibility at the very time when state legislatures, functioning within the traditional democratic process, are debating the proposed Amendment." Brennan's opinion therefore did not show the proper "respect for duly prescribed legislative processes."

    Rehnquist agreed with the District Court's ruling that the military would have required all members to prove dependency of a spouse, as it required all members to prove dependency of other adults, if that were administratively feasible. Because it was not, the military was simply trying to curb the excess of benefits on the basis of probability. It was highly probable that the wives of servicemen were in fact dependent upon their husbands for primary support, but it was unlikely that the husbands of servicewomen were primarily supported by their wives. Probability, not sex, therefore, was the determining factor. See Frontiero v. Laird, 341 Federal Supplement 201 (US Dist. Ct. 1972).

13. "Sexequality: Impact of a Key Decision," *US News & World Report,* 28 May 1973, p. 69.

14. Schlesinger v. Ballard, 42 L.Ed. 2d 610.

15. Hébert's first claim to fame was as city editor of *The New Orleans Times-Picayune* when the paper broke the Huey Long scandals in 1939.

16. Defense Advisory Committee on Women in the Services, "Recommendations made at the 1974 Spring Meeting," 25 April 1974, p. 2.

17. Albert P. Clark, "Women at the Service Academies and Combat Leadership," *Strategic Review,* Fall 1977, p. 67.

18. Hearings before the House Armed Services Committee, 94th Congress, "Eliminate Discrimination Based on Sex for Admission to the Five Federal Service Academies" (Washington, D.C.: GPO, 1974), p. 165.

19. Hearings, p. 137.

20. Hearings, p. 256.

21. Hearings, p. 265.

22. Judith Hicks Stiehm, *Bring Me Men and Women: Mandated Change at the U.S. Air Force Academy* (Berkeley, Calif.: University of California Press, 1981), p. 38.

CHAPTER IV

Eighty's Ladies

*The great thing about those first ten weeks [at Sandhurst] was
that although one was being treated like mud it was at least
grown-up mud. We were treated like men for the first time in
our lives, and as men we were expected to react.*

DAVID NIVEN[1]

POETRY GREETS each year's crop of young civilians entering the
United States Air Force Academy at Colorado Springs, Colorado. As
the ragged formation of new recruits marches down the ramp into the
cadet living area, all eyes are afixed to three words proclaimed in
stone from the granite roof overhead: BRING ME MEN. So begins
the poem entitled "The Coming American" by Sam Walter Foss:

> Bring me men to match my mountains,
> Bring me men to match my plains,
> Men with empires in their purpose
> And new eras in their brains. . . .

In 1976, when the entering class included not just men but women,
the Air Force Academy rejected a suggestion that the offensive
phrase be revised. The rejection was, however, a rare departure from
the Academy's policy of easing the process of sexual integration by
thoroughly accommodating the first female cadets.

The award for the worst performance by a service academy in the first year of sexual integration can only be given to the United States Air Force Academy. It was the only academy where attrition rates for men exceeded attrition rates for women. The Air Force Academy Class of 1980, the first sexually integrated class, lost 23.5 percent of its male cadets in the first year alone, but only 19.7 percent of its female members. The same class graduated with barely half of its original men: 44.4 percent of those who started in the summer of 1976 did not finish, compared to 37.8 percent of the original women. Both men and women exceeded the average dropout rate of 35 percent among pre-integration classes. Today, the Air Force Academy remains the only academy where men have left in greater numbers than women, despite innovative attempts to reduce attrition.[2]

The Air Force Academy had, nevertheless, shown the most enthusiasm of all the academies for the task of integration. It had begun planning for integration in 1972, when congressional passage of the ERA made integration seem inevitable to some Academy administrators. By the summer of 1975, with the integration bill still pending, the Air Force Academy had already formulated a comprehensive plan for the admission of women.

Unfortunately for the Academy, its headstart was in the wrong direction. Early on in its planning, the Academy misidentified the chief problem of integration as one of easing women into the Academy without driving too many of them away. A visit by the Academy's planning committee to Lackland Air Force Base in 1974 reinforced fears that the sensitivity of the first women admitted posed the principal threat to integration. At Lackland, the committee noted that female Air Force recruits responded better to encouragement, or "positive motivation," than to the harsh discipline applied to male recruits, yet even the comparatively relaxed atmosphere of Air Force basic training was described by most female recruits as "stressful."[3] Convinced that the much more stressful environment of the Academy's fourth-class system would be too much for most women, the committee incorporated in its draft plan several special measures to protect the women from the worst of cadet life.

Even if the committee had been right about the principal threat to integration, it incorrectly anticipated the passage of the integration law. PL 94-106, as finally passed, specified only "minimum essential adjustments" to academy standards to accommodate "physiological differences" between men and women. The Academy's plan, however, was designed to make life as pleasant as possible for the first female cadets in a number of non-physiological ways. Congressional overseers might have saved the Academy considerable trouble had they held the Academy to the letter of the law. But the spirit of the law was another matter. As long as extra adjustments were intended to favor the female cadets, no one—least of all, Congress—cared. The Academy was therefore allowed to continue along its pre-set course of accommodation and protection, the law notwithstanding.

Few changes were made to the draft plan before implementation. The only significant change placed women in 20 of the 40 squadrons of the Cadet Wing, instead of concentrating the women in a separate women's squadron, thus avoiding the appearance of a policy of separate-but-equal without spreading the women so thin throughout the wing that they were deprived of peer support. For privacy, the women were still to be quartered together on the same floor of the same building, off-limits to all males during certain hours. To protect the women from the usual harassment endured by fourth-class cadets, upperclassmen were still to be instructed to use positive motivation on the women. Fifteen female Air Force lieutenants were still to be chosen as Air Training Officers (ATOs) to act as "surrogate upperclassmen" and role models for the female cadets.

In the fall of 1975, while scrambling to attract qualified young women for the class of 1980, the Academy began its search for 15 qualified female Air Force lieutenants or captains to volunteer to serve as ATOs. Hundreds of records were reviewed, but only a handful of women who were physically and professionally qualified were also interested in the assignment. The following spring, fifteen female surrogates entered the Academy as ATO candidates to undergo special training, including a three-week "mini-academy" to introduce them to life as an air cadet. During the training, the ATOs made a dismal showing for their sex. Unaccustomed to intense physical exertion, they suffered an embarrassing rate of injury and fatigue. Two dropped out of the program before the end of training. The rest fell woefully short of Academy standards.

Fortunately for the Academy, the first female cadets were a different breed—younger, more athletic, with a somewhat better idea of what they were getting into and better reasons for being there. From over a thousand applicants, the Academy selected 157 of the most athletic, most scholarly women in the country.[4] Eighty-four percent were in the top 10 percent of their high school class. Seventy-nine percent were members of the National Honor Society. Their average SAT and ACT scores were slightly above the men's average in verbal skills, slightly below the men's in math skills.

Fourteen hundred and thirty-six male cadets also entered the Air Force Academy that year. They too were among the most scholarly, most athletic young adults in the country. But despite their numbers, they seemed nonexistent to the flocks of journalists who flew in and out of the Academy that summer like pigeons in a park, clucking and clustering around the fledgling female cadets.

In addition to the journalists, the Academy played host to several academicians who stayed for extended periods to observe the event. Among them were Dr. Lois B. DeFleur, professor of sociology at Washington State University, and Judith Stiehm, professor of political science at the University of Southern California. Dr. DeFleur would become a mainstay of the Academy's efforts to monitor its progress, participating in nearly every official study of integration conducted at the Air Force Academy for the next ten years. Stiehm, a philosophical feminist, would later write a not-too-flattering book about the first year of integration.

An initial survey of entering cadets found that the only significant difference between the outlook of new male and female cadets concerned the role of women in society and in the military. On such issues, the male cadets were found to be "significantly more traditional" than civilian males at other institutions, while female cadets were found to be less traditional than civilian females.[5] The Air Force Academy was drawing men from one end of the spectrum and women from the other end. This polarity was bound to inhibit the assimilation of women, even if they had been men, but the blame for the lack of affinity between male and female air cadets regularly fell on the men, since their traditional opinions were officially out of favor. Years later, Dr. DeFleur would recommend easing the assimilation of women by recruiting "a wider variety of people," preferably fewer of the more traditional males, the very men who have historically shown the greatest interest in the Academy.[6]

Though the survey showed that most of the male cadets, particularly the upperclassmen, held more traditional opinions, it also showed that the men of the Class of 1980 were initially neutral with regard to the presence of women at the Academy, willing to wait and see before passing judgment. They did not have to wait long. By the end of the summer, the attitudes of male "doolies" had begun a long shift toward the negative.

Life as an Air Cadet begins long before the start of the academic year. While other recent high school graduates are working to save money for college or still cavorting about at the beach, cadet-recruits are beginning two months of military regimentation known as Basic Cadet Training, or BCT. Modeled after West Point's "Beast Barracks," BCT is designed to turn high school kids into Air Cadets.

There was nothing novel in the Air Force Academy's approach to this task. Throughout the ages, tribes of warriors have performed the same task with similar rituals. Almost all societies have recognized the necessity of such rituals. Only in our Western culture in relatively recent years have both the mechanics of the process and the rationale for the transformation been forgotten.

Neither were lost upon the Air Force Academy after the first year of integration, however. A draft report produced in 1977 by the Academy's Department of Behavioral Science and Leadership showed a clear understanding of the role of BCT in initiating young cadet-recruits into the Cadet Wing. "The Integration of Women into a Male Initiation Rite: A Case Study of the USAF Academy," by Dean H. Wilson and David C. Gillman, was perhaps the only official study of the Academy's integration not heavily influenced by Lois DeFleur. Instead the authors followed the thinking of Arnold Van Gennep, whose work pre-dated the feminist takeover of the field of sociology. In his 1908 book entitled *The Rites of Passage,* Van Gennep divided the initiation rites of aboriginal Australian and African tribes into three phases. Wilson and Gillman used the same phases to describe the process of BCT.

Van Gennep's first phase, the Rite of Separation, signalled the separation of the initiates from everything they had known until then—families, friends, all that was a part of their past life. At the Air Force Academy, it begins immediately upon arrival of the new cadet-recruits. That very day, the recruits lose much of their personal identity by having their heads shaved, donning uniforms, and marching for the first time in formation with other recruits. They are assigned rooms and roommates and are grouped into flights and squadrons under the complete control of the Academy's officers and upperclass cadets. The rite of separation ends late the same day when the recruits are ceremoniously sworn in as Air Cadets.

The next phase, Van Gennep's Rite of Transition, begins after the swearing-in and lasts the duration of BCT. The first half of BCT is conducted in the cadet living area and consists of instruction in close-order drill, cadet regulations, military customs and courtesy, Air Force Academy traditions, and physical conditioning. The second half is conducted at the Jack's Valley encampment and consists largely of combat and survival training. Cadets learn land navigation, patrolling, marksmanship, weapons maintenance, tactical operations, and survival techniques. At Jack's Valley, new cadets are subjected to intense physical and mental pressure. It is supposed to be a grueling experience involving demanding and sometimes dangerous assault and obstacle courses, and no doubt for many cadets prior to 1976 it was. The emphasis throughout this phase is on commonality of experience. Having put their personal lives behind them, the cadets must learn to live, act, and think as a group.

The last phase, the Rite of Incorporation, comes at the end of BCT, when the cadets who have not dropped out are awarded the uniform shoulder boards of full-fledged doolies and accepted into the Cadet Wing.[7]

These rites of passage are intended to impress upon new cadets three things: the irreversibility of their separation from their past, the significance of their own transformation, and the value of their future status as cadets of the United States Air Force Academy and ultimately as Air Force officers. With these firm impressions, cadets will commit themselves utterly to the pursuit of an Academy education, enduring years of repeated academic trials and demanding military training. But the impressions depend upon the seared memory of the initiation experience. The rites must be attended not only by stirring ceremony but also by the sharp experience of physical and mental pain. Without it, the rites will fail. The cadets will not feel the break between their lives before entering the Academy and their lives after, nor will they think their status as cadets too valuable to give up.

These things the Air Force Academy knew instinctively prior to the summer of 1976. Twenty times since its founding it had successfully repeated the process. Yet for the first integrated class, Basic Cadet Training failed to achieve its higher purposes. It achieved neither the commonality of experience necessary to bind the integrated class together nor the intensity of experience needed to bind the new cadets to the Academy. And its failure would forever curse the Class of 1980.

Behind the failure of BCT was a brazen double standard. That BCT was to be one thing for women and another for men was plainly evident to all on the very day the new class of cadet-recruits arrived. Flight by flight, cadet-recruits were marched into the base barber shop. Male recruits came out with stubble; female recruits escaped with neat and stylish trims. Women retained both their individuality and their femininity, while men suffered the embarrassment and dehumanization of fuzzy pates and radically altered self-images. There being nothing physiological about the length of one's hair, the integration law would have required the women's heads to be shorn also, but no one dared ask that much of these daring women.

Next, the cadet-recruits were assigned rooms. All of the women were assigned to the sixth floor of Vandenberg Hall, off-limits to male personnel mornings and evenings. There the female cadets enjoyed the easy tutelage of their surrogate sisters, while real upperclassmen applied intense harassment to the bald-headed males on the floors below. Even if the ATOs had tried to match the male upperclassmen in ferocity of harassment, there were simply not enough of them to do so. Though male upperclassmen matched male recruits roughly one-for-one during the first summer, the ratio of ATOs to female recruits was one to ten.

Then came physical training. The Academy's physical fitness test included pushups, pullups, a standing broad jump, and a 600-yard run, but since very few of the women could perform one pullup or complete any of the other events to male standards, different standards were devised for women. The female standards allowed more time for the run and required less distance on the jump and fewer pushups. Instead of pullups, female cadets were given points for the length of time they could hang on the bar. If a woman could do one pull-up, she earned herself considerable extra credit. [8]

Though the female cadets performed somewhat better than the ATOs had earlier, their record was not impressive. They fell out of group runs, lagged behind on road marches, failed to negotiate obstacles on the assault courses (later modified to make them easier), and could not climb a rope, sometimes breaking down in tears when confronted with their own limitations. The rate at which the female cadets sought medical attention could hardly have allowed them to keep up the pace of training. The women averaged eight visits to the medical clinic per female cadet; the men average only 2.5 visits. Eighty-five percent of female cadets received medical treatment during the eight weeks of BCT, compared to 70 percent of male cadets. On the average, women suffered nine times as many shin splints as the men, five times as many stress fractures, and more than five times as many cases of tendonitis. [9] With time off for sick call and with their participation limited by medical restrictions of their physical activity, many female cadets must indeed have only watched a lot of BCT.

Such performance would have earned male cadets considerable harassment from upperclassmen, but because upperclassmen were enjoined to use "positive motivation" on female cadets, their abuse was concentrated on the males who were, for the most part, performing satisfactorily. Ironically, the men of the first integrated class received the brunt of the upperclassmen's disgust with integration. They were constantly derided as "Eighty's Ladies" and reminded that their BCT was easier than that of every class before. Upperclassmen felt that overall standards for men and women had been lowered and referred to the first integrated BCT class as the "coke-break BCT" and the "Burger King Basics" with "Have It Your Way" as their theme.

At the same time, some upperclassmen faulted the new males for not looking after their female classmates, though there was no real incentive for them to do so. Stragglers in earlier all-male classes tended to draw the fire of upperclassmen away from the rest of their class, receiving in return the support of the class, which had an interest in keeping the stragglers from falling out altogether. The women of the Class of 1980 provided no such relief for their male classmates and therefore received little support. When men did endeavor to pull the women along with them, they often found themselves not meeting performance standards. This no-win situation caused resentment among the men towards the women, and harboring such resentment, few men saw any reason for helping the women do what everyone (except the upperclassmen) said the women could do on their own.[10]

Most of the women did succeed in BCT, but largely because the Academy overlooked their poor performance. Wilson and Gillman's survey of those who finished the summer revealed an increase in the women's confidence in their ability to survive at the Academy. If BCT was not as hard on the women as it was on the men, it was still harder than anything the women had experienced before. More likely to have been editor of the high school newspaper than captain of the football team, female cadets reported finding the physical and combat training of BCT much more demanding than they had expected.

Their male classmates, however, were not impressed. Most reported that BCT had not lived up to their expectations and was no more physically or mentally demanding than high school football practice:

> The male initiates, on the other hand, felt the physical and mental challenges of BCT were either easier or no different from what they had expected. The worth of the cadet status for the males had not been increased by the discomforts of BCT as much as for the females. The males' perception that BCT was easier led to a less established inner sense of identity and less pride in being a cadet.[11]

Wilson and Gillman went on to conclude that the few experiences actually shared by both male and female cadets served to diminish rather than increase the attachment of males to the Academy and to their class, particularly to their female classmates. Though shared experiences do serve to bond men together when "the major social value of a military society is a warrior image, particularly a masculine warrior image," at the Air Force Academy "a new social value of an androgynous warrior was pressed upon the members of the institution." The sharing of experience by men and women in order to mold androgynous warriors would necessarily have made the women more masculine and the men more feminine, had not the men resisted this loathsome imposition on their inner self. Instead of growing closer through shared experiences, male and female cadets grew farther apart.[12]

The Air Force Academy never acknowledged that the poor performance of female cadets was the chief complaint of male cadets against the first women at the Academy. Indeed, the Academy repeatedly insisted that standards had not been changed and that the negative shift in male attitudes was attributable to sexist upbringing and "negative emotional support" from faculty and upperclassmen. Nine years after the first females struggled through BCT, however, Dr. DeFleur, ever the accommodator, recommended that physical events in which women did not do well should be abandoned altogether.[13]

The start of the academic year did little to improve the acceptance of women at the Academy. One mistake was corrected. At the beginning of the second semester, the Academy decided to integrate all 40 squadrons of the Cadet Wing to eliminate the advantage of all-male squadrons in intramural sports competition. Intramural sports are a chief means of developing squadron *esprit de corps,* but the women's participation in intramurals handicapped the integrated squadrons in competition with all-male squadrons, causing male cadets to view female cadets as liabilities on the playing field. The integration of all squadrons placed all squadrons on an equal footing, but it hardly improved the males' opinions of female physical abilities. Seven years later the Air Force Academy discontinued integrated intramurals altogether after discovering that neither male nor female cadets thought integrated sports conducive to the assimilation of women.

Many other mistakes in planning went uncorrected, most of which were intended to shield women from harassment. Harassment did not end with BCT, but the policy of "positive motivation" continued to protect the women from the worst of it. Though some women wailed to the Academy and to the press of sexual harassment in the form of insults and openly expressed opposition to integration, nothing the women knew came close to the fierce and sometimes physical harassment doolies traditionally faced throughout the doolie year. Insults had always been the daily fare of doolies, and every one of them had felt at one time or another that he had been singled out for persecution by some sadistic upperclassman who, for unknown reasons, had it in for him. Pain was the price one paid to belong. Positive motivation spared the women such pain, but it also barred their acceptance into the Cadet Wing.

Also inhibiting the assimilation of women was the mistake of concentrating the women on the sixth floor of Vandenberg Hall, instead of quartering them with their assigned squadrons. During the school year, doolies put themselves in harm's way anytime they entered their squadron area. They were often rousted out of bed at an early hour by screaming upperclassmen, who dogged them constantly during the five or ten minutes they had to prepare for the morning run. After the run, they had to hurry again to shower and dress before the breakfast formation. Harassment was a frequent interruption of these meager moments of personal time. Just as frequently, doolies were grabbed to form a detail to clean the day rooms, police the squadron area, or turn in laundry. Other details in the evening took them away from their studies.

The women, however, were spared such interruptions. Upperclassmen could not roust the women out of bed and send them scurrying up and down the halls in their skivvies, as they did the men. After a squadron run, the women returned immediately to Vandenberg Hall, escaping further harassment as well as the morning details. Out of sight and out of mind, they were usually left alone in the evenings also. This arrangement produced the Academy's intended result of making life easier for the women, but it also produced the unintended result of making their male classmates resent them more. Absent from so much of daily squadron life and shielded from even mild harassment, the women never earned membership in their assigned squadrons.

The task of supervising the women in their own area was left to the fifteen female Air Training Officers, but none of the male cadets trusted the ATOs to do the job properly. To upperclassmen, the ATOs were not and had never been cadets and therefore had no business training doolies. The Air Force Academy had used surrogate upper-classmen before in its first few years of existence, but those surro-gates had all attended other military academies and had acted in the absence of upperclassmen, not in their stead. The female ATOs, however, had no valid academy experience and were entrusted with duties which could have been performed by male upperclassmen, as indeed was the case at the other service academies. To upperclass-men, the ATOs were unnecessary and unwelcomed intruders, whose poor performance in training only proved that they did not belong at the Academy.

Through the year, the ATO program caused more harm than good. Male cadets generally believed that the ATOs treated female cadets more like little sisters than doolies. Though the ATOs struggled to present the impression that they were as hard if not harder on the women as the men were on the men, most male cadets suspected that it was all an act which ended when the women returned to their sanctuary on the sixth floor. Indeed, Stiehm recounts one incident in which an ATO and a female cadet deliberately staged a dressing down, complete with tears, to impress male onlookers.[14]

If the ATOs themselves were not easier on the women, they did ensure that male cadets were. When ATO's were present, male cadets took care not to treat female cadets too roughly, and having ATOs present whenever possible was standard policy. For their own protec-tion, the cadets began including their squadron's Air Officer Com-manding (AOC), an Air Force officer who shepherds cadets through the Academy, in any event in which women were likely to be sub-jected to harassment or physical stress. Fostering an atmosphere of distrust was another effect of the ATO program. The very existence of the ATOs was proof that the Academy did not trust the Cadet Wing with the task of initiating the first female cadets. The cadets in return distrusted the women, both ATOs and cadets, and altered the way they conducted training to protect themselves. Where once it was common for upperclassmen to take the time to work one-on-one with a doolie on some point of performance, group instruction became more and more the only way to train, as male cadets were uneasy dealing with female cadets in private.

One unacknowledged good the program did accomplish, from the Academy's standpoint, was to lower male expectations of female ability prior to the arrival of the Class of 1980, so that when the first female cadets performed somewhat better than the ATOs, upper-classmen were forced to admit that the female cadets had performed better than expected. This of course did not improve the ATOs reputation among male or female cadets. Upperclassmen still de-spised them for upsurping their authority within the Cadet Wing, and female doolies would have preferred to do without them. The Acad-emy discontinued the program a year earlier than planned, pretend-ing for the press that the program had met its objectives ahead of schedule and was therefore "successfully concluded." Dr. DeFleur was more candid. "There was an abortive attempt to bring female officers to the Academy as ATO's," she wrote, eight years later, "but this turned out to be an untenable role and both male and female cadets rejected them."[15]

Some inequities of integration were unintentional, such as the different experience of male and female doolies during meals in the cadet dining facility. Every infamous "square meal" in Mitchell Hall was an ordeal for doolies. After reciting the menu and serving the upperclassmen at their table, doolies sat stiffly on the edge of their seats, chin up, back straight, eyes always level. When they were not responding to questions or requests from upperclassmen, they ate in a mechanical manner, conveying food to their mouths via right angles above their plates. The amount of food a doolie was able to ingest under these conditions was governed by the whim of upperclassmen and reflected the doolie's performance of the required tasks. Doolies who performed poorly went hungry.

Most female doolies escaped this torture by joining one or more of the Academy's many women's athletic teams. With more slots on teams than female cadets to fill them, women who had never partici-pated in organized sports in their life became instant collegiate athletes. One advantage of their official status as athletes was that it frequently took them away from the pressures of the Academy for weekend games or meets. Another advantage was that it permitted them to sit with their teammates at separate "jock ramps" during meals, where harassment was forbidden and even doolies ate like normal people. The women therefore rarely went hungry. Many developed what the cadets called "CHD," or Colorado Hip Disease, caused by the high caloric value of meals in Mitchell Hall. (West Point cadets noticed a similar phenomenon and dubbed it "Hudson hips.") At least one member of the women's cross-country team was also enrolled in the Academy's weight-control program.

Other persistent inequities were deliberate results of the Academy's policy of special protection. Those charged with making integration work were not about to risk their careers by taking seriously their own boasts about equal treatment and able young women. To protect themselves from failure, they devised a number of ways to uphold the appearance of success and keep the female attrition rate down. Double standards on physical tests hid the poor comparison of female performance to male performance. Higher ratings for women from AOCs made up for the lower scores they received in peer ratings and military studies, thus ensuring that women ranked as high as men on the Military Order of Merit. Even in academics, where they hardly needed it, women were allowed special protection. In class, women as a group performed nearly as well as the men, slightly less well in the hard sciences. Even so, male doolies with low grades were boarded for dismissal and sent home, while female doolies with lower grades remained.

The Academy's reluctance to let women leave contrasted sharply with its lack of concern for retaining men, a source of much regret later. The custom had always been that doolies who wanted to leave were sent packing with little effort on the Academy's part to change their minds. Traditionally, the very act of quitting revealed a weakness of character that confirmed that a doolie did not belong at the academy. For males, this custom continued, but for females indicating a desire to leave, the Academy required mandatory counselling by Academy officials intent upon persuading them to stay. One unprecedented exception allowed a female doolie who voluntarily left the Academy before the end of the first year to return the very next year as a sophomore. Such exceptions made men of the Class of 1980 feel that the Academy considered it more important for a woman to graduate than for a man.

Individual acts of insensitivity further irritated the Cadet Wing. According to Judith Stiehm, male cadets were offended by the inclusion of females in the squadron selected to march in President Carter's inaugural parade. The squadron that won the honor during the first semester was originally all-male, but by the time of the inauguration, the squadron had been integrated. When a number of cadets were cut from the squadron to reduce the size of the formation, not one of the new female squadron members was among them. Knowing that the new Commander-in-Chief was keen on women in the military, Academy officials then arranged the formation to place women conspicuously in the front rank and on the left flank, contrary to military custom and Air Force regulations which require the shortest in a formation to march in the rear.

The unkindest cut of all, in the eyes of male cadets, was the Academy's dissemblance on the subject of integration. Many inequities would have been more tolerable if the Academy had been willing to admit that they existed. Instead, the Academy consistently denied the existence of double standards or serious difficulties with integration. The official line was that, yes, a few cadets were having a hard time accepting the change, but they would adapt, and, no, the essential nature of the Academy was not in the least affected by the integration of women. Changes to Academy standards were "insignificant." The Academy needed only a little more time to modify a few outdated or misconceived policies and everthing would work out fine. And of course, the women performed superbly.

The worst offender was the Academy superintendent himself, Lieutenant General James R. Allen. Stiehm quotes upperclassmen saying, "The guys at West Point and Annapolis *knew* their 'supe' didn't want girls, but our 'supe' didn't back us."[16] Allen repeatedly annoyed cadets with public proclamations of the Academy's success. In October, cadets were shown an Air Force promotional film that included scenes of female cadets in BCT, with Allen saying, "The women are undergoing the same training program that the men are undergoing . . . with some insignificant changes." Later in the year,

Allen told *The Denver Post,* "The only problem we've had is finding that there's no way to hold the women back to equal effort . . . . They've been working harder than the men all summer."[17] Male cadets were outraged by what they read as both a lie and an insult. Attempts by the Academy cadre to explain away the affront did little good. What was needed was a confession and an apology from the superintendent himself.

Cadets were limited in the ways they could express their disgust at the Academy's hypocrisy. The December issue of *The Dodo,* a cadets-only humor serial, mocked the policy of positive motivation and the public relations line that "all is well." A later issue poked fun at the Academy's crack-down on squadron nicknames that eliminated the sexually suggestive and otherwise unsuitable. A few cynical comments appeared elsewhere in cadet publications, but the official reading of the Wing's pulse was taken by Dr. DeFleur, whose surveys showed male approval of integration dropping throughout the academic year. By spring, the attitudes of male cadets, particularly upperclassmen, were "significantly less positive" toward women at the Academy and in combat and significantly more traditional toward women in general.[18]

Some male cadets, however, did grow to like having women around. By the end of the first year, there was one wedding, one engagement, and an unknown number of romances, many of which were violations of the rule forbidding fraternization between doolies and upperclassmen. Some cadets avoided discovery by exchanging letters through the mail or, in one case, communicating by two-way radio. Others were less careful. Seven percent of the Commandant's Disciplinary Boards dealt with fraternization, and 17 frat offenders were on conduct-probation.

The first female cadet to leave the Academy for pregnancy was apparently not the victim of a ramp-side romance, however. She probably entered the Academy pregnant, for, according to Stiehm, she planned to have the baby while on leave during spring break and to return to the Academy afterward. Six days before the cadet would have started leave, she went swimming, acted in a school play, and ran several miles. Her condition was discovered when she was admitted to the hospital later the same day. This remarkable story was reported only in *The Denver Post,* which, giving none of the details, noted only that the Academy had officially admitted to experiencing what the paper called an "inevitable first."[19]

As a rule, the nation's media ate up everything the Academy fed it and regurgitated nothing but hurrahs for both the bastion-breaching women and the breached academy. The serious press was committed to heralding a feminist triumph. The not-so-serious press was infatuated with delightfully boyish coeds in their spiffy little uniforms. Both saw everything about the first year of integration through rose-colored glasses provided by the Academy. "So Far, So Good," said *US News & World Report's* headline. The story beneath it quoted a female air cadet testifying, without contradiction, that male cadets were finally growing warm to the idea of women at school.[20] It wasn't true, but everyone who wanted to believe it did.

At least one article did report that integration had been less than satisfactory at the Air Force Academy. *Science News* called it "a rough start" and linked the high rate of male attrition to the presence of women.[21] Wilson and Gillman were right. Basic Cadet Training failed to foster sufficient pride and a strong sense of belonging among many male doolies, and the rest of the year only made things worse by undermining the cadets' respect for both the Academy and the Air Force. The result was that when things got tough many male doolies saw little reason to stay.

Ironically, because the Academy never openly admitted its mistakes, the shame of high attrition rates, the blame for the failure of the women to assimilate, and the fault for much of the difficulty with integration fell upon those men who stayed to graduate. For not "going along with the program" in the beginning, the Class of 1980 never quite earned the full confidence of the Academy staff. Eighty's Ladies were branded a troubled class, to be used later by Academy cadre as a negative example for succeeding classes not to follow. Don't be like the Class of '80, they counselled, it's got problems.

By its own narrow measure, the Academy's plan for integration was a success. The Academy got what it wanted: the percentage of women to finish the first year was the highest of any Defense academy. The Academy's success, however, was the Air Force's loss. The women who finally graduated with the Class of 1980 did not make up for the loss of men. The Air Force got far fewer pilots, navigators, missilemen, science officers, and administrators for the increased trouble and expense of educating the Class of 1980.[22]

But the real losers were the men of the first integrated class. All of the men who entered the Academy in the summer of 1976 were cheated out of much of the pride they might have felt in their status as air cadets. Those who finished the first year were betrayed by some of the very officers who talked to them of honor and integrity. Those who finally graduated were so burned by the bungling of integration that it is hardly likely they share with earlier classes the same fondness for and devotion to the Air Force Academy. At least one graduate of the Class of 1980 was so embittered by the experience that he applied for and received, upon graduation, a service-transfer to the United States Army.

NOTES ON CHAPTER IV

1. *The Moon's a Balloon* (New York: G.P. Putnam's Sons, 1972), p. 64.

2. Office of Institutional Research, "Women in the Classes 1980-1990: The First Decade" (Colorado Springs, Colo.: U.S. Air Force Academy, September 1986.) The Air Force Academy Class of 1986 was the only other class where male attrition exceeded female attrition, 35.9 percent to 32.1 percent. It was also the only other Academy class where the female rate was below 40 percent. The only classes with male rates above 40 percent were 1980 and 1982, with 44.4 and 42.3 percent respectively.

3. Judith Hicks Stiehm, *Bring Me Men and Women: Mandated Change at the U.S. Air Force Academy* (Berkeley, Calif.: University of California Press, 1981), p. 99.

4. At the time, only five percent of Air Force officers were women, but expecting a higher rate of attrition among female cadets and an increased requirement for women officers in the future, the Air Force decided that 11 percent of the Class of 1980 would be female.

5. Lois B. DeFleur, Dickie Harris, and Christine Mattley, "Career, Marriage and Family Orientations of Future Air Force Officers," p. 20. DeFleur and William Marshak, "Changing Attitudes Toward Women's Roles and Women in the Military at the U.S. Air Force Academy," p. 13.

6. Lois B. DeFleur, Frank Woods, Dick Harris, David Gillman, and William Marshak, *Four Years of Sex Integration at the United States Air Force Academy: Problems and Issues* (Colorado Springs, Colo.: U.S. Air Force Academy, August 1985), p. 168.

7. One might extend this analysis to the entire experience at the Academy. BCT would be the rite of separation, four years of education and training would serve as the rite of transition, and the rite of incorporation would be the commissioning of new Air Force second lieutenants.

8. Lois B. DeFleur, David Gillman, and William Marshak, "The Development of Military Professionalism Among Male and Female Air Force Academy Cadets," p. 168. Upon entry, cadets were given physical aptitude tests. Males averaged 11 pullups. Females averaged 24.1 seconds of the "flexed arm hang."

9. Lois B. DeFleur, David Gillman, and William Marshak, "Sex Integration of the U.S. Air Force Academy: Changing Roles for Women," *Armed Forces and Society,* August 1978, p. 615.

10. David Gillman and William Marshak, "The Integration of Women into a Male Initiation Rite: A Case Study of the USAF Academy," p. 16.

11. Gillman and Marshak, p. 15.

12. Gillman and Marshak, pp. 18, 23.

13. *Four Years of Sex Integration at the United States Air Force Academy: Problems and Issues,* p. 168.

14. Stiehm, p. 264.

15. *Four Years of Sex Integration at the United States Air Force Academy: Problems and Issues,* p. 167.

16. Stiehm, p. 83.

17. Quoted by Stiehm, pp. 257–259. In a 1988 interview, Allen said integration "went very well" and cited as proof the praise the Air Force Academy received from Congress, the press, and the Carter Administration. He insisted that male and female cadets were held to the same standards, which were merely "applied differently."

18. Lois B. DeFleur and William Marshak, "Changing Attitudes Towards Women's Roles and Women in the Military at the U.S. Air Force Academy," p. 13.

19. "Air Force Academy Has Inevitable First—Pregnant Cadet Quits," *The Denver Post,* 11 March 1977, p. 3.

20. "So Far, So Good: A Report Card on Coeducational Military Academies," *US News & World Report,* 11 July 1977, p. 30.

21. "Female Cadets: a rough start," *Science News,* 15 September 1979, p. 182.

22. With an actual male attrition rate of 44.4 percent, the Class of 1980 graduated 798 men and 97 women, for a total of 895. If the male attrition rate had been 35 percent, the average rate of previous classes, the Class of 1980 would have graduated 933 men alone. If the number of women had stayed the same, the graduating strength would have been 1030.

CHAPTER V

The Last Class with Balls

*Your mission remains fixed, determined, inviolable—it is to
win our wars. Everthing else in your professional career is but
corollary to this vital dedication. All other public purposes
. . . will find others for their accomplishment; but you are the
ones who are trained to fight; yours is the profession of arms.*

GENERAL DOUGLAS A. MACARTHUR TO THE
WEST POINT GRADUATING CLASS OF 1962.

THE U.S. MILITARY ACADEMY at West Point and the U.S. Naval
Academy at Annapolis avoided some of the early mistakes made by
the U.S. Air Force Academy, but after the first year of integration
none of the academies could resist pressure for greater accommodation of women. In a very short time, the academies were converted
from "bastions of male chauvinism" to institutions officially dedicated to the feminist principles of equality and androgyny. Those
principles were pushed upon the men at the academies with little
success. Though opposition to integration outside the academies was
routed and scattered, inside the conquered and occupied academies
opposition went underground.

One difference in the first year of integration at West Point and
Annapolis was that male cadets and midshipmen believed academy
officials were opposed to integration. They knew that some academy
officials had opposed integration before the congressional mandate,

and those who supported integration somehow managed to avoid offending the cadets and midshipmen with exaggerated public pronouncements of integration's success. West Point and Annapolis intended to make as few adjustments as possible to accommodate women and adopted a policy of equal treatment, in contrast to the Air Force Academy's policy of special protection.

This is not to say that the first women at Annapolis or West Point experienced the same torture that men traditionally endured. A survey of male and female midshipmen at Annapolis showed that less than 5 percent of both sexes thought female plebes were treated the same as male plebes. Almost two-thirds of the male midshipmen said upperclassmen showed favoritism toward women. Three-quarters said women received favoritism from physical education intructors (a third of the women agreed), and half said company officers, academic instructors, and executive department officials showed favoritism toward women. Naturally, most of the women thought men received favoritism, especially from upperclassmen. Certainly some upperclassmen deliberately harassed the women more than men with the intention of making them quit the academy. Most, however, found it difficult not to be gentlemen. "It's tough to discipline a soldier when she blinks her baby-blue eyes or slips you a dimple," explained an Army colonel at West Point.[1]

Women performed less well academically and suffered higher rates of attrition than did men at West Point and Annapolis. At Annapolis, the first year's attrition rate for women was 22.2 percent, twice the rate for men. At West Point, the first year's attrition rate for women was 28.6 percent, compared to 23.8 percent for men.

Despite the disparity between the attrition rates of men and women, the first year of integration seemed a success to many observers. Proponents of integration were relieved that the women's attrition rates were not higher. The Carter Administration publicly praised the Air Force for its "success" and kept criticism of the Army and Navy quiet to avoid giving the impression that integration had failed. To many critics of integration, the results of the first year were a psychological defeat. Underestimating both the kind of women admitted in the first year and the academies' willingness to accommodate them, many old soldiers and sailors had expected most if not all of the "ladies" to wither like roses in the desert. When that didn't happen, and life at the academies seemed to go on as before, some gave up and joined supporters in proclaiming integration's success, while others retired in silence, privately bemoaning the brave new world.

Of course, nothing short of mutiny among male cadets and mid-shipmen would have qualified the first year of integration as a certain failure. The question answered by the experience of the first year of integration was not whether integrated academies would succeed or fail, but how the presence of women would change the academies. Male students at all of the academies registered overwhelming disapproval of the changes. Surveys of midshipmen at Annapolis showed that 81 percent of upperclassmen and 74 percent of plebes still opposed integration. The survey also showed a slight shift toward a less traditional view of women in society among male midshipmen, but the report of the survey warned "the more the situation touched these men personally, the less likely they were as a group to endorse equal opportunity for women."[2]

The most common complaint heard from male cadets and mid-shipmen was that the integration of women had lowered the aca-demies' physical standards. Physically, the women simply could not keep up. The dropout rate on morning runs during West Point's "Beast Barracks" was 23 percent for women and less than 3 percent for men. In the seventh week of training, 26.3 percent of female cadets reported for physical "reconditioning" instead of the morning run, compared to 5.6 percent of men. Women reported for sick call an average of 6.8 times per female cadet, compared to the male average of 1.7 times. They suffered more than ten times as many stress fractures as men. Attrition during the first summer was 16 percent for women, 9.7 percent for men. Even after a year of regular physical training, West Point women in the first integrated class suffered five times as many injuries as men during field training. The following year, the injury rate for women in field training was 14 times the rate for men.[3]

Even when the women were healthy, they could not perform to male standards. On their first timed two-mile run, 85 percent of the female plebes at West Point received a score of D or lower according to the male standard. When 61 percent failed a complete physical test, compared to 4.8 percent of male plebes, separate standards were devised for the women. Similar adjustments were made to other standards. At Annapolis, a 2-foot stepping stool was added to an indoor obstacle course to enable women to surmount an 8-foot wall. At West Point, women carried M-16 rifles for rifle-runs and bayonet drills, while men continued to carry much heavier M-14s. On parade, West Point women were initially allowed to brace the M-14 on their knee when drawing back the bolt for inspection. Later, the bolt springs were shortened to reduce tension, making the bolt easier to draw.

Like the Air Force Academy, West Point and Annapolis also made allowance for some differences between the sexes that were not based on physiological differences, as the law required. Women were thought to require more privacy than men and so were issued shower curtains though men were not, and of course none of the women had their heads shaved. Likewise, the substitution of classes in karate and self-defense (and "interpretive dancing" at the Coast Guard Academy) for classes in boxing and wrestling had more to do with what the academies thought becoming of women, than what physical risks the sports presented to them. It didn't seem to matter that the purpose of training men to box and wrestle was to develop physical courage and aggressiveness, neither of which was achieved by most of the alternatives offered to women.

These differences were not missed by the male cadets and midshipmen. In her book *Mixed Company,* Helen Rogan explains how men at West Point felt:

> The separate grading scale on the obstacle course and the three-mile run meant that a female cadet could get a low score and pass, while a male who got the same score had to go to summer school to make up—and this in an institution that was making so much triumphant noise about equality. . . . Furthermore, since the women learned neither to box nor to wrestle, and their close-quarters training emphasized self-defense, they never had bloody noses. The men were outraged, since deep down they knew war was about bloody noses.[4]

To combat the "misconception" among male cadets that separate standards meant lower standards, the academies tried to point out that standards for men had not changed since the admission of women. Later, they developed the doctrine of "equivalent training," which held that physical training was intended to elicit from each cadet "equal effort rather than equal accomplishment."[5] Since women tried too hard to meet male standards when so required and were often frustrated by their failure, "dual standards" were said to be necessary to challenge them to attainable levels of performance.

Male cadets saw little difference between dual standards and double standards, a term never used by academy officials. They overwhelmingly rejected the doctrine of equivalent training as another strained attempt to accommodate women. No such doctrine had existed prior to the arrival of women, and it applied only to physical requirements and only to differences between the sexes. Short males were still expected to meet the same standards as tall males. Effort only mattered if you were female. Otherwise it was performance that counted.

Some requirements still embarrassed and frustrated women despite double standards. In those cases, it was easier to eliminate the requirement than to manipulate the standards. One such requirement was West Point's Enduro run. The Enduro run was a timed event requiring a cadet to run 2.5 miles wearing combat boots and a helmet and carrying a rucksack, rifle, canteen, and poncho. Coming near the end of summer training for third-class cadets, the run was the last event a cadet was required to complete successfully to be awarded the Recondo patch.

Since the run was viewed as essentially a combat task and women were not being trained for combat, West Point cadre debated over whether to devise a double standard for the Enduro run or simply excuse female cadets from the requirement. For the Class of 1980, they decided that women would participate in the event but their performance would not be used to determine who received the Recondo patch. Only 42 percent of the women completed the run on time, but 73 percent were awarded the Recondo patch. Eighty-nine percent of the men passed the run, but only 75 percent received the patch. Naturally, the men were not happy with the devaluation of a once coveted award.

The next year, the Academy sought to avoid the outrage of male cadets by requiring female cadets to complete the Enduro run to the same standards as the men in order to receive the Recondo patch. Forty-two percent of the women of the Class of 1981 passed the Enduro run, but only 32 percent qualified for and were awarded the Recondo patch. Ninety-seven percent of the men passed the run, and 82 percent received the patch.

In the third year of integration, the Academy changed its mind again, this time to spare female cadets the stigma of failure by eliminating the Enduro run from the training program altogether, for both men and women. The final official report on integration at West Point hailed this as a good example of "the Academy's attempt to normalize physical requirements."[6] Dual for double, normalize for lower—anything could be fixed to accommodate women if only a suitable euphemism could be found to veil the attempt.

The doctrine of equivalent training was bound to undermine the importance of physical activity at the academies. It held that men (but not women) were required to perform pullups, not because pullups were of any value in themselves, but because the academy wanted the men to exert themselves physically—it wanted to see them sweat. Sooner or later, cadets would have asked why they should sweat over something that was not itself important.

Before the doctrine's effect could be fully felt, however, officials were already asserting the preeminence of academics over all else at the academies. Defenders of integration insisted that nothing had changed. "Academics have never taken a backseat to military education at the Academy and certainly never should," wrote Rear Admiral William P. Lawrence, superintendent at Annapolis.[7] But critics like James Webb, a 1968 Naval Academy graduate later to become Reagan's second Secretary of the Navy, charged that making men combat leaders had always been the academies' central concern until the admission of women relegated that purpose to the periphery. In 1979, Webb wrote, "Havard and Georgetown and a plethora of other institutions can turn out technicians and intellectuals *en masse;* only the service academies have been able to turn out combat leaders *en masse,* and they have ceased doing so."[8]

Perhaps ironically, the new emphasis on academics coincided with the liberalization of the academic curriculum. To cadets, this meant more electives, more courses in the humanities and social sciences, fewer courses in military science, fewer required courses in the hard sciences, and academic majors in fields other than engineering. At all three Defense academies, it also meant the end of the Order of Merit, the age-old practice of ranking each class by academic record. "We want to recognize that each individual has his own academic profile," explained West Point's second superintendent after integration, Lieutenant General Andrew Jackson Goodpaster. "It is no longer possible to reach a high level of competence across the board... I do not want to stereotype or categorize a man according to a single number. Everyone has more dimensions than that."[9]

Liberalization was a boon for women, who usually performed less well in the hard sciences than the men, but it was not initiated merely to accommodate their presence. The trend began after World War II, proceeding with stops or starts for thirty years with each change of superintendents.[10] The admission of women, however, accelerated the process precipitously by freeing the hands of the superintendents to make whatever changes they desired. Changes made to accommodate women first diminished the respect of academy officials for the established way, which had protected the academies for more than a century from the vandalism of petty reforms that each new chief made so that he could leave his mark on the place. Thus unbound by respect for the way the academies had always been, each superintendent felt free to make his academy what he wanted it to be, without regard for traditions older than his great grandfather.

Goodpaster had replaced Lieutenant General Sidney B. Berry as West Point superintendent after the first year of integration, ostensibly to restore integrity to the Academy's educational program after the 1976 cheating scandal. Berry had accepted the task of integration with soldierly stoicism. "We have our orders, and it is our responsibility to implement them to the best of our ability," he told the academy's alumni in 1976.[11] Nevertheless, much of the criticism of

West Point's handling of integration from within the Carter Pentagon was directed at Berry, who had openly opposed integration prior to the congressional mandate.

Goodpaster was another kind of soldier. Second in his class at West Point in 1939, with two masters degrees and a doctorate from Princeton University, he had retired as a four-star general in 1974 after serving as Supreme Allied Commander in Europe. He returned to active duty with one less star to assume the superintendency in 1977. To some, he was a scholarly intellectual in the mold of Maxwell Taylor, an ideal choice to lead the Academy through coming changes. To male cadets at West Point, he was the kill-joy dean of the movie *Animal House.*

Goodpaster initiated the most sweeping reforms in West Point's history, many of which had little to do with academics. To West Point alumnus James Salter, writing for *Life* magazine, it was "a ruthless pruning of outmoded traditions."[12] There were fewer parades and formations. Gym shoes replaced combat boots on morning runs, and rifle runs were much less frequent. Plebes were sent home for Christmas and were no longer required to recite a litany of useless trivia about the Academy before being allowed to eat their fill at mealtime. Breakfast was made optional for upperclassmen. Shouting in plebes' faces was replaced with "eyeball to eyeball instructing in a firm voice." Mental pressure at the Academy should be academic, not abusive or demeaning, explained Goodpaster.

Academy officials passed many of these reforms off as fallout from the 1976 cheating scandal, in which 94 third-class cadets were expelled and 44 resigned after a cadet honor board found them guilty of cheating on a take-home engineering examination. The scandal prompted a thorough review of the cadet honor code, which critics said was unrealistically rigid. Changes were made to the code, and those who were forced out were allowed an opportunity to re-enter. Still, the breadth of reforms instituted by Goodpastor far exceeded the expectations of many at the Academy. Even critics of the Academy's harsh discipline thought the Academy was over-reacting. Cadet Timothy Ringgold, a central figure in the scandal who had filed suit in U.S. District Court to get the honor code ruled unconstitutional, told *The New York Times* in 1978, "The Academy may have gone overboard on easing military discipline."[13]

The same thing was happening at the other academies. At the Air Force Academy, the doctrine of positive motivation was extended to apply to all cadets, not just women. At the Naval Academy, traditional forms of harassment were losing their sanction among the officer staff. Many were outlawed entirely. Plebes no longer "braced up" anytime they entered Bancroft Hall, nor reported to upperclassmen for "come-arounds," nor ran off demerits during extra duty, nor even sat at attention during meals.

The common denominator among the academies was the presence of women. Some reforms were intended specifically to improve the performance of female cadets. Peer ratings, a reliable means of gauging the respect a cadet or midshipman had earned among his peers, were discontinued at the Naval Academy when the Academy saw that women consistently received lower ratings than men. Without peer ratings, the selection of midshipmen for leadership positions within the Brigade of Midshipmen depended entirely upon the evaluation of the officer cadre and was thus susceptible to manipulation by the Academy to advance women. Many male midshipmen felt that women needed only "good grades and a modicum of professionalism," in Webb's words, to make rank at the Academy. One middie told Webb, "The Academy has used a lot of pressure to establish women as stripers. Women are groomed from plebe year. The scary thing is that it's creating the presumption that women can command troops."

Other reforms were the result of a growing feminine sensibility among academy officials. Female cadets and midshipmen had shown little sympathy for the practice of hazing and even less understanding of its purpose. To the women, hazing was either a deliberate attempt to drive them from the academy or a childish and unnecessary display of malicious *machismo*. As upperclassmen, the women never indulged in the more severe forms of hazing. As plebes, they sometimes tearily reported incidents of relatively mild harassment to the academy cadre. Webb tells of one such incident in which a senior at Annapolis ordered a female plebe to eat with oversized utensils as punishment for poor table manners. The woman cried to her room-mate, the roommate complained to her company commander, and her company commander reprimanded the senior for harassing the woman. At West Point, two third-class cadets, a man and a woman, resigned after the woman was goaded by her classmates into biting the head off a live chicken. They made their resignations public during a press conference at which they denounced the sexist nature of hazing at the Academy.

Actually, biting the head off a chicken was a routine event during survival training at West Point. After demonstrating any of the various ways to decapitate a chicken, the instructor, usually a non-commissioned officer, would offer a bird to the class. In the absence of volunteers, the class often pushed forward the most squeamish among them to do the deed. In this particular case, the woman claimed that she was selected because her classmates disapproved of her romantic relationship with the cadet who later joined her in resigning.

To the press, such an event was sensational, and when accompanied with charges of official toleration for sexist harassment, it was scandalous. "West Point Concedes Some Hazing Tactics Have Become 'Sexist,'" read the headlines. An interview with Superintendent Goodpaster relieved anyone's doubts about the Academy's official line. Goodpaster denounced such "sophomoric antics" as no longer appropriate for Academy cadets, saying "the time for foolishness over the matter of women at West Point is long past."[14] It seems he would have preferred male cadets to act more like women.

For the academies to side so regularly with plebes against upperclassmen was a serious blow to the fourth class system. "The whole place has been pulled down to the level of the women," a midshipman told Webb. "And look what it's done to this place. The word came down not to shout at plebes anymore. Treat them with courtesy, they said."

It was bad enough when the academy cadres began interfering in what were traditionally student affairs. It was worse when uninitiated outsiders began second-guessing the decisions of duly appointed student committees. In 1978, a federal judge in Brooklyn issued an injunction to stop the expulsion of a West Point senior accused of fraternization with a female plebe and lying. The following year, the Secretary of the Army Clifford L. Alexander intervened on behalf of a sophomore also charged with fraternization and lying. Upon the recommendation of a cadet honor committee, Goodpaster had ordered the cadet dismissed, but Alexander countermanded the order and had the cadet reinstated, an unprecedented act which incensed the Corps of Cadets, as well as many officers at the Academy.[15]

Like hazing, fraternization was an issue over which male cadets and the rest of the world seemed hopelessly at odds. A minority of men considered any social contact between male and female cadets fraternization. Many more thought romantic relationships between members of the same company or squad inappropriate. Most supported a conservative interpretation of the official policy, which defined fraternization as social or romantic contact between upperclassmen and plebes and between cadets or midshipmen and members of the academy staff.

Female cadets and midshipmen were decidedly more liberal on the issue than the men. More than a third of West Point women favored relaxation of the ban on fraternization, while almost none favored tighter restrictions. Those who favored the status quo did not consider fraternization a serious offense. Male cadets complained that women often failed to fully support the ban by neglecting to enforce it.

Women had much more to gain from relaxing the ban on fraternization than men. With a male to female ratio of better than 9 to 1, many more women than men could expect to start both a career and a family upon graduation. Half of the women graduating with the first integrated class at West Point were married within a year or two of graduation, the great majority to other Academy graduates. At the Air Force Academy, 90 percent of the women of the Class of 1980 had been romantically involved with someone at the Academy (officer, cadet, or civilian) during their four years there. Of course, some women did not have to stay the full four years to find a man. Of the first 25 women to drop out of the Naval Academy Class of 1980, 20 married former midshipmen.

The academies gradually accepted the view that social relations between the sexes were another proof of integration's success. In the absence of general acceptance among male cadets, a handful of Love's devoted converts could comfort the alienated women and tip the balance of male attitudes in the desired direction. Marriage had always been desirable for career officers, and everyone assumed that it would have the same stabilizing effect on the women as it had on the men. Romance in the ranks was thus seen as a healthy social development, and academy officials seemed not to mind when pictures of tearful female cadets embracing male cadets at graduation began appearing in the newspapers and magazines.

The academies were looking on the bright side. As everyone knew, unhealthy social developments were impossible to prevent as long as men and women lived in close quarters. The best the academies could do was to keep them quiet. The number of times a cadet walked into his room to find his roommate in bed with another cadet cannot be counted. But between 1977 and 1981, the Naval Academy punished 29 midshipmen of both sexes for sexual misconduct. The worst offense was committed by five men and one woman who videotaped themselves having intercourse in Bancroft Hall, while a crowd of middies cheered from outside the window. A 1984 study at the Air Force Academy found an "exceptionally high rate of pregnancy among women cadets" and widespread concern for what the cadets derisively called "the USAFA dating game."[16]

Originally, all of the academies dismissed women for becoming pregnant. West Point and Annapolis also dismissed men for causing a pregnancy. The Air Force Academy, however, as early as November 1977, changed its policy to allow a pregnant female to take a leave of absence, have the baby, and then return as a cadet in good standing. Subsequent recommendations by the Air Force Academy staff have shown the same willingness to do anything but discourage sexual promiscuity. One report recommended the following: a liberal dorm-room visitation policy for both sexes to stop cadets from "sneaking around"; mandatory courses in human sexuality; assertiveness training which must "clearly address 'date rape' from both the male and female perspective"; an assault and rape hotline; and widespread dissemination of information on hospital and clinic services and the availability of "contraception, rape management and counselling, and sex education." Such information "must be common, firsthand knowledge to *every* cadet. . . . There is no way we can oversaturate this information." [17] (Original emphasis.)

What such recommendations do not address is the effect of fraternization and sexual promiscuity on the cadets' respect for the academies. "All summer we were lectured about the high standards we were expected to meet," one midshipman told Webb. "Our squad leaders talked about honor, performance, and accountability. Then before you knew it, they were going after the women plebes, sneaking some of them away on weekends." When the academies were unable or unwilling to deal effectively with such violations, the cadets turned cynical. Sometimes it seemed as if only the male cadets were willing to defend their academy's honor by prosecuting other male cadets.

But aside from the problems of fraternization and sexual immorality, the integration of women had a much more general effect on the social nature of the academies. A new factor had entered the equation. A force more powerful than the call of duty, the pride of honor, or the bonds of comradeship so completely reversed the polarity of social relationships at the academies that even when men contained themselves they could not rest indifferent to its presence. Wrote Salter:

> There were women in the barracks. There were cadets with beautiful, boyish hair, like that of a shipmate on a cruise. It was an appeal that touched fantasies—on a clear autumn morning or in the winter dusk, the image of a tender cheek beneath a military cap, the trace of a smile, the womanly figure in rough clothes. . . . [18]

The men were charmed. They could never see the women as just cadets, and they could never treat the women just as they treated other men. Men who remained critical of women in general could not be so critical of individual women they had come to know. The women were just too hard to hate. Some men could bluster threats and insults from behind or from a distance, but when they came face to face with the enemy, they quailed out of natural affection and decency. If they were sticklers for equal treatment and especially careful of themselves, the men could succeed in bringing pressure to bear on a female plebe, but not without careful scrutiny of their own feelings and actions, and they were never sure if they had been too tough or too easy.

The academies were also charmed. They were no longer the strange and cold conclaves of unsentimental militarism, where young men first learned the pain of separation, where love was delivered in sealed envelopes at distant intervals, where alienation made plebes on leave feel like strangers at home, where cadets could prepare for lives of sacrificial hardship and deprivation, where they could learn leadership and gain confidence without the fearful disruption of suddenly running into someone with whom they were falling in or out of love.

Women brought the world into the academies, the world with all its mystery, romance, jealousy, and pain, with all its delights of gazing at feminine forms from afar, of flirting, of fumbling in a private darkness. Women were not just one part of the world hitherto excluded, as black males had once been excluded; women were the world itself, they were what life was all about. In comparison, the ancient military glory of the academies seemed parochial and quaint, and the traditions that attended that glory seemed purposeless and anachronistic. Their virtue and distinction was gone. They would never again mean as much to those who went there. Never again would a graduate's last conscious thoughts be of "the Corps, and the Corps, and the Corps."[19]

"The plebe experience, in particular, was not modified in the slightest because of women and remains as intensive today as during my time as a plebe 30 years ago," wrote Admiral William P. Lawrence, Superintendent of the Naval Academy, responding in 1980 to James Webb's charges to the contrary.[20] It was the standard, official response: nothing of consequence had changed, the women were doing everything the men were doing, and they were doing it as well or better than the men.

Still, those embarrassing attrition rates had to be explained. Attrition rates for women at graduation exceeded rates for men for all classes at all of the Defense academies, except for the Air Force Academy classes of 1980 and 1986. Just why more women quit than men no one at the academies confessed to knowing. Surveys of those who quit revealed little, as women gave the same answers as men. Some suggested that maybe the academies were recruiting the wrong kind of women, or maybe women came to the academies without an accurate expectation of what life would be like there. West Point proposed to seek new sources of qualified women and advise female candidates to expect the worst.

The only other possible answer given by academy officials was that the lack of acceptance by the men drove the women out, and if that were the case, "then strong negative sanctions must be enforced to discourage this from happening."[21] Sanctions included punishment for cadets (and officers) who voiced opposition to integration or whose words or actions revealed sexist tendencies.

But it wasn't enough for cadets to keep their opinions to themselves; they had to become believers. The academies became fervid propagandists for the very beliefs they had so staunchly resisted only a few years before. West Point's "Institutional Plans to Overcome Sexism" called for tighter controls on the gathering of data related to integration to "avoid research activities which have sexist consequences." The plans also proposed stopping publication of all documents and manuals containing such words as "gentlemen," "star man," and "he." Air Force Academy cadets were taught the supposed "male penalties of sexist behavior (heart attacks, repressed emotions)." At all of the academies, classes on sexism and sex-role socialization, taught solely from the feminist perspective, were mandatory. Feminism was the official orthodoxy, the measure of morality, and if cadets or cadre were not among the faithful, "then they're in the wrong line of work," warned General Goodpaster.[22]

The academies' campaigns to win the social conscience of male cadets and midshipmen showed a crusader's contempt for whatever beliefs the men already possessed. Like barefooted boys from the backwoods of Borneo, cadets were assumed to be ignorant, superstitious primitives. They were not allowed opinions, only "attitudes." If they did not support the doctrine of equivalent training, it was because they did not "understand" it. If they were "helped to understand the women's perspective," they would be more "open-minded" to "pluralistic beliefs" and therefore more accepting of integration. No study produced at any of the academies suggested that women needed to understand the male perspective, except, as mentioned earlier, on the subject of "date rape." Only the men needed to be open-minded because only the men needed to have their minds changed. If male cadets "myopically" shunned contact with female cadets and failed to respond to indoctrination, they were considered morally defective.

It was all for naught. The academies' efforts to indoctrinate male cadets in the evils of sexism only succeeded in suppressing overt expressions of opposition to integration. The absurdities of dual standards and equivalent training were too obvious, and the defense of such absurdities only incited resentment, disrespect, and cynicism, though of course cadets were smart enough to keep such things to themselves, at least most of the time. The Naval Academy Class of 1979 chose *Omni Vir* as its class motto. The West Point Class of 1979 proudly professed to be "the last class with balls." A picture in *The Howitzer,* West Point's yearbook, showed members of that class holding a variety of balls: footballs, baseballs, basketballs, balls for golf, tennis, and billiards.

Opposition to women at the academies did not end when the Class of 1979 graduated, as many who supported integration had predicted. When Kristine Holderied received her diploma as valedictorian of the Naval Academy Class of 1984, there was only polite applause from the crowd and the class, nothing to compare with the ovation Dean Miller received as salutatorian. The midshipmen knew and the spectators knew who should have been first in the class. That same year, surveys of cadets and midshipmen revealed widespread opposition to women at all of the academies. Administrators were shocked. Three out of five midshipmen said women were not accepted at Annapolis. A study group at the Air Force Academy, addressing the surprising finding, admitted that many preconceived notions of the success of integration were "inaccurate, unfounded, misguided and/or shallow."[23]

If any male cadets had hoped that by revealing their opposition their grievances might be redressed, they were surely disappointed. The grip of radical feminism on the academies was too strong. The response of the Air Force Academy was reflexive. It was only interested in redressing the grievances of female cadets, and the solution for that was even greater accommodation. "Are certain tasks in basic training or some of the athletic competitions really central to the primary goals of the Academy?" one Academy researcher asked. If not, then those tasks should be eliminated because "as males observe and 'learn' that young women do not perform well in some areas, there is an immediate decline in favorable orientations towards women." Other suggested solutions included admitting more women to the Academy, recruiting a "wider range of people" with fewer traditionally-minded males, and making "the entire Academy milieu" less military, "less discontinuous" from the rest of society.[24]

The results of an eight-month investigation by a committee of Academy faculty members came up with similar recommendations. The committee called for: a standing watchdog committee to meet monthly to discuss the status of integration; classes on "power relationships" and "powerless to power broker" to assist the "socio-sexual development" of "well-adjusted human beings"; the segregation of integrated intramural sports to prevent men from learning the wrong things; an expanded definition of combat which would include duties to which women are assigned; greater emphasis in the classroom on Air Force support functions and less emphasis on its mission to "fly and fight"; and a crackdown on "expressing 'anti-woman in the military' feelings." The committee's report stated, "The intent is for everyone to be aware of potential anti-woman feelings and to insure people do not *consciously or unconsciously* contribute to it."[25] (Emphasis added.)

None of these recommendations is likely to change things at the academies. Men and women remain essentially different both physically and psychologically. Though the academies prefer to look at similarities between the sexes, the purpose and nature of the academies only highlight sexual differences.

The biggest difference is that men and women do not come to the academies with the same interest in the military. Their higher attrition rates, both before and after graduation, and their consistently poorer performance in history and military science prove that women at the academies simply do not want to be soldiers or sailors or airmen as much as men do. Nothing can explain why women score lower in history except that history does not much interest them.

Nothing can explain why 60 to 70 percent of the women at West Point score below the mean in easy military subjects like map reading, military heritage, and tactics, except that they do not much want to be soldiers.

Surveyed after graduation, many male West Point graduates said the Academy should have required more courses in military history; none of the women made the same recommendation. Because the academies now teach less military history than they did before integration, officers learn most of what they know about the history of their profession from what they have read on their own. Because few young girls grow up reading *Landmark Classics* about D-Day or the Battle of the Bulge, and few develop such an interest later, female academy graduates are likely to be dangerously ignorant of the history, art, science, and psychology of war.

When the first of these women graduated from West Point, 20 percent of them had decided already that they would leave the Army after serving their initial commitment. Only 2 percent of their male classmates also planned to resign. Six years later, the attrition ratios for the women and men of the classes of 1980 were 40 percent to 25 percent for West Point graduates, 23 percent to 11 percent for Air Force Academy graduates, and 32 percent to 24 percent for Annapolis graduates who had entered the Navy. Of the first women to enter the Marine Corps from Annapolis, more than half (57 percent) had left the Corps by 1986. Only 27 percent of similar males had also left.

Academy officials have minimized the import of these statistics, which they say may not reflect significant trends. The Class of 1980 was not typical of other classes because they bore the scars of blazing the trail. Fewer men were eligible to resign in 1986 because of extended service commitments for flight training and other assignments. Lastly, the first women were encouraged to expect too much from the services and may have become disappointed as the years passed when they found their opportunities limited by combat exclusion laws.

There is, however, ample evidence to show that differences between male and female graduates will persist in all classes of all academies for the foreseeable future. Interviews and surveys of West

Point graduates found that women rarely listed any positive aspect of their West Point education except physical training; they were more likely to say that there should be less infantry training at West Point; they were more likely to have had more trouble as cadets dealing with noncommissioned officers; and they were more tolerant of unethical behavior at the Academy, preferring to live and let live in most cases.

Of life in the Army, the women were less tolerant of adverse conditions like long hours and unpleasant surroundings and much more concerned about the imposition of work on their personal lives. When asked to talk about their jobs, three-quarters of the male graduates interviewed mentioned positive aspects of their jobs as sources of satisfaction, but less than a quarter of the women mentioned any source of satisfaction on the job. Men were most likely to list "successfully completing a job, seeing a job done right, completing a mission, doing a good job" as their primary source of job satisfaction. Women were much less likely to agree. The number one reason for job satisfaction among women was "working with troops, helping troops."

Asked about sources of "life satisfaction," most men and women cited marriage and family as primary sources, but in varying degrees: 26 percent for men and 18 percent for women. Men were next most likely to say their job (12.5 percent). Women were next most likely to say travel, sports, and their job (all 7 percent). Thirty-five percent of women officers felt negative about their Army careers, while only 2 percent felt positive.

Marriage, which had a stabilizing effect on male officers, had the opposite effect on female graduates of the academy. Of those who were married within five years of graduation, almost all married other officers. Problems with joint-domicile assignments, conflicting work schedules, and family priorities made married life much more difficult for the women than for the men. "Problems of spouses' commitment seem to be much more severe among females than males," the surveys found. One third of the husbands of female graduates of West Point did not want their wives to stay in the Army.[26]

Not surprisingly, children also increase dissatisfaction with military life among women. One 1981 graduate of the Air Force Academy had five children within five years of graduation. Generally, the families of female graduates had fewer children than the families of male graduates, but even one child is enough to radically alter a woman's desires for the future. Many resign. Others accept less demanding assignments in order to be with their families. "When Rebecca was born, I knew I could never go back to sea," said Liz Belzer, now Liz Semcken, a 1980 graduate of the Naval Academy. According to her male classmates, Belzer was one of the women who were "groomed for stripes" by the Academy staff. After graduation, she married a Navy pilot of the Class of 1978 and became a surface warfare officer because officers at the Academy had convinced her that that was the place to be to excel in the Navy. She left the Navy in 1987. "To the world, being in the first class was probably the most significant thing I've done," she said in 1985. "But in my own life, there's no question—it's Rebecca."[27]

A report by the U.S. Military Academy on the post-graduation beliefs of male and female graduates recommended a more sophisticated joint-domicile assignment system to relieve the stress of family separation for "dual career couples," and greater career opportunities to prevent women from becoming discouraged with their careers. Some would add expanded military child-care to the list. The report contained an admission that was unremarkable for its truth but astounding for its frankness. The services rarely say things so plainly:

> All of these [suggested] changes are in the direction of accommodating the Army to the officer, rather than the other way around. Changes in the other direction, requiring accommodation by female officers, are likely to accentuate the negative aspects of an Army career and drive more women out.[28]

There are two kinds of cadets and midshipmen at today's federal service academies. One is male: aggressive, strong, daring, and destined for combat; the other is female: none of the above. Both are resigned to live with what they cannot change. The men accept women individually as women but reject them collectively as cadets. The women cannot assimilate into the corps of cadets because they cannot become men. They have stopped trying.

The thoroughly feminized academies continue to live by a double standard. Wherever necessary, allowance is made for the unsuppressed girlishness of female cadets. There was a time when uncontrollable fear was called cowardice by military men, but now "intellectual discipline" is more important at the academies than physical courage or discipline of any other sort. A female first-class midshipman can flatly refuse to complete a mandatory requirement for graduation because of her fear of a 34-foot jump into the water, a task simulating abandoning ship. One woman who did so was granted a waiver, allowed to graduate, and commissioned as an unrestricted line officer in the United States Navy.

The benefits of sexual integration of the service academies are few. "The place looks quieter," one observer has said. Others have spoken of an improvement in the quality of students. Today's cadets and midshipmen are cleaner, better behaved, and more refined than the brutes of yesteryear. "If there was one thing that was irrelevant to my preparation for combat it was refinement," Webb wrote. As Secretary of the Navy, Webb directed that Naval Academy graduates on orders to the Marine Corps will attend "Bulldog" training, formerly required only of Marine officers from other sources of commission. His concern was that Marine officers needed to develop a certain toughness they no longer develop at the Naval Academy.

There are women at the academies who, like Webb, wish the academies still prepared cadets and midshipmen for combat. They are ambitious women who are not happy with the combat exclusions. Though Congress took a different view when it integrated the academies, these women see little reason to keep them from combat when the services spend so much time and money on their education as officers. In 1981, when an admiral at the Naval Academy, speaking to an assembly of midshipmen, told a female middie why women were excluded from combat, the woman interjected, "Maybe women shouldn't be here at all!"[29] The mostly male assembly responded with vigorous and prolonged applause. The Class of 1979 was not the last class with balls after all.

NOTES ON CHAPTER V

1. "So Far, So Good: A Report Card on Coeducational Military Academies," *US News & World Report,* 11 July 1977, p. 26. West Point officials had been warned by female drill sergeants at Fort Knox, Kentucky, and Fort McClellan, Alabama, that female recruits often took advantage of male drill sergeants, who tended to treat them less roughly than they treated the men.

2. Kathleen P. Durning, *Women at the Naval Academy: The First Year of Integration* (San Diego, Calif.: Navy Personnel Research and Development Center, 1978), p. 20.

3. Department of Behavioral Sciences and Leadership, *Project Athena: Report on the Admission of Women to the U.S. Military Academy* (West Point, N.Y.: U.S. Military Academy, 1 June 1979) Volume I–IV.

4. Helen Rogan, *Mixed Company: Women in the Modern Army* (New York: G.P. Putnam's Sons, 1981.), p. 199.

5. Lieutenant General Sidney B. Berry, "Women Cadets at West Point," Address to the Defense Advisory Committee on Women in the Services, Washington, D.C., 16 November 1976.

6. *Project Athena,* Vol. IV, p. 48.

7. Rear Admiral William P. Lawrence, Letter published in *The Washingtonian,* January 1980.

8. James H. Webb, Jr., "Women Can't Fight," *The Washingtonian,* November 1979.

9. James Feron, "West Point '78 Closing Book on Cheating '76," *The New York Times,* 5 June 1978, p. D9. The General Order of Merit was not so sinister as it was made out to be. The last man to graduate in each class was honored as the "goat" at West Point, the "anchorman" at the Annapolis, and "Tail End Charlie" at the Air Force Academy. Tradition held that the last man received a dollar from each of his classmates. Famous goats include George A. Custer, George E. Pickett of "Pickett's charge," and one superintendent of the Academy.

10. See John P. Lovell's "Modernization and Growth of the Service Academies: Some Organizational Consequences," in *The Changing World of the American Military,* Franklin D. Margiotta, ed. (Boulder, Colo.: Westview, 1978). Lovell says that prior to World War II, the academies were essentially "military seminaries," run faithfully as they had been since founding, with knowledge of the fourth-class system passed from class to class. The growth of the military bureaucracy in America forced the academies to codify their policies, taking control of the class

system out of the cadets' hands and putting it into the hands of the academy administrators.

11. Rogan, p. 188. Rogan says that Berry almost resigned rather than accepting the mission of integrating West Point. In an interview, Berry said he might have mentioned resigning in an off-hand remark but he never seriously considered it.

12. James A. Salter, "It's Not the Old Point," *Life,* May 1980, p. 76. Salter is a 1945 graduate of West Point.

13. Feron, "West Point '78 Closing Book on Cheating '76."

14. James Feron, "West Point Concedes Some Hazing Tactics Have Been 'Sexist,' " *The New York Times,* 10 November 1979, p. 25.

15. In the first case, the Academy dropped the charges and allowed the cadet to graduate with his class to avoid a court ruling that might have had far-reaching effects on the cadet honor system. In the second case, Alexander had first requested that Goodpaster simply review the case before taking action. Goodpaster did so and concurred with the honor committee's recommendation for dismissal. Alexander then overruled Goodpaster's determination on the basis of an unstated "colateral issue." The cadet was reinstated with a lesser punishment.

16. Committee on the Integration of Women into the Cadet Wing, "Recommendations: Report on the Integration of Women into the Cadet Wing," U.S. Air Force Academy, July 1984, pp. 13-15. Oddly, after months of interviews and surveys, the committee produced no written findings, only 30 pages of recommendations.

17. Committee on the Integration of Women into the Cadet Wing, pp. 12–18, 27.

18. Salter, p. 76.

19. General Douglas A. MacArthur, "Duty, Honor, Country," Address to the Corps of Cadets of the United States Military Academy on 12 May 1962.

20. Lawrence, p. 18.

21. *Project Athena,* Vol. III, p. 12.

22. Feron, "West Point '78 Closing Book on Cheating '76."

23. Committee on the Integration of Women into the Cadet Wing, p. 1.

24. Lois B. DeFleur, Frank Woods, Dick Harris, David Gillman, and William Marshak, *Four Years of Sex Integration at the United States Air Force Academy: Problems & Issues* (Colorado Springs, Colo.: U.S. Air Force Academy, August 1985).

25. Committee on the Integration of Women into the Cadet Wing, p. 23. The committee also recommended making miniature Academy class rings unavailable to anyone but female cadets. For decades, "miniatures" have been given as engagement rings to fiancées and as special gifts to mothers. The committee deemed this a devalua-

tion of identical rings worn by female graduates, but the Academy rejected the recommendation.

26. Jerome Adams, *Project Proteus* (West Point, N.Y.: U.S. Military Academy, 1984), Vol. II, pp. 3-19 and 3-20.

27. Esther B. Fein, "The Choice: Women Officers Decide to Stay In or Leave," *The New York Times Magazine*, 5 May 1985, p. 45.

28. Adams, p. 3-38.

29. C. H. "Max" Freedman, "Navy Valedictorian and Feminism Stole Male Cadet's Award," *The New York Tribune*, 1 June 1984, p. 2B.

CHAPTER VI

Damn the Services, Full Speed Ahead

*The first quality of a soldier is the ability to support fatigue
and privations. . . . Poverty, privation, and misery are the
school of the good soldier.*

NAPOLEON BONAPARTE[1]

ON 18 AUGUST 1976, a detail of American soldiers was pruning a tree
in the Joint Security Area separating North and South Korea when
they were suddenly attacked by a truckload of axe-wielding North
Korean guards. Two American officers were killed. Nine other soldiers were wounded.

An appropriate response to the attack was hotly debated at all
levels. "There was no question in the minds of anybody in Korea that
we had decided to take limited military action," recalls Major General John K. Singlaub, then chief of staff of U.S. forces in Korea.
Neither was there any doubt that a military response, however limited, might be misinterpreted by the North. While the White House
weighed the risk of provocation with the necessity for some show of
force, United Nations forces in South Korea prepared for the worst.
Ground units assembled and moved forward into battle positions, and
air forces were called in from Alaska and Japan. On the night of
August 20, U.N. forces in Korea stood at DEFCON 1, with B-52s

winging their way toward the North Korean capital, fighters warming their engines on the runway, and helicopter gunships hovering above the border. "We had rounds up the spout and hands on the lanyards, and every weapon had a target," says Singlaub. For all that anyone in the ranks knew, they were going to war.

Early on the morning of August 21, American soldiers cut down the half-pruned tree and dismantled a few unoccupied shacks built by the North Koreans in the Joint Security Area. The timid response provoked no one, and the emergency soon passed, but not before U.S. Army commanders observed a disturbing reaction among their troops. As soon as it became clear that the alert was no ordinary training exercise, commanders throughout Korea were flooded with requests from female soldiers for transfers to the rear. War was more than these women had bargained for when they had joined the Army. Most fully expected to be evacuated in the event of hostilities, but when the question of evacuation was raised at higher headquarters, Singlaub nixed the idea immediately and ordered all soldiers to their posts.

Later, when the emergency was over, Singlaub learned that his order was not strictly obeyed. Many women had abandoned their posts near the border and headed south on their own. Some turned up later in units well to the rear. Others had reported for duty with dependent children in tow, since their arrangements for child-care did not cover the event of war. In some instances, male noncommissioned officers had left their posts temporarily to tend to the safety of their wives and girlfriends in other units.

The Korean emergency dramatized the growing concern among commanders in the field for the presence of women in the ranks. Four years after the marriage of the All-Volunteer Force to the Equal Rights Amendment, the honeymoon was over and the debilitating effects of integration had begun to show. Social and sexual relationships between male and female service members defied bans on fraternization between ranks. Marriages between service members were on the rise. Incidents of sexual assault soared. For the first time ever, commanders and supervisors throughout the services were confronting problems with sexual harassment, dating, pregnancy, single parenthood, in-service couples, and joint-domicile. Most had never served with women and were just beginning to wonder about the vastly different art of managing women. Their knowledge and experience as leaders of men were of little use.

In December 1976, the Army completed the first of several studies of the problems relating to integration. The report, entitled simply *Women in the Army,* drew much criticism from proponents of integration, for while it identified and explored most of the problems caused or aggravated by the presence of women in the ranks, it did not compare the advantages and disadvantages of women versus men. One whole chapter discussed problems caused by pregnancy among Army women, but there was no discussion of the disciplinary problems caused by men, though it was widely known that men presented much higher rates of indiscipline.

Worse than the report's omissions was the report's timing. Jimmy Carter had just defeated Gerald Ford in the race for the presidency, and no study, however valid, would have altered the president-elect's commitment to the feminist movement. "I am fully committed to equality between men and women in every area of government and in every aspect of life," declared candidate Carter in July 1976. As president, he recited the same oath of commitment to securing for women "every choice" and an "equal role" whenever the occasion and the women around him called for him to do so.

The Carter Administration vigorously supported any program that White House feminists thought would advance their cause, from special federal grants to schools that provided "non-sexist" education and girl's football teams, to programs under the Comprehensive Employment and Training Act (CETA) that trained and encouraged women to become plumbers and welders instead of secretaries or nurses. The President and First Lady took a very active role in pushing the states to ratify the stalled Equal Rights Amendment, so much so that Phyllis Schlafly accused the Carters of violating the constitutional doctrine of separation of powers by interfering in the ratification process. The Carters personally telephoned pro-ERA state legislative leaders to offer encouragement and sometimes to dangle federal funds as a lure for ratification. When these efforts failed and time ran out on the proposed amendment, Carter met monthly with pro-ERA leaders to plan strategy to win an extension.

Feminists could not have asked for a more loyal president, but they might have asked for a more effective one. Carter's biggest help to their cause was his personal program of affirmative action whereby he appointed women, usually ardent feminists, to high-level government positions. Of 2,110 political appointments handed out by the Carter Administration, 22 percent went to women, including 28 federal judges, 4 cabinet heads, 3 undersecretaries, 20 assistant secretaries, 5 heads of federal agencies, and 13 ambassadors. Heading up this network of federal feminists was Sarah Weddington, Special Assistant to the President for Women's Affairs, chairwoman of the Interdepartmental Task Force on Women, and publisher of a newsletter touting Administration achievements for women and of a network directory, *Your Guide to More Than 400 Top Women in the Federal Government.*

The Defense Department was by no means exempt from the infiltration of feminists. Those near the top in the Pentagon included: Kathleen Carpenter as Deputy Assistant Secretary of Defense for Equal Opportunity; Deanne Siemer as Defense Department General Counsel; Antonia Handler Chayes as Undersecretary of the Air Force for Manpower, Reserve Affairs, and Installations; Jill Wine Volner and Sara Elisabeth Lister as General Counsel of the Army; Mitzi M. Wertheim as Deputy Undersecretary of the Navy; Patricia A. Szervo as Deputy General Counsel of the Navy; and Mary M. Snavely-Dixon as Deputy Assistant Secretary of the Navy for Manpower. None of the above had ever served in the military. Most had no connection with the Defense Department before 1977. All were committed to expanding opportunities for military women even if it meant drafting women for combat.

Not all feminists in the Pentagon were women, however. Both Secretary of Defense Harold Brown and Secretary of the Army Clifford J. Alexander, Jr., distinguished themselves by expanding the prerogatives and privileges of military women. One week after taking office, Secretary Brown ordered an appraisal of women in the services. The task fell to another man much impressed with modern women, Navy Commander Richard W. Hunter. In the course of his study, Hunter consulted Martin Binkin and Shirley Bach, who were already at work on an independent study of the same issue. Binkin was a fellow at the Brookings Institution, a liberal think-tank in Washington, D.C., for which Hunter had worked in the early 1970s while on loan from the Navy. Bach was a lieutenant colonel on loan to Brookings from the Air Force. Their study, though unfinished, had piqued the interest of the new civilian chiefs in the Pentagon, as it was known already that the study would conclude that the services could make greater use of women.

Based largely upon the findings of Binkin and Bach, Hunter's report, entitled *Use of Women in the Military,* reduced the entire issue to a simple matter of cost and quality. High quality female recruits were less expensive to attract than high quality male recruits, wrote Hunter, and high quality female recruits were more desirable than low quality male recruits, so to save money and improve the quality of the enlisted force, the services should recruit more women and fewer men. Hunter figured the services could save $1 billion annually by 1982 by doubling the number of women in service. He considered valid only two factors which might limit the number of women the services could employ: women are physically weaker than men, and women are excluded from combat. All other arguments against employing more women were dismissed as "centered on emotionalism" or "supported by unsubstantiated generalities, or isolated examples."[2]

The Hunter study gave the Defense Department the green light for expanding the number of women in the services, but the study that laid the foundation for all future arguments in favor of women in the military was Martin Binkin and Shirley Bach's *Women and the Military,* published by the Brookings Institution later in 1977. Still widely cited today in support of integration, the Binkin and Bach study invalidated a crucial assumption of the Gates Commission regarding the supply of young males eligible for enlistment. Whereas the Gates Commission had counted on the population of enlistment-eligible men increasing through the 1970s, Binkin and Bach showed that that population had already begun a long decline which would continue into the 1990s. The post-World War II baby boomers were growing up and moving out of the ages of eligibility. If the AVF needed to attract one in eleven eligible males in 1977 to maintain a force of two million plus, by 1992 it would need to attract one in eight. On that fact alone, the study concluded that the AVF would be forced to make greater and greater use of women to sustain current levels of manning.[3]

Another important contribution of Binkin and Bach to the argument for expanding the use of women in the military concerned the issue of how many women could be absorbed by the services without degrading the services ability to accomplish their missions. Given that the military was becoming increasingly dependent upon technology and that the ratio of combat troops to support troops was shrinking, Binkin and Bach figured that women could fill more than 600,000 positions, almost a third of all military jobs, without degrading mission accomplishment. On the other hand, the statutory ban on women in combat and at sea and the number of women interested in military service made that level of participation unattainable. Binkin and Bach suggested 22 percent as a more realistic level.

Binkin and Bach also argued that women were cheaper to attract, more intelligent, and better behaved than most men. Female recruits scored higher on entrance tests, were more likely to have finished high school, and were more likely to have had some college. They were generally older and much less prone to disciplinary problems than men. All of which, argued Binkin and Bach, made them a better investment of defense dollars and better qualified for many of the more technical jobs in the modern military, in which brains were assumed to be more important than brawn.

Despite the study's definitive success, the Binkin and Bach study did have its faults. The authors wrongly assumed that the mental quality of female recruits would remain the same no matter how many women were recruited. Later studies would find that as the number of female recruits increased, their "quality" dropped precipitously. When the services were forced to equalize entrance standards for men and women, the advantages of recruiting women over men evaporated. Four years after publication of the Brookings study, women were still older, better behaved, and more likely to have high school diplomas, but test scores had evened out, and dramatically higher rates of attrition among low-quality women made men the better investment.

Naturally the study gave short shrift to all objections to integration. A single chapter handled the problems of attrition, pregnancy, menstruation, physical strength, fraternization, emotional and psychological differences, effects on group performance, and the military's prestige abroad. The study did not address the impact of single parents and in-service couples on the services. It did not substantiate the assumption that technology had alleviated the need for physical strength in the many jobs that women were supposed to fill. It ignored evidence that the greater aggressiveness of men is rooted in biology and not solely the product of socialization. It doubted whether women interfere with the process of male-bonding in groups, noting that terrorist groups enjoy intense camaraderie despite the active inclusion of female terrorists, a worthwhile observation only if the minds of Abu Nidal and G.I. Joe are more alike.

Most problems mentioned in the study were dismissed simply for lack of documented evidence that they actually existed. Again and again the authors confront the limitations of social science: "Virtually no information is available . . . evidence is far from conclusive . . . largely unknown . . . inadequately researched and poorly understood." An exclusive reliance upon the work of other sociologists led to absurd admissions of ignorance when common knowledge would have sufficed. "Precious little is known about the effects of combining men and women," the authors wrote. Such holes of knowledge did not prevent Binkin and Bach from drawing optimistic conclusions about the use of women by the services, however. Though Binkin now insists the study was meant to determine how many women the services *could* employ given the combat exclusion policies, not to recommend how many women the services *should* employ, most of those who used the study to buttress their agrument for expanding the use of women never made that distinction. The failure of the study to warn of potential problems allowed them to do so.

In the years following the publication of the Binkin and Bach study, the Carter Pentagon tried to "paper over," in the words of one critic, the holes of knowledge with tests and studies showing the apparent ability of women to perform all kinds of tasks without degrading unit performance.[4] The Army led the way in 1977 with two tests of women in combat support units in a field environment.

The first test, called MAX WAC, lasted only three days, hardly enough time to properly evaluate any unit for any purpose. The second test, called REF WAC 77, lasted only 10 days and employed 50 "observers" to evaluate the effects of integration during RE-FORGER operations in West Germany. A number of difficulties were observed during the test. First, 29 percent of the women assigned to units scheduled to participate in the test were excused from going to the field for "personal reasons," though only 15 percent of the men were likewise excused. Many of the women who did participate were not required to perform much of the physical labor of loading and unloading trucks and setting up and tearing down equipment. The women complained about the absence of shower facilities and disliked using field-expedient slit-trench latrines. Some refused to leave their tents at night for fear of the dark. Male co-workers resented doing the women's share of heavy lifting and dirty work, and most supervisors identified 18 support specialties as being too physically demanding for women. Still, the official bottom line of both MAX WAC and REF WAC was that no evidence had been found that the presence of women degraded the performance of units in the field.

Another test designed to support the Carter Administration's pre-determined policy of expansion was the Army's Female Artillery Study conducted in 1979. Thirteen handpicked female volunteers, all over 110 pounds, were given extensive physical conditioning and additional training and were then tested on their ability as gun crews to meet standard rates of fire for 105mm and 155mm howitzers. The study's conclusion, as summarized later by the Department of Defense, was that the women "showed the ability and aptitude to perform all the artillery assignments *given them.*"[5] (Emphasis added.) In other words, the women achieved the standard rates of fire with both weapons.

If achieving minimum standard rates of fire were all that gun crews are required to do, the Army's artillery study might have served a legitimate purpose. But gun crews are tested on their ability to do much more. One common task is called a "hipshoot." A battery on the move is suddenly ordered to stop and fire a few rounds down range. The crews must hurriedly emplace the gun, unload the ammunition, fire the mission, and pack it all back up. Speed is essential, and physical strength is a must for crews to be able to move a gun rapidly into action. The women were not required to emplace or move their guns, or even to unload their ammunition. They were tested only on their ability to adjust elevation and deflection by means of a handcrank, load a round into the breech, close the breech block, and pull the lanyard. The test was conducted under ideal conditions, with the women unbothered by the strain of combat or fatigue or simple boredom. Even so, only pairs of the tallest women were able to perform the test's most difficult task, loading the 95 pound projectile into the breech of the 155mm howitzer.

The artillery test's extremely limited scope guaranteed the women's success, thus enabling the Carter Pentagon to marvel at yet another demonstration of female ability. Its real purpose was to encourage the notion that women can fill combat roles as well as men, at a time when the Carter Administration was trying to persuade Congress to repeal the combat exclusion laws. With a cursory knowledge of artillery, however, a careful look at the test report will reveal that testing women on rate of fire alone is like putting women on a rifle range to prove that they can be infantrymen.

Armed with a battery of such studies defending the expanded use of women by the military, Secretary of Defense Harold Brown, in 1978, ordered the services to double the number of women in uniform to 200,000, 11 percent of the total force, by 1983. The following year, the goal was raised to 236,000 by 1984 and 265,500 by 1987. This meant 99,000 women for the Army, 53,700 women for the Navy, 9,600 for the Marine Corps, and 103,200 for the Air Force. The Air Force would have both the most women and the highest percentage of women: 18.7 percent.

The Air Force presented the least resistance to expansion. Only 10 percent of all Air Force personnel billets were closed to women under Section 8549, Title 10, United States Code, which prohibited Air Force women from flying combat missions. Far fewer jobs in the Air Force than in the other services involved physically demanding work, and most jobs presented a relatively pleasant work environment. Not surprisingly, the Air Force experienced the least difficulty attracting female recruits. From 1977 to 1980, the Air Force added 20,000 women to its rolls, a 50 percent increase. By 1981, women made up 11 percent of the Air Force's enlisted force and 9 percent of its officer corps.

Most advances for Air Force women under the Carter Administration affected only female officers. Since Air Force women were barred by Title 10 from flying combat missions, the Air Force in the past had not trained women for flight duty because doing so was not considered cost-effective. The Carter Administration quickly persuaded the Air Force to change its mind and begin training female officers as both pilots and navigators. The Air Force also began assigning women to all-female Titan II missile crews and was under pressure to open Minuteman crews to women also.

In the rush for expansion, the Air Force disappointed the Carter Administration only once. In 1979, it closed the security specialist field to women after a three-year test program showed exceptionally high rates of attrition among female security specialists. Less than half of the women admitted to the field remained after one year, compared to 71 percent of the men. The closing brought howls of protest from Administration feminists, but the field remained closed to women until it was reopened by the Reagan Administration in 1982.

Unlike the Air Force, the Navy presented formidable obstacles to increasing its number of women. From 1972 to 1977, the number of enlisted women in the Navy had already more than tripled. Since Section 6015, Title 10, U.S.C., barred Navy women from serving aboard ship, Navy women were concentrated in the Navy's "rotational base" of shore billets. For Navy men, this meant fewer billets open to them when they returned from sea duty and therefore more time at sea. The Carter Administration's planned increases of women in the Navy would only make things worse, except that the Administration's solution was to open sea duty to women.

The Navy had experimented with women aboard ship before. In 1972, the unconventional Admiral Elmo R. Zumwalt, then Chief of Naval Operations and author of the notorious "Z-grams" which ordered sweeping changes in the Navy way of doing things, welcomed the new day dawning for Navy women with the promulgation of Z-gram 116, which opened the door for Navy women to a host of opportunities in the civil engineers' corps, the chaplains' corps,

Naval ROTC, and command of shore units. Z-gram 116 also initiated an experiment involving 424 Navy men and 53 thoroughly screened volunteer Navy women aboard the hospital ship USS *Sanctuary*. Publicly, the Navy claimed the test went very well, but press reports and the Navy's own official report told another story. The ship was only underway for 42 days of the 400-day test, and while the women performed most of their shipboard duties well, they often required the assistance of men to perform physically demanding tasks. Romantic relationships developed between crew members. Several women became pregnant and public displays of affection, or PDA, became demoralizingly common. "The situation was becoming serious and was definitely detrimental to the good order and discipline of the ship's company," reported the ship's commanding officer. A ban on PDA was announced and the ship's company assumed a more professional appearance, which satisfied the commanding officer that all was well.[6]

The Navy itself, however, was not so easily satisfied. Many senior officers, including the director of the Women's Naval Reserve, doubted whether the *Sanctuary* experiment proved anything, except that putting women on ships would cause problems that ships' captains could very well do without. Besides the effect of integration on a ship's crew, a commanding officer had to consider the reaction of Navy wives, many of whom were opposed to women on ships for obvious reasons. It seems that everyone, except Martin Binkin and Shirley Bach, knew enough about men and women to predict what would happen on a sunny cruise through the South Pacific. The *Sanctuary* spent most of its time in port as a floating dispensary before being quietly decommissioned in 1975.

To the Carter Administration, however, no inconvenience was too great to limit the opportunities of a handful of women. In 1977, to make room for more women, the Department of the Navy sponsored an amendment to Title 10 to permit women to serve permanently aboard non-combat ships such as hospital, transport, and supply ships, and temporarily (up to six months) aboard all other ships. In 1978, the amendment was added to the Defense Authorization Act of 1979, which was still under consideration by Congress when a federal district court in Washington, D.C., threatened to preempt the democratic process by judicial fiat. In the case of *Owens v. Brown,* a group of Navy women seeking assignment aboard ship had brought a class-action suit against the Department of Defense. In July 1978, Judge John J. Sirica of Watergate fame ruled that the statutory ban on women at sea wrongly denied women their right of equal protection under the 14th Amendment of the U.S. Constitution. The ban, wrote Sirica, "tends to suggest a statutory purpose more related to the traditional way of thinking than to the demands of military prepared- ness." His assumption was that traditional ways of thinking about the sexes never justified democratic legislation and were always uncon- stitutional. Sirica dismissed all practical reasons for wanting to keep women off ships, saying, "whatever problems might arise from integrating shipboard crews are matters that can be dealt with through appropriate training and planning." He stopped short of ordering the Navy to integrate its ships, however, noting imminent approval of pending legislation.

In the summer of 1978, Admiral James L. Holloway, Chief of Naval Operations, issued a call for Navy women to volunteer for sea duty, and in November, the first female sailors were piped aboard the repair ship USS *Vulcan.* Within a year, the *Vulcan* was christened the "Love Boat" by the press, when three pregnant sailors were returned to shore before the ship put to sea.

The Navy's female enlisted strength increased 53 percent from 1977 to 1980. Most Navy women remained concentrated in shore billets, as very few women volunteered for sea duty. Later, when the call for volunteers failed to provide as many enlisted women as the Navy had hoped, the Navy was forced to send women to sea involun- tarily. The problem of sea/shore rotation improved very little, and many young women who had enlisted without any expectation of going to sea soon found themselves retching over the railing, a long way from land.

In the same three years, the Marine Corps' female enlisted strength almost doubled, though the number of women Marines remained relatively small. Since a greater proportion of Marines were consid- ered combat troops and Marine units went to sea aboard combat ships, the Marine Corps was better able to defend its desire to keep down the total number of women Marines. By 1980, women still made up only 3.7 percent of enlisted Marines and 2.7 percent of Marine officers, the lowest levels of participation among the services.

The Army, however, was in some ways more vulnerable to expansion efforts than even the Air Force. No law excluded Army women from combat. When the exclusion laws were written in 1948, the authors could easily keep Navy and Air Force women out of combat by keeping them off ships and aircraft, but they could not decide where to draw the line in the Army's case. That task was left to the Secretary of the Army, with the understanding that Congress intended combat to be off-limits to women. For twenty-five years, the Army had lived by the understanding, making sure women were kept as far as possible from the battlefield.

The influx of women into the Army in the early 1970s forced women into many jobs and units previously closed to them, so that by the time of the Korean emergency in 1976, women were already serving in units which operated regularly within the wartime "combat zone," defined by Army doctrine as anywhere forward of the rear boundary of a corps in the field. When the Carter Administration proposed further increases in the number of women in its ranks, Army leaders balked and raised concerns about combat. Soon calls came from Carter appointees in the Department of the Army and the Defense Department for a new definition of the word *combat*. War had changed, said many who had never known it. There were no more friendly lines or enemy lines, they said. The modern battlefield was much too fluid to base exclusion policies upon unit boundaries.

Did this mean that the Army needed a broader, more inclusive definition of combat? Did it mean that units which once operated safely behind friendly lines should be closed to women because they were now endangered by the fluid nature of modern combat? On the contrary, the same civilians who argued that war was now more fluid also argued that war was now more technical, more tidy, and thus more suitable for women. Modern war meant pushing buttons in an air-conditioned bunker. Since decades of typing operation orders had proven that women could push buttons as well as men, the new definition of combat, said the activists, must allow for expanding the role of women in the Army.

To make room for more women, the definition of combat was

narrowed drastically. It no longer made any reference to boundaries or distances. It had nothing to do with where one was in relation to the enemy or how close one was to the fighting. The single definitive factor of the new term combat was an individual's or unit's primary duty or mission. If a soldier's primary duty was to engage the enemy with lethal force, he was considered a combat soldier. If a unit's primary mission was to engage the enemy with lethal force, the unit was designated a combat unit. As for women, the Army's new combat exclusion policy stated: "Women will be excluded from units and positions which have as their primary mission or function crewing or operating direct or indirect fire weapons."[7] This policy allowed the Army to make the widest possible use of women while still pretending that Congressional intent and the will of the American people protected women from combat.

The only issue remaining concerned the size of the unit to be included in the designation combat. Infantry and armored divisions could have been considered combat units, as indeed they always had been, because they exist only to maneuver against and engage the enemy. On the other hand, the Army's 1978 Evaluation of Women in the Army (EWITA), interested primarily in expanding opportunities for women, defined a unit as any element company-size or smaller and recommended opening to women thousands of positions in maneuver battalions and closing to women only 20 of the Army's 350 military occupation specialties (MOS). If this had been the policy of the Army in World War II, women would have landed by parachute in Normandy on the night of June 5, 1944. The Army, however, settled on the policy of barring women from all combat units battalion-sized and smaller.

Having solved the problem of combat, the Army continued to expand its recruitment and use of women. During the Carter years, the Army's female enlisted strength increased 40 percent. At the end of 1980, the Army was burdened with more women than any other service, with 61,351 enlisted women and 7,609 female officers. Army enlisted women were 9.1 percent of the Army's total enlisted strength. Because many Army women were still concentrated in traditional career fields, some support units were as much as 40 percent female.

Opportunities for women in the Army were wide open. Only 4 percent of enlisted specialties were closed to women by the new combat exclusion policy, and there were no limits on the number of women who could enlist for any of the remaining 96 percent. Potential female recruits were, in fact, encouraged to select nontraditional career fields, and many were steered into a nontraditional MOS when they were told that their first choice of MOS was not available. The deactivation of the Women's Army Corps in 1978 and the administrative integration of women into the Regular Army brought Army women as close as they have ever come toward absolute equality with Army men. Even basic training was integrated at the squad level.

The Army would have added even more women if it had had greater success recruiting them. It was the only service to fail to meet the Carter Administration's recruitment quotas for women. High quality women were not as easy to attract as Binkin and Bach had predicted, so the Army twice lowered its standards for female recruits. In 1979, after Army General Counsel Jill Wine Volner settled out of court a suit brought by the American Civil Liberties Union, the Army equalized entrance standards for men and women, dropping the requirement for women to have a high school diploma. It also made available to women special enlistment options like the buddy plan which allowed three or four recruits to enlist together for the same training and the same assignment.

Recruiting barely improved. The Army fell short of its quotas for women in three consecutive years from 1978 to 1980. It achieved 91.5 percent of its 1979 goal and 95 percent of its 1980 goal, once it began accepting women without high school diplomas. Later, the Army realized that its attempts to channel women into nontraditional jobs had turned many women away. Women of both high and low quality preferred more traditional jobs, jobs with no heavy lifting, no dirty fingernails, no days in the motor pool, no rainy nights in the field. Of all the services, the Army had more to offer of just such discomforts, and the recruiter's pitch could only hide so much.

Nevertheless, the ease with which the Army, unhindered by Title 10, was able to make room for women was an inspiration to women's rights activists in the Pentagon. As early as February 1978, the

Defense Department formulated a proposal to repeal the statutory combat exclusions. In May 1979, Deanne Siemer, the Defense Department's General Counsel, sent a letter to Thomas "Tip" O'Neill, the Speaker of the House of Representatives, offering to submit legislation in draft for amending Title 10 to repeal the combat exclusions if such legislation did not originate in the House. The offer was later backed by the recommendation of Defense Secretary Harold Brown.

Much had changed since 1967, when Congress and the Department of Defense had assured each other that combat was still for men only and that greater opportunities for women in the services would not mean sending women into combat. Still, the ultimate goal of feminists in the Pentagon, putting women in the infantry, was too much for Congress and the general public to accept, even in 1979. The request for repeal was draped with assurances that women would not be placed in direct combat roles, that repeal would not necessitate putting women anywhere, and that the suggested amendments to Title 10 would only grant the secretaries of the Navy and the Air Force the same authority already vested in the secretary of the Army. Each service secretary would have the authority to "set policy for, monitor, and review the assignment of women within their respective departments."

During hearings held by the military personnel subcommittee of the House Armed Services Committee in November 1979, Defense Department representatives made the usual remarks about how national security, of course, always comes first. After testifying that the need to provide greater "flexibility and efficiency" in the use of military manpower was the primary reason for requesting repeal, they then mentioned that repeal was also a matter of fairness and equality.

The weight of testimony, and the persons giving it, suggests that things were actually the other way around. Anytime the Defense Department finds itself allied with the American Civil Liberties Union, something is likely to be wrong. The ACLU was represented by Diana A. Steele. The Defense Department was represented by Kathleen Carpenter, Deputy Assistant Secretary of Defense for Equal Opportunity, who had earned a reputation as "the unguided missile" of the Defense Department. Carpenter once told author George Gilder in an interview that "while men have greater upper-body strength, women have greater midsection strength," so the services were restructuring jobs to make better use of the female midsection, thereby "enriching the work experience for all."[8] Others who testified for repeal included Antonia Handler Chayes as Undersecretary of the Air Force, Sally K. Richardson as chairwoman of the Defense Advisory Committee on Women in the Services, and Jeanne Holm, recently retired from the Air Force.

Such a line-up is not likely to make the strongest case for military necessity in any debate. Flexibility and efficiency received only brief mention before being abandoned in favor of an endless refrain of careerism and equality. "There must be policy changes to assure women that they can satisfy personal career goals and ambitions by moving up the ladder to senior management," argued Chayes. "What we achieve by barring women from combat roles is an obstacle to career advancement."[9]

On the other side of the issue was a hastily organized battery of witnesses, called to arms with just four days notice by Phyllis Schlafly's Eagle Forum, the organization that had led the STOP ERA movement to many recent victories. Besides Schlafly herself and retired Army Brigadier General Andrew J. Gatsis, Eagle Forum's military advisor, witnesses against repeal of the combat exclusions included General William C. Westmoreland, former Army Chief of Staff; Admiral Jeremiah A. Denton Jr., a former prisoner of war in Vietnam and future senator from Alabama; Dr. Harold M. Voth, a psychiatrist with the Menniger Foundation and an admiral in the Naval Reserve; and Brigadier General Elizabeth P. Hoisington, a former director of the Women's Army Corps.

Dismissing the supposed need for flexible and efficient use of manpower as a fig leaf for the feminist agenda, the witnesses against repeal concentrated their fire on the issue of women in combat. They repeatedly referred in their testimony to James Webb's article "Women Can't Fight," which had just appeared in the November issue of *The Washingtonian* magazine. Of the Carter Administration's efforts to prove that women could fight, General Hoisington said, "Studies cannot duplicate the realism of battle in a Vietnam jungle, in the cold Korean hills, the trauma from killing or witnessing death and terrible wounds."[10] General Westmoreland and Admiral Denton attested to the misery and horror of war and captivity. Dr. Voth explained the physiological and psychological differences between men and women. Mrs. Schlafly targeted the politics behind the Defense Department's campaign for sexual equality. "What a way to run the armed forces!" she said. "We must be the laughing stock of the world."[11]

The subcommittee closed the book on the request for repeal and never reported the bill out of committee. The anti-repeal side had won, but they would not know how important their victory was until two years later.

Undaunted by defeat on one front, the Carter Administration tried again in January 1980 to radically expand the participation of all American women in the national defense. The coincidence of the takeover of the American embassy in Teheran and the Soviet invasion of Afghanistan caused the Carter Administration its first serious concern for the nation's security. In his 1980 State of the Union address, President Carter called for the resumption of the requirement for young men to register for selective service. When the request for registration went forward to Congress one week later, the proposed legislation included young women on an equal basis with young men. In defense of the request, Carter stated, "There is no distinction possible, on the basis of ability or performance, that would allow me to exclude women from an obligation to register. . . . My decision to register women is a recognition of the reality that both men and women are working members of our society."

Having just heard numerous witnesses denounce the Carter Administration's understanding of women and war, the House Armed Services Committee was not receptive to the Administration's request and did not include women in the bill reported out of committee. A motion made before the full House to include women in the bill was defeated by voice vote.

In the Senate, however, feminist activists pressured Senator Nancy Kassebaum of Kansas to sponsor an amendment to include women in the Senate version of the bill, but before the Senate could hold hearings on the bill, Schlafly's Eagle Forum had formed the Coalition

Against Drafting Women, consisting of prominent military, religious, and civic leaders, and had collected 200,000 signatures on "Don't Draft Women" petitions.[12]

The inclusion of women found more friends in the Senate but not enough. After hearings and debate, the Kassebaum amendment was defeated 51 to 40 in June 1980. Senators Sam Nunn, Jake Garn, Roger Jepsen, and John Warner had led the fight against inclusion. Among those who voted to register women were Senators John Glenn, Howard Metzenbaum, William Proxmire, and William Bradley. Senators Edward Kennedy, George McGovern, Frank Church, and Joseph Biden, though reliable supporters of feminist causes, did not vote.

Both the ACLU and the National Organization for Women had testified for requiring women to register. Both opposed registration and the draft on principle but regarded a men-only draft as a greater evil. The difference, they said, was between a law that was evenly unjust and one that was unevenly unjust. When a men-only registration law was enacted, the ACLU assembled sixteen draft-age males to file a class-action suit in federal court challenging the constitutionality of the law on the grounds that it violated the Due Process Clause of the Fifth Amendment by discriminating on the basis of sex. Not to be out-flanked, Eagle Forum assembled sixteen draft-age women, each with her own reasons for opposing a genderless draft, and petitioned the same court for the opportunity to present opposing arguments.

Then, to the surprise of all concerned, a federal district court in Philadelphia exhumed a ten-year-old unresolved suit involving two men who had challenged the constitutionality of the draft law in 1971, using the same argument of sex discrimination. The suit had been tabled by the court when the draft was discontinued in 1973 and had remained inactive until 1979, when it was brought up for routine dismissal in 1979. A further delay brought the suit new relevance when draft registration resumed in 1980. In July, the three-judge panel in Philadelphia, without hearing additional arguments, finally ruled in favor of the plaintiffs that the registration law unconstitutionally discriminated on the basis of sex. The case of *Rostker v. Goldberg* was then brought to the U.S. Supreme Court on appeal.

The defense of the men-only registration law before the Supreme Court was officially the responsibility of the Justice Department, which, under the Carter Administration, was less than enthusiastic about the task. *US News & World Report* noted that "some Justice Department officials hope the Supreme Court strikes down the draft-registration law that their agency is formally defending." The Justice Department's lame brief, filed the day before President Carter left office, used only the weakest of arguments in defense of the law. Defense of the law depended solely upon the brief of Eagle Forum's sixteen young women, filed by eminent constitutional lawyer Nathan Lewin as an *amicus curiae.*

NOW filed its own *amicus* brief calling the men-only draft law "blatant and harmful discrimination" against women. The NOW brief held nothing back, however implausible. Excluding women from the draft, NOW argued, deprives women of "politically maturing experiences," consigns women to a second-class status, increases "the incidence of rape and domestic violence," and "causes harm to women by increasing the prospect of violence in their daily lives."

The *amicus* of the Women's Equity Action League (WEAL) was less extreme. WEAL argued that true equality required the "equal division of societal obligations and duties," without which the gains women have made would be viewed as "magnanimous concessions to women's demands instead of as prerogatives justly due to equally productive members of society." WEAL added that the combat exclusion laws were also discriminatory and therefore unconstitutional, but since the original plaintiffs had not raised the issue of the combat exclusions the Court did not address it.

With the fate of all future generations of American women in the balance, the nation's media was conspicuously silent. Only *The Washington Post* seemed interested. Members of Congress showed greater concern. While the Court deliberated, they moved to fix the case by proposing legislation to withdraw jurisdiction from all federal courts over laws and regulations treating men and women differently with regard to military service. Congressman Billy Lee Evans introduced the Women's Draft Exemption Act in the House, and Senator Strom Thurmond, then chairman of the Senate Judiciary Committee, promised to introduce a similar Senate bill if necessary. A finding against the government might have inspired the first serious check of judicial power in the history of the Constitution.

In June 1981, the Supreme Court reversed the lower court's decision and ruled that the men-only registration law was constitutional. The majority opinion written by Justice William Rehnquist reasoned that men and women were "not similarly situated" because women were barred from combat by Title 10 of the U.S. Code. Rehnquist reasoned that because a draft exists for the purpose of raising combat troops, women could be constitutionally excluded from the registration law. A dissenting opinion filed by Justice Byron White, joined by Justice William Brennan, argued that men and women were similarly situated with regard to non-combat positions which would also have been filled by a draft. A second dissenting opinion filed by Justice Thurgood Marshall, also joined by Justice Brennan, argued that the Court had failed to separate the issue of registration from the issue of the draft and that there was no constitutional reason to exclude women from registration.[13]

To feminists, the ruling was "tragic" and "outrageous." The ACLU called it "a devastating loss for women's rights and civil rights generally." Eleanor Smeal, then president of NOW, said the Court had "taken away our voice of protest. We can't even say, 'Hell no, we won't go.' "

To Phyllis Schlafly and the unbeatable Eagle Forum, it was another brilliant victory, but one which, to their surprise, hinged upon their earlier victory against repeal of the combat exclusion laws. No one had expected that women would have been included necessarily in any future draft if the service secretaries had been granted the flexibility that the Carter Administration had requested. No one had guessed that the desire of a tiny minority of female officers to fill combat slots in peacetime would have made all women subject to compulsory military service and possibly combat duty in time of war.

NOTES ON CHAPTER VI

1. Napoleon's Maxim No. 58, quoted by Conrad H. Lanza, *Napoleon and Modern War* (Harrisburg, PA: Military Service Publishing Co., 1943) p. 78.

2. Office of the Assistant Secretary of Defense for Manpower, Reserve Affairs, and Logistics, *Use of Women in the Military* (Washington, D.C.: Department of Defense, May 1977). Binkin and Bach estimated saving as much as $6 billion annually.

3. Martin Binkin and Shirley Bach, *Women and the Military* (Washington, D.C.: The Brookings Institution, 1977).

4. Michael Levin, "Women as Soldiers: the Record So Far," *The Public Interest,* Special Edition, 21 August 1984, p. 32.

5. Office of the Assistant Secretary of Defense for Manpower, Reserve Affairs, and Logistics, *Background Review: Women in the Military* (Washington, D.C.: Department of Defense, 1981), p. 144.

6. Memorandum from the Commanding Officer, USS *Sanctuary,* to the Chief of Naval Operations, "Evaluation of Women Aboard the USS *Sanctuary,*" 19 November 1973, p. 13-2.

7. *Final Report: Evaluation of Women in the Army* (Ft. Ben. Harrison, Ind.: Department of the Army, 1978), p. 1-18.

8. George Gilder, "The Case Against Women in Combat," *The New York Times Magazine,* 28 January 1979.

9. Quoted by Seth Cropsey in "The Military Manpower Crisis: Women in Combat," *The Public Interest,* Fall 1980, p. 66.

10. Hearings before the Military Personnel Subcommittee of the House Armed Services Committee, 13–16 November 1979 and 11 February 1980, p. 232.

11. Hearings, p. 238.

12. The Coalition Against Drafting Women included, among others: Sen. Jesse Helms, Rep. Marjorie Holt, Rep. Richard Ichord, Marine Corps Gen. Lewis W. Walt, Army Lt. Gen. Daniel O. Graham, Army Maj. Gen. Henry Mohr, Army Maj. Gen. John K. Singlaub, Rabbi Herman N. Neuberger, Dr. Bob Billings, Dr. Gregg Dixon, Dr. Bill Pennell, the Rev. Jerry Falwell, and representatives of the National Council of Catholic Women, the American Security Council, the Conservative Caucus, Young Americans for Freedom, Family America, and the Moral Majority. All of the military men were retired.

13. Rostker v. Goldberg, 69 LEd 2d 478.

CHAPTER VII

DACOWITS 1, Army 0

Our Army is not a "corporation." Defending this nation is not
an "occupation." And being a soldier is not a "job." There is
no other business firm anywhere that has, as its foremost
objective, the requirement to fight and win the land battle.

COLONEL DANDRIDGE MALONE,
AN ARMY OF EXCELLENCE

IN EARLY NOVEMBER 1980, Ranger Class 2-81 bid good-bye to the
world and disappeared into the woods of Fort Benning, Georgia. The
class was composed of a few junior enlisted men assigned to the
Army's two Ranger battalions and many more brand-new second
lieutenants, mostly infantrymen and mostly West Point graduates of
the Class of 1980. For the next three months, they would have no
rank, no names, no hair, no rest, and nearly no news from the
outside.

At ten o'clock in the evening of the first long day, the class was
struggling to stay alert after hours of patrolling instruction when
a bull-faced Ranger instructor stepped forward and announced
that Ronald Reagan had just defeated Jimmy Carter in the presidential election. The class erupted into a riot of fist-pounding, boot-
stomping, hat-throwing, war-whooping joy. While their instructors
stood by grinning, the would-be Ranger lieutenants and privates

abandoned military courtesy and classroom decorum to join each other in cheering the defeat of their commander-in-chief.

Never in this century has a president earned less respect from the uniformed men under him. From the top down, the American military despised Jimmy Carter as much for what it regarded as his weak personal bearing and cowardly foreign policy as for his opposition to defense improvements and penchant for putting politics before military preparedness. His departure was an occasion for celebration in the field and sighs of relief in the Pentagon. At last, the chiefs of staff could candidly address the problems that confronted them, not the least of which was the hasty expansion of the role of women.

The United States entered the 1980s leading the world in the use of women in the military. In ten years, the number of women in the military had increased sixfold. In the last year of the Carter Administration, the services were recruiting more new women each year than the total strength of the women's components eight years earlier. In 1981, women accounted for 14 percent of all new recruits and 9 percent of the total force. Numbers aside, American military women were more widely employed than military women anywhere else in the world. Ninety-five percent of all military jobs were open to women, and 28.5 percent of all women were employed in nontraditional jobs. In every possible way, the Defense Department had attempted to equalize the treatment of men and women, so that by 1981 all of the services except the Marine Corps had integrated basic training. No other country in the world had gone so far.

While Jimmy Carter was in office, the nation's top military leaders were under great pressure to portray integration and expansion as completely successful and to support repeal of the combat exclusions. Dissent was not tolerated. Carter had proven his willingness to sack anyone who differed openly with Administration policy by chastizing General Donn A. Starry for speaking too plainly about the Soviet threat in Europe and by firing Major General John K. Singlaub for criticizing Carter's plan to pull troops out of Korea. But though the services were officially muzzled, the civilian press freely turned up story after story exposing problems with integration. Letters to the editor from female servicemembers complained of being "defeminized to the point of depression." Junior officers complained to reporters that fraternization and pregnancy were increasingly common. One article reported that nine out of twenty women assigned to a military police company in Germany had become pregnant within nine months, and only two of the women were married. Publicly, the Army advised commanders to treat pregnancy as a temporary disability and to work around it as they would work around casualties or desertions in wartime. Privately, Army commanders complained to the Chief of Staff, General Edward C. "Shy" Meyer, that something had to be done.

Meyer himself was well aware of the problems with integration. As commanding general of the 3rd Infantry Division in 1975, he had witnessed the dismay and confusion of officers and NCOs when the first batches of women were dumped into unprepared combat support units. Soon after taking over as chief of staff in 1979, Meyer had asked a trusted personal friend, retired Lieutenant General Arthur S. Collins Jr., to take a firsthand look at the Army in the field and deliver his personal assessment of its present condition. Author of the book *Common Sense Training*, Collins was widely respected within the Army for his insight and judgment. His informal report added other problems to those raised during the 1980 Commanders' Conference and strengthened suspicions that the presence of women was sapping the Army's strength.

Meyer did not wait for Jimmy Carter to leave office before advising Defense Secretary Harold Brown and Army Secretary Clifford Alexander that a thorough review of women in the Army was needed before the Army proceeded toward the Carter Administration's goal of 87,000 enlisted women in the Army by 1986. Though not enthusiastic about anything likely to reduce opportunities for women, Brown and Alexander acquiesced in the fall of 1980 to Meyer's proposal to freeze the strength of Army women at 65,000 until completion of a review. One month after Reagan's inauguration, formal notice of the Army's freeze, or "pause" as it was called, was delivered to the new Defense Secretary, Caspar W. Weinberger. In May 1980, Meyer established the Women in the Army (WITA) Policy Review Group, a four-man, one-woman team of handpicked Army experts. Their initial report would take a full eighteen months to prepare.

Shortly after the announcement of the Army's "pause," the Defense Department initiated its own study of women in the services, adding to the public impression that the Reagan Administration was out to roll back the Carter Administration's advances for women. In March 1981, Deputy Secretary of Defense Frank C. Carlucci directed the services to conduct a joint background review on the impact of present and projected numbers of women on readiness and on the ability of the services to accomplish their missions. Completed in October, the review confirmed the existence of a number of problems that commanders in the field already knew too much about. Women suffered higher rates of attrition, medical "noneffectiveness," and single parenthood. Their presence had resulted in a rapidly growing number of couples in which both partners were in service, about a third of which were with children. They were not suited for physically demanding duties and were more prone to injury than men. They joined the services for different reasons than men and were not attracted to nontraditional jobs. Both their morale and their opinion of the services were lower than that of the men.

Yet the background review made ominous efforts to minimize the seriousness of these problems. Not enough was known about their impact on the military, said the review, echoing Binkin and Bach. There was "no concrete evidence" that single parents adversely affected readiness. The testimony of officers in the field did not count unless it was backed by some study, and most of the studies available for review were the work of the Carter Administration. MAX WAC, REF WAC, and a number of other ideologically tainted works were all given the benefit of the doubt in the absence of anything else. Data collected by the Carter Administration was accepted at face value, though it had sometimes been manipulated to support established policy. The Army under Carter had included servicemembers paying child support in its tally of single parents to show that most single parents were men. The background review used the Army's tally to conclude that single parenthood was not "a female issue" because men accounted for three quarters of all single parents. It did not point out that Navy statistics showed that women were seven times more likely than men to be single parents *with custody* of their children.[1]

The background review did make several original contributions to the study of women in the military, though these were not noted in the review's executive summary. Digging past the executive summary, one discovers that the services' market share of eligible male high school graduates dropped steadily as the services concentrated on recruiting more and more women. In 1972, the services attracted 17 percent of all eligible men with high school diplomas; by 1980, they were attracting only 13 percent of such men. Only the Marine Corps had concentrated its efforts on recruiting "a few good men," and only the Marine Corps was able to increase its share of the market in that time.

Also without note in the review's executive summary was the discovery that, for the second time in the history of the AVF, the experts had been fundamentally wrong in their assumptions and predictions. Just as the Gates Commission had wrongly assumed that the supply of eligible males would increase through the 1970s, the experts at the Brookings Institution had wrongly expected that the advantages of recruiting women would withstand dramatic increases in the number of women recruited.

Women on average were still older than men, but, said the review, "all other selected characteristics have either narrowed or been reversed." Binkin and Bach had figured that women were cheaper to enlist because they were less likely to be married and thus less likely to be encumbered with dependents, but the review found that by 1980 female recruits were more likely than males to be married. Commander Hunter had argued that women were preferable to men because women were smarter and therefore higher in quality, but the mental quality of female recruits sank when entrance standards were lowered. Test scores among female recruits plummeted until there was "no appreciable difference" between the scores of men and women, and though women were still more likely to have graduated from high school, the percentages of men and women in the lowest mental category were very nearly the same.

The only remaining advantage of recruiting women over men was that women were better behaved and missed fewer duty days for medical reasons than men missed for disciplinary reasons. Even this was not true for the service which made the greatest use of women. Air Force women had slightly higher rates of absenteeism, courts-martial, and desertion than Air Force men. After comparing the number of duty days lost by both men and women for all reasons, the Air Force figured:

> If the FY 1980 force were all male, end-strength could be reduced over 600 spaces. FY 1986, end-strength cost of female nonavailability will be more than 1000 spaces. This equates to nearly 12 million dollars at 1980 prices. [2]

All told, the Air Force expected to incur additional costs of 20 to 30 million dollars per year to meet the Carter Administration's 1986 objective for female strength. The background review's executive summary did not mention this additional cost.

Though the background review did recommend that the services be given greater latitude to establish their own policies regarding women, the portents apparent in the review did not favor the use of that latitude for anything other than minor adjustments to accommodate further expansion. Clearly there were still some in the Defense Department who shared the Carter Administration's see-no-evil regard for integration and many who were more concerned about integration's political sensitivity than about the trouble it caused the services. The review was, in fact, prepared by the office of Dr. Lawrence J. Korb, Assistant Secretary of Defense for Manpower, Reserve Affairs, and Logistics. Years later, after leaving the Defense Department and joining the Brookings Institution, Korb became an outspoken proponent of expanded use of women in the military.

Unlike the Defense Department's background review, which was intended merely to provide Defense executives with information they would need to do their jobs, the Army's Women-in-the-Army (WITA) Policy Review Group was charged with the dual task of reviewing the issues and formulating policy. General Meyer's guidance was that the Army should be prepared to go to war tomorrow with what it has today. He took a personal interest in the review's progress, often stopping by its office in the Pentagon for informal updates. Sometimes members of the review group doubted whether their recommendations would be politically acceptable, but they never doubted Meyer's desire that they confine themselves to considering what was for the good of the service.

To narrow its focus, the review group began by categorizing issues related to women into those which were institutional and those which were "soldier specific." Institutional issues were those that involved all soldiers regardless of the presence of women in the ranks. They included problems with attrition, clothing, hygiene, medical care, child care, single parents, physical ability, lost time, career development, and sexual harassment, though many of these were never considered problems until integration. Soldier specific issues were those that resulted directly from integration. They were further categorized as those specific to women only and those relating to men and women together. Initially only pregnancy was considered "female specific," but later the review group added combat exclusion policies to the category. Male and female issues included fraternization and intra-Army and inter-service marriages.

The WITA review group referred all of the institutional and male-female issues to other Army staff activities, except the issue of physical requirements for the Army's many Military Occupational Specialties (MOS). A brief examination of the problem of pregnancy revealed that 16 percent of Army women (10,577) were pregnant in 1980. Defense Department policy prohibited pregnant women from entering service, but if a woman became pregnant after entering, the option to stay in or get out was hers. Of the Army women who became pregnant in 1980, one third aborted their babies at their own expense and remained in the Army, a third chose to have their babies and remain in the Army, and a third chose to leave the Army. The WITA review group noted commanders' concerns that pregnancy conflicted with the Army's mission and fostered the view that the peacetime Army was unprepared for war, but because the policy was established by the Defense Department, the issue was out of Army hands. The review group therefore confined its work to the issues of physical abilities and combat exclusions.

The problem with the Army's combat exclusion policy was that it did not exclude anyone from combat. The definition of combat upon which the exclusion policies were based did exactly the opposite of what it was intended to do: it limited job opportunities for women in the Army without providing women much protection from danger. The authors of the Army's 1978 combat exclusion policy had ignored the realities of war, in which many soldiers assigned to so-called "non-combat" jobs work shoulder-to-shoulder with others assigned to "combat" jobs. Intelligence personnel operate ground surveillance radars collocated with front-line grunts, engineers are responsible for blowing bridges after combat units have withdrawn to the rear, and military police are often the last to leave an evacuated area. Additionally, many dangerous Army jobs have safe-sounding civilian job titles. An Army plumber, for instance, is responsible for laying and clearing minefields and priming and emplacing explosives. Army doctrine also stresses the responsibility of support personnel to "fix and fuel forward," requiring maintenance and recovery, supply, and communications personnel to service combat troops as close as possible to their battle positions. All of these conditions made the Army's MOS-based combat exclusion policy nonsensical. Women could not serve in specialties primarily responsible for killing the enemy, but they could serve in specialties that exposed them to an equal opportunity of being killed.

Instead of excluding women from combat, the 1978 combat exclusion policy pushed women right up to enemy lines. In July 1981, when the Army surveyed the assignment of women to the United States V Corps in West Germany, it found 175 women assigned to units belonging to the Corps Covering Force, which operates well forward of friendly lines and maintains constant contact with the enemy. Seven hundred and twenty-seven women were assigned to units that operate in the Main Battle Area (forward of the brigade rear boundary). A total of 3,799 women were assigned to units operating in the "combat zone," according to pre-1978 Army doctrine.

To restore some integrity to Army policy, the Army had two choices: it could drop the combat exclusions, admit that women were already filling combat roles, and either integrate all units or attempt to exclude women from some units for reasons other than excluding them from combat; or, it could make the combat exclusions meaningful by reducing the involvement of women in combat and removing them from many of the positions they then filled. The first option was politically impossible at the time. Congress could not admit to the American people that it was allowing the Army to commit young women to mortal combat, though it knew that Army doctrine had done so already. Even if the Army were allowed to drop the combat exclusions, it would not have wanted to unless it could exclude women from certain units on other grounds. That was also impossible, because the nation's courts did not recognize any other grounds as constitutionally sufficient, so convinced was the judiciary of the truth of feminist social theory.

The second option presented the problem of arbitrariness. Reducing the involvement of women in combat entailed reducing opportunities for women, but if the Army appeared to reduce opportunities for women arbitrarily, it left itself open to accusations that it was using the combat exclusions to resist integration for other reasons. The only truly non-arbitrary way of excluding women from combat was to exclude women from the theater of operations, eliminating any chance that women would see combat, but this too was politically impossible because it would drastically reduce opportunities for women. The Army's problem was to devise a method of arbitrarily drawing a line that did not appear arbitrary. The WITA review group solved the problem by creating Direct Combat Probability Coding, a seemingly scientific way of determining which jobs should be closed to women and which should not.

Direct Combat Probability Coding (DCPC) involved assessing each and every position in the Army for the probability that the soldier filling the position would see "direct combat," an unspecific term used for years in the debate over the combat exclusions to connote a situation generally considered too dangerous for women. The WITA review group made the term official and gave it essentially the same meaning as the term *close combat:*

> engaging an enemy with individual or crew-served weapons
> while being exposed to direct enemy fire, a high probability of
> direct physical contact with the enemy's personnel, and a sub-
> stantial risk of capture.[3]

To ascertain the probability of direct combat for each position, the WITA review group asked the Army's doctrinal authorities to respond to questionaires concerning the position's assigned duties, the parent unit's mission, its place on the battlefield, and tactical doctrine. The results were then calculated to produce for each position a numerical probability code of 1 to 7. Positions with the highest probability of involving a soldier in direct combat were coded P1, and those with the lowest probability were coded P7.

The line was drawn by General Meyer, who decided that women would be excluded only from positions with the highest probability of direct combat, those coded P1. This included 53 percent of Army enlisted positions. Based upon the recommendation of the WITA review group, Meyer closed 23 specialties, in addition to 38 already closed to women, because they would require assignment to P1 positions. Together, the MOS closings and P1 exclusions would not prohibit women from ever serving forward of the brigade rear boundary or from ever seeing direct combat, but they would prohibit women from serving in the brigade area "habitually" and from "routine" engagement in direct combat. Many Army leaders favored a more complete exclusion, but the politics of the issue made the P1 exclusion, in Meyer's view, the best the Army could do.

The next great accomplishment of the WITA review group was the establishment of physical strength requirements for each MOS. Army commanders had long complained that women were unable to perform many routine physical tasks associated with their assigned specialties. Their complaints were substantiated by a 1976 study of the utilization of women in the military by the General Accounting Office (GAO). The GAO found that women trained as ammunition storage specialists had trouble handling rounds of ammunition that weighed between 58 and 120 pounds. Female medical specialists assigned as ambulance drivers had trouble loading and unloading patients, braking and steering ambulances, and changing tires on ambulances. Similar difficulties faced women trained as wheeled vehicle mechanics. When women were unable to perform routine duties for which they had been trained, they were often assigned clerical or administrative duties instead, while male soldiers picked up the slack.

The GAO's recommended solution was a simple one: gender-free strength testing of potential recruits to enable recruiters to match the man or woman to the MOS. The solution was so simple that the 1978 Evaluation of Women in the Army (EWITA) made the same recommendation, saying, "The Army cannot be assured of accomplishing the ground combat mission if women are randomly accessed into positions with physically demanding tasks exceeding their capabilities."[4] The Defense Department's 1981 background review repeated the recommendation, praising similar tests in use by the Air Force. The Army, however, had never gone beyond preliminary research begun in 1977 because the Carter Administration was not interested in anything that would lead inevitably to limiting opportunities for women.

In 1981, members of the WITA review group verified the GAO findings with their own eyes. At Aberdeen Proving Grounds, Maryland, they were amazed that women being tested and certified as ammunition handlers appeared to have no trouble completing a test of their proficiency at moving and sorting large crates of ammunition, until they discovered that the women were only required to move empty crates because full crates were too heavy for them. At Fort Hood, Texas, they found that more than half of the female track vehicle mechanics assigned to some units were working outside their MOS because they were dissatisfied with the job and frustrated with their inability to perform routine tasks, such as separating the links in a vehicle's track with a 68-pound track wrench.

The WITA review group then began the task of constructing a means of matching the physical abilities of each recruit, regardless of sex, to the physical requirements of each MOS. It started with the Department of Labor Occupational Classification System, devised in 1939, that divided jobs into five categories according to physical demand: sedentary, light, medium, heavy, and very heavy. Each category was defined as requiring the following:

	Maximum Lifting	Frequent Lifting
Sedentary	10 pounds	—
Light	20	10 pounds
Medium	50	25
Heavy	100	50
Very Heavy	in excess of 100	50

When the review group found that many Army jobs fell into the upper half of the medium category but short of the heavy category, it eliminated the sedentary category and added a category called "moderately heavy," defined as requiring maximum lifting of 80 pounds and frequent lifting of 40 pounds.

Next, the review group set about categorizing each MOS using four simple physical tasks: lift, carry, push, and pull. This involved extensive field research to consider every task, explicit or implicit, that a soldier in an MOS would be required to perform. After observing soldiers at work, interviewing the soldiers and MOS experts, and consulting official publications, the review group assigned 132 of the Army's 351 specialties to the very heavy category requiring lifting in excess of 100 pounds and frequent lifting of 50. This category accounted for 64 percent of all positions in the Army. Twelve percent of the Army's positions were rated heavy, and the remaining quarter of all Army positions were distributed evenly among the moderately heavy, medium, and light categories.

The next step was to develop a test to be administered to potential recruits to determine their ability to meet the physical demands of their preferred MOS. The Military Enlistment Physical Strength Capacity Test (MEPSCAT) was designed to test a recruit's strength and stamina. The test consisted of four components: a skinfold measurement to determine body fat content, a handstrength test using a dynamometer, a dynamic lifting test, and a stress test for cardiovascular fitness.

Before either the MEPSCAT or the categorization of an MOS could be trusted to accurately predict a recruit's ability to perform in an MOS, the entire system required "validation." To ensure the accuracy of the results of validation, the system would be validated by both the Army Research Institute and a commercial research contractor with extensive experience in the study of physical performance but no previous involvement in the WITA project. The validation process was expected to take more than a year to conclude. It had just started when the WITA review group released its final report in the fall of 1982.

If valid, the MEPSCAT system offered several advantages to the present practice of randomly assigning recruits to an MOS. Obviously it would provide the Army with soldiers who were better able to perform their assigned jobs, but the Army also expected the system to reduce attrition, job migration, and "malutilization," particularly among women. Women assigned to MOSs too physically demanding for them attrited at higher rates than those assigned to less demanding jobs. Forty-nine percent of women in jobs rated heavy and very heavy did not complete their three-year enlistments. Supervisors often assigned them duties unrelated to their MOS, and the women were more likely to change specialties to find less demanding work.

The disadvantage of the MEPSCAT system was that it would concentrate the great majority of Army women in a fraction of the Army's positions. No job or position would be closed to all women on the basis of physical demands, but tests at Fort Jackson, S.C., had shown that very few Army women were likely to be able to perform work rated heavy or very heavy. Only 3 percent of Army women were expected to be able to qualify for very heavy work, and only 8 percent for heavy work. This meant that approximately 89 percent of Army women would be concentrated in 24 percent of Army positions. If the level of enlisted women in the Army remained at 65,000, women would fill almost half of all positions rated light to moderately heavy.

Before the results of WITA were ever announced, the study had found strong enemies. The Army's Recruiting Command was very much opposed to anything that would add to the hurdles recruiters must overcome to successfully enlist a man or woman. Besides making it harder for recruiters to please potential recruits with their choice of jobs, the MEPSCAT test would completely disqualify some men and women who were physically weak. The review group had considered this a plus for the MEPSCAT because it would turn away such men and women before the Army became liable for injuries they were likely to suffer during training, but the Recruiting Command seriously questioned its ability to achieve recruiting objectives if recruits were required to meet the MEPSCAT standards. Meetings between the Recruiting Command and the WITA review group, championed by the Deputy Chief of Staff for Personnel, General Maxwell Thurman, were tense contests between the best of both camps. Resident experts from the Recruiting Command picked and poked at any angle of the review they thought vulnerable, while the Chief of Staff and the Vice Chief of Staff looked on. In the end, the review group prevailed. General Meyer, a man with little patience for incompetence who was known to order the immediate retirement of officers who disappointed him, was thoroughly satisfied that the recommendations of the WITA review group were for the good of the service.

When the Army announced, in August 1982, that it would begin to implement the recommendations of the still unpublished WITA review, the review group found other enemies. Hundreds of women held specialties recommended for closing, thousands were assigned to P1 positions, and more than half of all Army women were working in jobs rated heavy or very heavy. Naturally WITA was very unpopular among the many women who were to be involuntarily reclassified or reassigned, but the strongest opposition to WITA came from women not in the least affected by the changes, women outside the Army whose concerns were strictly ideological. Leading the fight to quash WITA's counterrevolution against feminism's dominance of military manpower issues was the Defense Advisory Committee on Women in the Services (DACOWITS).

There was no special reason why the Army should have feared the opposition of DACOWITS. The committee's thirty-year career was an unremarkable one, beginning with its failed attempt to draw women into the Korean War. After the war, DACOWITS attracted little attention with modest recommendations for improving the standard of living among servicewomen and for enhancing career incentives for nurses and medical specialists. The military in those days was no longer interested in expanding the ranks of military women, and the directors of the women's components disliked the kibitzing of 50 civilian women with no military experience. DACOWITS survived for many years as little more than an opportunity for the wives of prominent Washington men to hobnob with famous women. Early members included anthropologist Margaret Meade, actress Helen Hayes, Vassar's president Sarah Blanding, and Dr. Lillian Gilbreth, the mother portrayed in the book and movie *Cheaper by the Dozen.*

DACOWITS's one triumph in its early years was the passage of PL 90-130 in 1967, after which the committee's enthusiasm waned rapidly. As the Vietnam War's unpopularity grew, members of DACOWITS lost interest. The year the first women were made generals, only 31 of DACOWITS's 50 members bothered to attend its fall meeting. By 1972, DACOWITS had earned a reputation as "a nice little group that doesn't do very much."[5] The article in *Army Times* pointing this out quoted a reporter saying, "I hope you tell the truth about DACOWITS because they don't do much at all." As a result of its inactivity, its authorized strength shrank from 50 to 40, then to 30 in 1975, and then to 25 with only 23 actually appointed in 1976.

Another reason for the committee's shrinking membership was the shifting consensus among DACOWITS members. Radical members wanted revolutionary change within the military and began pushing DACOWITS to become more politically active. "This group has got to become an action group," argued Sarah McClendon, a Washington correspondent and columnist appointed to the committee by the Nixon Administration. Complaining that many committee members knew little about the military, McClendon, who had served as a WAC officer in World War II before being discharged for pregnancy, worked to bring in retired female officers who shared her revolutionary dreams. McClendon also agitated to open DACOWITS meetings to the press and public, a move opposed by many more conservative committee members who feared becoming a "focal point of the women's rights movement." DACOWITS did open its meetings to the public in late 1973, but only after the radically feminist Center for Women Policy Studies filed suit in federal court to force the issue.

Opened to outside influences, DACOWITS meetings became semi-annual *schutzenfesten* providing feminist organizations the opportunity to hurl abuse both at the military for oppressing women and at DACOWITS for not doing enough about it. The committee began to make regular headlines in military newspapers not for what committee members said or did, but for what its audience complained about. In 1974, outsiders were already calling for the repeal of the combat exclusion laws and the integration of the service academies. That year, the committee passed on the issue of combat but did recommend that the services begin planning for the "inevitable" integration of the academies. The committee also recommended that the Defense Department submit legislative proposals to Congress to "equalize [promotion] opportunities for women . . . regardless of available billets." DACOWITS wanted more female generals and admirals whether the services needed them or not.[6]

Thereafter the committee's recommendations to the Defense Department were merely modulated renditions of the demands of professional feminists. When the Center for Women Policy Studies complained that the absence of women at the academies "seriously compromises their military career opportunities," DACOWITS strengthened its call for the services to integrate the academies without waiting for legislative authorization. When the National Organization for Women (NOW) complained that enlisted Army women were handicapped by their inability to win decorations for battlefield bravery and combat service, DACOWITS asked the Army to "clarify" its definition of "combat duty" and "combat assignment," with an eye to opening more jobs to women.[7]

Quickly the committee's less radical members faded away or joined the party, so that by 1976 the takeover was complete. By driving away opponents, the feminist minority had become the majority. In a classic demonstration of the dynamics of revolutionary politics, the former military advisory committee was reborn as an active antimilitary lobby with legislative and "civic action" subcommittees.

DACOWITS stepped off the deep end in 1976, calling the combat exclusion laws "arbitrary and unnecessary." Barely two years after exposing itself to organized feminism, the committee recommended:

> That laws now preventing women from serving their country in combat and combat related or support positions be repealed.
> Rationale: Self-explanatory.[8]

In the same meeting, DACOWITS condemned the Veterans of Foreign Wars for discriminating against women and asked the Defense Department to sever ties with the organization. It also asked the services to review their physical standards,

> to ascertain if height and physical standards are valid requirements and necessary for job performance . . . or should they be replaced with other job related qualifications.[9]

The qualifications the committee had in mind were high school diplomas and entrance exam scores, often used as easily measurable proof that women make better soldiers and sailors. The committee's rationale for this recommendation included the following knot of nonsensical prose:

> In keeping with current changes in the military as well as in the civilian work world, it has been proven that an individual, regardless of sex, can fulfill the requirements of jobs on the basis of their capabilities. According to medical science it is commonly known that women are shorter in height and have other physical differences but have proven they have the capabilities to do a given task.

What has been proven? That *all* individuals can fulfill *all* requirements of *all* jobs regardless of sex? Or that *some* individuals can fulfill the requirements of *some* jobs regardless of sex? If it is some and not all, then so what? Some people have always been able to do some jobs. And why does a committee of thirty prominent women need "medical science" to tell it what is "commonly known"? If women can perform "a given task" despite their sex, does this mean that women can perform all tasks given to them as members of the military? Some members of DACOWITS seemed to believe so. Indeed, what the committee seemed to be saying was that women were just as capable as men of doing anything in the military, their physical limitations notwithstanding. Certainly, that was what it seemed they were saying to the editors of *Air Force Times,* whose headline of the event read: "Women Can Do Anything Men Can Do."[10]

Ironically, the Carter Administration posed a greater threat to the continued existence of DACOWITS than any presidential administration before or since. In its enthusiasm for advancing the cause of women in the military, the Carter Pentagon hardly seemed to need the advice of DACOWITS, and some committee members were concerned that DACOWITS would be disbanded as unnecessary. As it happened, the Carter Administration bolstered DACOWITS with increased membership appointments and additional full-time administrative support. Among the members appointed in 1977 was retired Air Force Major General Jeanne Holm, always an advocate of the advancement of women. As director of the Women's Air Force in 1972, Holm testified before Congress in favor of integrating the service academies, though the directors of the Army, Navy, and Marine Corps women's components testified against integration.

During the Carter years, DACOWITS knew no restraint. It called for the assignment of a general officer to head the predominantly female Army Medical Specialist Corps, for no better reason than that without one "the implication is that the corps mission is not as important as other medical corps." It wanted women appointed to the Court of Military Appeals and assigned to Minuteman missile silos. It demanded the elimination of sex bias in recruiting literature, which it faulted for being "predominantly male-oriented." It denounced open bay barracks, cushion-sole boot socks, and the ban on abortion in military hospitals. It endorsed tube socks instead, private entrances to officer quarters, and the Equal Rights Amendment. DACOWITS attacked and tried to suppress the Air Force study upon which the Air Force based its decision to close the security specialist field to women. It blamed all of the medical problems that women experienced on poorly designed clothing and equipment and continued to recommend repeal of the combat exclusion laws.

The defeat of Jimmy Carter inspired new fears that the Reagan Administration would silence DACOWITS by packing the committee with anti-feminists. Such fears proved unfounded. The committee maintained remarkable ideological continuity during the change from Carter to Reagan, partly because members are appointed by the Secretary of Defense for three year terms and partly because new members are often selected upon the recommendation of old members, but mostly because the Reagan Administration never showed the will to oppose feminists in any significant way, except on the issue of abortion. There was no attempt to stuff DACOWITS with the friends of Phyllis Schlafly. Many of the women the Reagan Administration appointed were establishment Republicans who may not have described themselves as feminists but nevertheless supported most feminist aims. Under pressure from senior members of the committee, the audience at DACOWITS meetings, and especially the committee's pro-feminist military advisors, the new members quickly found themselves caught up in the committee's enthusiasm for radical reform.

Nevertheless, in the early Reagan years, DACOWITS's paranoia manifested itself in new complaints. In 1981, it blamed the services for too successfully promoting the view that women were needed to make the AVF work:

> The services' focus on the expected shortage of available males in the next 10 years fosters the perception that women are merely "fillers" and not professionals contributing to the defense effort.[11]

Never mind that DACOWITS had itself done much to foster the same view. It also reported sinking morale among military women, particularly Army women, as a result of "gender specific actions." The Army's "womanpause," as the press rendered it, and the WITA review were of special concern. General Meyer had tried to allay the committee's apprehensions by enlisting several present and former DACOWITS members as advisors to the WITA review group, but somehow the review group neglected to keep the advisors informed of the review's progress. Formal briefings given by the review group to the full committee on the progress of the WITA review explained the origin, scope, and conduct of the review in such a way that DACOWITS had no idea where the review was headed. One year after the review was begun, the Army was still keeping DACOWITS in the dark about the physical demands analysis and the combat probability coding. In April 1982, spokesmen for the WITA review group talked instead about problems related to pregnancy, which the review group had long since given up as the responsibility of the Defense Department.

While the Army plotted major policy changes affecting women, the civilian leadership in the Pentagon hastened to assure military women that the Reagan Administration was not a threat to their careers and firmly supported equal opportunity for military women. In February 1982, Assistant Secretary of Defense Korb told a group of Navy women that the Defense Department was working "to break down any institutional barriers that still exist" within the services. In August 1982, the Army's new Assistant Secretary for Manpower and Reserve Affairs Harry N. Walters, told DACOWITS that the WITA review would be a "positive thing" for women. Assuring the committee that the Army was still committed to providing women "the same career advancement opportunities" available to men, Walters explained that the Army had "jammed an extra 55,000 women into the system without any thought being given to where they should be assigned." WITA was just trying to "unravel all the problems" caused by the hasty increases. Secretary of Defense Caspar Weinberger, who had been briefed on the results of the review by General Meyer and Army Secretary John O. Marsh, promised DACOWITS chairwoman Maria Elena Torralva that present Army policy would not change until the WITA review was approved by the Defense Department. Torralva was reassured. "I feel much better about what is happening," she told the committee. The study would be "a positive one for women."

No doubt owing to these assurances, the reaction to the release of the WITA review group's draft report, already approved for implementation by General Meyer and Secretary Marsh, in late August 1982 was mixed and relatively mild. Carolyn Becraft of the Women's Equity Action League (WEAL) said that the report was better than she expected, that the review needed to be done, and that the Army had responded properly to "political pressure by women, DACOWITS, women's organization, and press reports." Sarah McClendon was "upbeat" about the report: "The report said women can do the job." Representative Patricia Schroeder of Colorado, a member of the House Armed Services Committee, was more cautious. "Every time there is a new study, it never helps morale," she said. Kathleen Carpenter, formerly Deputy Secretary of Defense for Equal Opportunity under Carter, called the report's unexplained recommendation that the Army add 5,000 enlisted women and 4,000 female officers a "public relations" move to divert attention from the review's impact.

Three months later, the mood had changed. "DACOWITS Rips Army Women Study," read the headlines in *Army Times* after a "stormy, confrontational" meeting in November, during which members and spectators railed against Army representatives with charges that the study represented "poor Army management" and was "nothing but a snow job." Sarah McClendon, one of the unused advisors, suddenly wondered "why the hell they wanted us to help." Jeanne Holm told committee members that the study had created morale problems for women who felt the Army was blaming its mistakes on them. An Army enlisted woman declaimed, "I'm not to be blamed for the problems. These are management problems."

Management's attempts to solve its problems were defended by William D. Clark, Deputy Assistant Secretary of the Army for Manpower and Reserve Affairs, and Lieutenant General Maxwell R. Thurman. They argued that WITA suffered from poor public relations, that the methodology employed was reliable, and that, in any case, the study still needed to be validated. If the validation process revealed problems with the study's findings, then changes would be made. Meanwhile the Army would make every effort to smooth the implementation of the recommended changes.

Specific criticisms of the review were fielded by the members of the WITA review group themselves. DACOWITS questioned everything, and for everything the review group had an answer. Many of the committee members' criticisms were made out of ignorance of the Army in combat. Margaret M. Scheffelin, an educational researcher charged with spearheading DACOWITS's attacks, could not understand why women were to be excluded from the job of air traffic controller (ATC) when civilian women supposedly made especially good ATCs. Reading from an Army manual describing the duties of an ATC, a member of the review group pointed out that Army ATCs are required to do much more than sit in front of a radar screen. Other duties include clearing airfields and landing zones and erecting runway lighting systems, sometimes behind enemy lines.

By the third day of the meeting, the Army's defense of WITA had been so successful that one member of the committee admitted privately that the Army had managed to "take the wind right out of our sails." An admission that DACOWITS was impressed with the Army's briefing was first added to the committee's official report and then deleted. The final report admitted only, "We are extremely concerned about the impact of this study on women in the military and on morale."

In the months following the meeting, members and friends of DACOWITS groped for ways to attack the study. The Labor Department's categorization of jobs according to physical demand was too old to still be valid, they said. The sampling of female recruits at Fort

Jackson was too small to accurately predict the abilities of Army women, they said. Of course, both objections are irrelevant, for even if they are true, the Army's determination of strength requirements for specific jobs still stands on its own. Other objections were equally weak. Even given more time, the critics of WITA could do no better. One critic complained that the creation of the "moderately heavy" strength category amounted to "statistical sorcery" and that long range weapons made close, physical contact with the enemy part of the Army's "historical memory, not its current operational concepts."[12] A 1985 study by the Air Force dismissed WITA's findings on physical strength because, it said, the WITA study group had assumed but not proved that soldiers who lacked the strength to perform their assigned tasks actually degraded unit effectiveness.

In April 1983, DACOWITS rallied its disheartened troops to another meeting, from which came recommendations that the Army establish an "objective panel," chaired by a retired female general officer and staffed with active and retired officers and senior non-commissioned officers, "with a predominance of women members." The proposed panel would review the WITA study and report its evaluation directly to the Secretary of the Army. Concerned again for the morale of military women, DACOWITS requested that all of the services disseminate articles and reports to the field "showing the positive performance of women in the military." The committee also decided that its executive board would draft a letter to send to the Secretary of Defense explaining the concern of DACOWITS for WITA's impact on morale and career progression.

Signed by DACOWITS Chairwoman Mary Evelyn Blagg Huey, president of Texas Woman's University, and dated June 6, 1983, DACOWITS's rambling letter abandoned most of the criticism that had been leveled at the study already. Instead, it fell back on the very arguments the committee had accused the services of over-using. WITA's probability-based combat exclusion "deprives our Army of many skilled soldiers" and "reduces available manpower." The effect of the combat exclusions on career development and promotion "poses concerns for morale, enlistments, and the continued success of the all-volunteer Army." DACOWITS would be remiss in its charge if it did not warn the Secretary that WITA's impact "upon our national security and the utilization of *all* personnel is seriously negative." (Original emphasis.)

The only specific criticism of the review was the charge that the Army's definition of "combat" was out of date. Modern combat, said the letter, is "of a fluid—and frequently remote—character." No mention was made of WITA's physical demands analysis, and no fault was found with the review's methodology. Nevertheless, the letter questioned the integrity of the review group and its motives:

> We have serious questions regarding the merit of the continual studying women's military participation. [sic] As a study reaffirms the positive performance and contribution by those of our gender, a new one seems to be ordered. This finally raises the question of whether objectivity or the "right answers" is the purpose.[13]

The letter also requested that a Marine Corps study of women marines be postponed indefinitely.

Secretary Weinberger's reply to Dr. Huey, dated 27 July 1983, was sympathetic and conciliatory. He assured Huey that the Defense Department was committed to ensuring that "women will be provided maximum opportunities to realize their individual potential" and that restrictions on women in the services were based solely on the intent of the combat exclusion laws. Regarding the Army's definition of combat, Weinberger agreed that the nature of combat is fluid, noting that "if hostilities break out, men and women in uniform are at risk no matter where they may be located," which is to say that combat is frequently not remote in character. He then politely pointed out that some soldiers are at greater risk than others and that the Army's desire to exclude women from positions with the highest probability of involving combat was consistent with the intent of the combat exclusion laws. Though the Marine Corps study would proceed, Weinberger promised that implementation of any policy affecting women would be closely monitored by Assistant Secretary of Defense Korb to ensure that "artificial or institutional barriers to career progression are systematically broken down."[14]

Weinberger's 19 July memorandum to the service secretaries, enclosed with his letter to Huey, put things more bluntly. Recent press reports, said the memo, had given the impression that the Defense Department had changed its policy toward women. That impression was wrong. Women would be provided full and equal opportunity with men to pursue military careers:

> This means that military women can and should be utilized in all roles except those explicitly prohibited by combat exclusion statutes and related policy. . . . The combat exclusion rule should be interpreted to allow as many as possible career opportunities for women to be kept open.[15]

The Army might have successfully defended WITA had it not been for two important changes of personnel that occurred before the summer of 1983. "Shy" Meyer had retired and was succeeded by General John A. Wickham Jr., and Delbert L. Spurlock Jr. had replaced Harry Walters as Assistant Secretary of the Army for Manpower and Reserve Affairs. Whereas Walters, who left to head the Veterans Administration, was a businessman with no use for the unconstructive advice of DACOWITS, Spurlock was a civil-rights lawyer with no military experience before becoming Army general counsel in 1981, no previous involvement with the WITA review, and no interest in defending it. After Weinberger talked to Korb, and Korb talked to Spurlock, Spurlock's recommendation to Wickham favored the emasculation of WITA. Wickham, who was not prepared to fall on his sword and end his stint as Chief of Staff so soon, dutifully presided over the greatest peacetime defeat in the history of the United States Army.

In the fall of 1983, Spurlock informed Korb that WITA had been "revalidated" after certain unnamed errors of methodology had been corrected. In fact, validation by an independent civilian agency, Advanced Research Resources Organization of Bethesda, Md., found no fault with the review.[16] In October 1983, the Army briefed DACOWITS on the changed WITA. Thirteen of the 23 specialties closed to women by WITA were reopened. The Direct Combat Probability Coding of many units was adjusted to keep as many positions as possible open to women. The physical capabilities test, so long the answer to the problem of recruits who were physically incapable of performing their required tasks, was reduced to a recruiter's "counselling tool." An Army representative suggested that it took courage to reassess the study, but a DACOWITS member replied, "I don't think it is an act of considerable courage to do what they should have done in the first place."

NOTES ON CHAPTER VII

1. Office of the Assistant Secretary of Defense for Manpower, Reserve Affairs, & Logistics, *Background Review: Women in the Military* (Washington, D.C.: Department of Defense, October 1981), p. 7. See p. 81 for data.

2. Background Review, p. 137.

3. Office of the Deputy Chief of Staff for Personnel, *Women in the Army Policy Review* (Washington, D.C.: Department of the Army, 12 November 1982), p. 4–9.

4. *Final Report: Evaluation of Women in the Army* (Ft. Ben. Harrison, Ind.: Department of the Army, 1978) p. 1–18.

5. Margaret Eastman, "DACOWITS: a nice little group that doesn't do very much," *Army Times*, Family Supplement, 15 March 1972, p. 11.

6. DACOWITS, Recommendations Made at the 1974 Spring Meeting, 21–25 April 1974, p. 2.

7. DACOWITS, Recommendations Made at the 1975 Spring Meeting, 6–10 April 1975, p. 2.

8. DACOWITS, Recommendations, Requests for Information, Commendations Made at the 1976 Fall Meeting, 14–18 November 1976, p. 1.

9. DACOWITS, Recommendations etc., 1976 Fall Meeting, p. 2.

10. "Women Can Do Anything Men Can Do," *Air Force Times*, 29 November 1976, p. 2.

11. "DACOWITS: 'Actions' Hurt Women's Morale," *Air Force Times*, 30 November 1981, p. 16.

12. M.C. Devilbiss, " 'Women in the Army Policy Review'—A Military Sociologist's Analysis," *Minerva*, Fall 1983, p. 95. Believers in WITA have nothing to fear from this "analysis."

13. Mary Evelyn Blagg Huey, Letter to Caspar W. Weinberger, 6 June 1983.

14. Caspar W. Weinberger, Letter to Mary Evelyn Blagg Huey, 27 July 1983.

15. Caspar W. Weinberger, Memorandum for the Secretaries of the Military Departments, Subject: Women in the Military, 19 July 1983.

16. David C. Myers, Deborah L. Gebhardt, Carolyn E. Crump, and Edwin A. Fleishman, *Validation of the Military Entrance Physical Strength Capacity Test* (Bethesda, Md.: Advanced Research Resources Organization, 1984). The report concluded that the MEPSCAT was "a valid predictor of performance on physically demanding tasks," p. viii.

CHAPTER VIII
Confidence Is High

My policy? Sir, I am a soldier. I do not have a policy.

FRENCH GENERAL HENRI GIRAUD[1]

NOT SINCE THE PASSAGE of PL 90-130 a decade and a half earlier had DACOWITS achieved a greater victory. In suppressing WITA, the committee had done more than merely overcome the apathy of lawmakers; it had overcome the Army. It had bullied and embarrassed an organized opposition through loud, persistent, and sometimes hysterical protest. In the end, the arguments of neither side mattered. The lesson learned was that the side that clamors loudest carries the day.

DACOWITS was exultant and emboldened. It emerged from the conflict full of fight, vowing to direct its appeals directly to the Secretary of Defense on other matters. Less than a year after questioning the objectivity and worth of repeatedly studying women in the military, DACOWITS was recommending that the utilization of women be "continually re-examined [but only] with a view to improving force readiness by making maximum use of this valuable human resource."[2]

New fears that the Reagan Administration would silence the successful committee by appointing more conservative members quickly faded. By 1984, all of the members of DACOWITS had been appointed under Reagan with no discernible shift in the committee's ideological bent. The only woman who regularly deviated from the committee's radical consensus was Elaine Donnelly, an Eagle Forum member who had led the fight against the ERA in her home state of Michigan. Donnelly fought hard against the push for repeal of the combat exclusion laws and often raised embarrassing questions about pregnancy, dual-service couples, and the lesser physical strength of women, but all too often she found herself alone and outnumbered.

In the year of the "gender gap," the Reagan Pentagon was interested only in deflecting criticism by pleasing the feminist lobby. The Defense Department spent $70,000 to dress the Pentagon's Military Women's Corridor with exhibits and propaganda. (The hall was soon dubbed "Broadway" by the sexist denizens of the Pentagon's shabbier corridors.) DACOWITS was treated to repeated pronouncements that women were an "integral part" of the nation's defenses and the committee itself was "an integral part of the Defense team." Such flattery was intended to dissuade members from seeking to make DACOWITS a statutory committee, responsible directly to Congress or to both Congress and the Defense Department. Assistant Secretary of Defense Lawrence J. Korb told the committee that a statutory committee would create "an investigative or adversarial relationship" between the committee and the military. "The effect would be polarization of women from the military community," said Korb.[3] Of course, both the polarization of women from the military community and an adversarial relationship between DACOWITS and the Defense Department already existed. The Pentagon nevertheless had good reason to fear closer ties between DACOWITS and Congress.

Both Korb and Weinberger strove to develop a more amicable relationship between the committee and the Pentagon. Korb, himself a true-believer in greater utilization of women, assured DACOWITS that "no issue has taken more of my time than women in the military."[4] Weinberger was described by a former DACOWITS chairwoman as "fatherly" and "almost sweet" in his desire to please the committee. He assured them of his personal commitment to the continued expansion of opportunities against the seemingly elastic combat exclusion laws, he praised the achievements of women whenever the occasion required him to do so, he created the Department of

Defense Task Force on Equity for Women, and he loudly called upon the services to accept more women into their ranks and open more jobs to them. Yet for all his efforts he never quite escaped the suspicion of insincerity. Some proponents of women in the military sensed that his policy was secretly one of appeasement: he was willing to give women an inch whenever they demanded one, but he showed no initiative to act without prodding and dodged the issue of combat at every turn.

The debate over women in combat was one battle Caspar Weinberger simply did not want to fight. His entire tenure in office was spent temporizing on the issue, trying both to please and protect his commander-in-chief, who was known to oppose women in combat, and to avoid angering the feminist lobby. He assured President Reagan that women could become "grease monkeys if they want to and things like that" but not combat soldiers.[5] He secretly advised the service chiefs not to worry about women in the combat zone because the President would order them withdrawn when the shooting started, an unsettling prospect for the chiefs because of the number of women in critical positions. He suggested in an interview on NBC's *Nightly News* that evacuation of women from a combat zone was a possibility but qualified the suggestion by adding that the "value of having women in those positions [in combat], the value of leaving all career avenues open, is greater than the problems of dealing with comparable small disruption." In fact, DACOWITS had already been told by Korb that evacuation was not a possibility: "We cannot afford to pull women back or protect them from the hazards of their duties. No one should expect otherwise."[6]

Weinberger would admit to being personally opposed to women in combat, but he always left his position conspicuously undefended. When pressed on the issue by DACOWITS, he proffered only flattery and a patronizing apology for his recalcitrant chauvinism:

> Either I'm too old-fashioned or something else is wrong with me, but I simply feel that that is not the proper utilization [of women]. And I think, again to be perfectly frank about it and spread all of my old-fashioned views before you, I think women are too valuable to be in combat.[7]

Whatever his reasons for opposing women in combat, he did not dare reveal them, not even to argue against repeal of the combat exclusion laws. Instead, he washed his hands of the issue and shoved it back at Congress, but only after surrendering all grounds for defending the exclusion laws as they already existed. The greatest favor Weinberger granted proponents of women in the military was the establishment of the Defense Department's current position that there are no military reasons why women should be excluded from combat, that present limitations on the role of women are based solely on present law, and that the law is based solely on the preference of the American public. As far as the Pentagon is concerned, the law's repeal is a matter properly decided by the public's elected representatives—strictly without benefit of military counsel.

Despite its boasts, the Defense Department under Weinberger did not lead the way toward greater use of women by the military, but it did allow itself to be goaded steadily in that direction by complaints from Congress and the feminist lobby. After its humiliating defeat, the Army buried WITA unceremoniously. Army leaders were so intimidated that they made no attempt to explain the study to the troops in the field, who knew nothing about WITA except what they read in *Army Times,* where criticism of the report grabbed all the headlines and charges of bias and faulty methodology were reported but never examined for their validity. Before retiring, General Meyer, who now says he would have resigned as Chief of Staff before allowing WITA to be emasculated as it was, had wanted to make a videotaped explanation of WITA for dissemination to the field, but he was persuaded to let General Thurman make the videotape instead. Thurman's videotape was never released. A member of the WITA review group prepared a painstaking explanation of the study for publication in Army journals, but that too was spiked. To have explained why WITA made sense would have placed Army leaders in the difficult position of having to explain why so many of its recommendations had not been implemented. The two-year study, they decided, was best forgotten.

By 1988, the Army had added more than 10,000 officer and enlisted women, raising the number of women to almost 11 percent of its total strength. As a counselling tool, the MEPSCAT physical test had no appreciable effect on the placement of personnel in specialties, as recruiters were not about to discourage potential recruits from entering the MOS of their choice. Direct Combat Probability Coding suffered gradual erosion as exceptions overrode the rule whenever P1 vacancies went unfilled. By 1986, 4,000 Army women in Europe were assigned to P1 positions. The following year, the coding system was "fine-tuned" to provide greater flexibility in personnel assignments and more command opportunity for female officers. Nearly 12,000 active duty positions were opened to women in forward support battalions, which provide direct support to combat units forward of the brigade rear boundary. More than 2,000 women are now assigned to such units.

The Air Force also continued to move towards greater and greater use of women. In five years under Reagan, the Air Force opened more than 30,000 new positions to women. Only 3 percent of Air Force jobs are now closed to women. With the reopening of the security specialist field in 1984, Air Force enlisted women may now serve in all but four career fields. All officer career fields are open to women. In 1984, women were assigned aboard Airborne Warning and Control System (AWACS) aircraft. In 1986, RC-135 reconnaissance aircraft and EC-130 electronic countermeasures aircraft were both opened to women. Also in 1986, the Air Force began assigning women to Minuteman missile crews, with plans for 20 percent of Minuteman crews to be all-female. Since 1980, the female share of total Air Force personnel strength has risen from 11 percent to 13 percent, and it continues to rise.

Not everyone, however, was satisfied with the Air Force's rate of progress. In 1984, members of Congress sought to force the Air Force to move faster toward increasing its number of female recruits, arguing that if the Air Force drew fewer recruits from the pool of qualified males, the other services might draw more. In the 1985 Defense Authorization Act, Congress included a provision requiring the Air Force to raise its recruitment quota for women from 14.7 percent of all recruits to 19 percent in 1987 and 22 percent in 1988.

The act also ordered the Air Force to study the effect of recruiting more women and to deliver its report to Congress. Written so as not to offend feminist supporters in Congress, the Air Force's report nevertheless concluded that the Congressionally mandated quota would lower mission effectiveness, increase manpower costs, and aggravate the problem of attrition. The report said that women were less available for daily duty, less available to travel for temporary duty because of personal reasons, and less likely to deploy quickly. The presence of women in large groups increased the rate at which members of the group were required to "work around" the absence of some members. As a result of the quota, the number of dual-service couples and single Air Force parents would double. Recruiting costs would increase because young civilian women showed less interest than men in military service. Training costs would increase because female recruits showed less aptitude for critical electronic and mechanical jobs and therefore would require additional training to replace men in those jobs.[8]

The report rejected the theory that forcing the Air Force to recruit fewer men would significantly increase the number of men available for recruitment by the other services. Citing behavioral and motivational differences between Air Force and Army recruits, the report estimated that only one out of twelve men turned away by the Air Force would join the Army as a second choice. The rest would seek civilian employment or educational opportunities. The report also predicted an increase in the number of quality male recruits for the Air Force by 1993.

Congress was not to be countered so easily and refused to back off on its mandated quotas. The report of the House Armed Services Committee on the 1986 Defense Authorization Act said repeal of the quota "would be premature at this time." The following year, the House committee recommended repeal of the 19 percent quota for 1987 but left in place the 22 percent quota for 1988. Later, Congress delayed the 22 percent quota until 1989. The Air Force finally succeeded in having a repeal amendment added to the fiscal year 1989 National Defense Authorization Bill. Nevertheless, it expects women to make up 19.6 percent of total Air Force accessions in 1989.

Like the Air Force, the Navy sailed ahead under Reagan with expanded opportunities for women, opening more jobs, more sea billets, and more command slots to women and increasing the total number of women in service. The number of Navy officer and enlisted women increased 52 percent from 1980 to 1986. In the fifth year of the Reagan Administration, 10 percent of Navy officers and 9 percent of Navy enlisted personnel were women. Plans called for adding another 4,000 enlisted women to reach the goal set by the Defense Department of 51,300 Navy enlisted women by 1989.

But, as with the Air Force, not everyone was pleased with the Navy's achievements. Female surface warfare officers found their opportunities for sea duty limited by their exclusion from ships of the Mobile Logistics Support Force (MLSF). When their complaints reached the sympathetic ears of DACOWITS, the committee began calling on the Navy to open these clearly labelled "support" ships to women. The Navy argued that MLSF ships fit the definition of combat vessels accepted by Congress when it amended Title 10 to allow women on noncombat vessels in 1978. That definition excluded women from permanent assignment aboard any "unit, ship, aircraft, or task organization" whose primary mission was to "seek out, reconnoiter, or engage the enemy." MLSF ships regularly moved as part of a battle group and therefore were classed as combat vessels. DACOWITS was unconvinced. "The Navy has to develop a more definitive determination of what constitutes a combat ship and what constitutes a support ship so that women will stay with that service and be fully utilized," said Constance B. Newman, DACOWITS chairwoman, in January 1986.[9]

Some women blamed the Secretary of the Navy, John F. Lehman Jr., for the MLSF restriction. A female naval officer at a DACOWITS meeting complained, "There are two words that explain why women aren't serving on MLSF ships: John Lehman."[10] Lehman himself told DACOWITS in November 1986 that opening MLSF ships to women was a "possibility, but we would need to adjust the legislation." Lehman belittled the problems of putting women aboard ship but said the move might provoke opposition from the wives of MLSF sailors. The Navy was "anti-family" enough without putting men and women together on ships, said Lehman. "That is the same excuse we heard about Air Force wives when women were being sent into silos," said Carolyn Becraft of WEAL. An aide to Senator William Proxmire of Wisconsin, a stalwart supporter of women in combat, observed that the National Military Family Association had endorsed the idea of women on ships, "so I think Mr. Lehman doesn't have to worry about Navy wives."[11]

Not long after Lehman's address to DACOWITS, the Navy reaffirmed its exclusion of women from the MLSF. Instead of opening the MLSF to women, the Navy renamed it the Combat Logistics Force. In March 1987, Vice Admiral Dudley L. Carlson, the Navy's chief of personnel, defended the name change before the Senate Armed Services Committee's subcommittee on personnel, showing the committee pictures of World War II ships burning and sinking after enemy attacks. "This is a picture of a combat logistics ship burning," said Carlson. "The people on that ship thought they were in combat." Not known for tact, Carlson tossed the grenade back into the lap of Congress, challenging Congress to do what it seemed to want the Navy to do. Said Carlson, "Our position is, if you want to change the combat exclusion law, fine. But, please don't mandate which ships are combat and which are not."[12] Congress backed off.

Other problems plagued the Navy during the years of expansion. The rush of women into the nation's sea service was not a rush to sea, as most female recruits preferred traditional jobs comfortably ashore to dirty work on the rolling waves. In 1983, three-fourths of Navy enlisted women were concentrated in one-fourth of Navy ratings, leaving very few sea billets in those ratings for women to fill. The Navy had opened more than 6,200 sea billets to women but could fill only 5,000 because there were not enough women in other ratings. Efforts to encourage women to pursue nontraditional jobs have met little success, and the preference of women for traditional jobs, not the reluctance of the Navy to open more ships to women, remains the largest stumbling block to putting more women to sea.

Because of this problem, the Navy was not enthusiastic about increasing its total number of women. More women only aggravate the problem of sea/shore rotation. When Congress tried to increase the Navy's female strength from 46,000 women in 1986 to 55,000 in 1987, Admiral James D. Watkins, as Chief of Naval Operations, made it known that the Navy had all the women it needed. Watkins' successor, Admiral Carlisle A. H. Trost, came to the same conclusion after several months in the job. In February 1987, Trost ordered a five-year freeze on the number of Navy enlisted women. Instead of proceeding toward the Reagan Administration's goal of 51,300, Trost intended to hold women to 46,796—9 percent of Navy enlisted personnel. Unfortunately for Trost, he had neglected to forewarn the Secretary of Defense or the Secretary of the Navy before making his decision public. Two days after the decision was announced, Weinberger met with DACOWITS chairwoman Jacquelyn K. Davis to hear her complaint about the effects of the decision on the Navy women, then brusquely countermanded the order.

Another defeat for the Navy involved civilian women employed by the Navy as technicians to work on Navy vessels. One such technician, Pamela Doviak Celli, was barred from going aboard a Navy submarine for sea trials and so filed suit with the Equal Employment Opportunity Commission (EEOC) charging the Navy with illegal sex discrimination. Celli's suit argued that Title 10 applied only to Navy servicewomen and not to Navy civilians and that excluding her from sea trials had inhibited her competition with male technicians for career advancement. The EEOC ruled in Celli's favor and issued an order to the Navy to rescind its prohibition on civilian women on combat vessels or pay Celli a substantial penalty. The Navy at first resisted the EEOC intervention on the grounds that the EEOC had no jurisdiction over the service, but on the last day before the EEOC's ultimatum was to expire, the new Secretary of the Navy, James H. Webb Jr., Naval Academy graduate, wounded Marine Corps veteran, bestselling author, and outspoken opponent of women at the service academies, ordered that Celli be allowed to participate in sea trials aboard submarines. Webb also ordered that decisions to allow anyone aboard ship should be left to ships' commanders, but "the basic policy that female employees shall have full opportunity to participate in sea trials still applies." Celli, who had received the support of the ACLU, called Webb's concession a "smokescreen" meant to avoid the sweeping consequences of a court ruling. Soon after Webb's decision was announced, female officers began complaining to DACOWITS that civilian women could now serve aboard ships closed to naval officers.

Webb's appointments first as Assistant Secretary of Defense for Reserve Affairs in 1984 and then as Secretary of the Navy in 1987 were anomalous blotches on the Reagan Pentagon's record on women. Feminist groups opposed his first appointment, as did some Pentagon officials, but Weinberger wanted him anyway. To better Webb's chances for confirmation by a Senate easily susceptible to feminist pressure, Weinberger submitted a letter to the Senate committee announcing that Webb had "reversed" his views regarding women in the military and was fully in line with Administration policy. To Webb, the announcement was a slap in the face. Though he admired and respected Weinberger greatly, he disliked being treated, in Webb's words, "like a reformed smoker." In fact, he did not recant his earlier views, though he did promise not to try to "turn back the clock."

Webb's appointment as Secretary of the Navy was less controversial because of his apparent good behavior as Assistant Secretary of Defense. Nevertheless, as if to test his sincerity, Jacquelyn Davis and DACOWITS toured Navy and Marine installations in the Far East in August 1987 and returned with a platter full of unappetizing issues that it served up to the Navy with great fanfare. On the menu were sexual harassment, fraternization, pregnancy, lesbianism, the burden of dependent children, problems with uniforms, troublesome male attitudes, the lack of decent housing, inadequate female medical care, insufficient promotion opportunity, poor communication between women and Navy leaders, and restrictions keeping women out of the CLF, the P-3 Orion anti-submarine aircraft, and the Marine Corps embassy guard program. The tone of the committee's report was that the Navy and the Marine Corps were inexcusably negligent in their duty to cater to the needs and demands of servicewomen. The report mentioned more than once that the "institutional hierarchies" of both services allegedly "continue to project attitudes that are biased against women."[13]

Secretary Webb had already ordered a comprehensive review of the "progress" of women in the Navy before DACOWITS's trip. The review was completed in December 1987, and Webb announced his approval of several of the review's recommendations in January 1988. More women would be allowed to compete to enter Navy ratings. More women would be assigned to aviation units and aboard P-3 aircraft. More women would be assigned to sea duty. Three kinds of CLF ships (oilers, ammunition ships, and store ships) would be opened to women, and the Navy's definition of *combatant* would be changed to include units, ships, aircraft, and task organizations which have as their primary missions "to seek out, reconnoiter, *and* engage the enemy." The 1978 definition required combatants to perform only one of the three tasks, instead of all three tasks.

Webb also had directed the Marine Corps to review its policies regarding the growing number of women Marines. In some ways, the Marine Corps remained the most conservative of the services. It still had fewer women as a percentage of its total force than any of the other services, and women Marines did not begin weapons training until 1987. But in six years under Reagan, the Marine Corps' female strength increased almost 50 percent, exceeding the Carter Administration's goal of 9,600 women Marines in service by 1987. The Women Marine Review of 1984 set the "ideal" strength of women Marines at 10,500, with 3,800 women in the Fleet Marine Force. The study also approved the deployment of women with a Marine Amphibious Force and with headquarters units and air combat elements of a Marine Amphibious Brigade, but kept them out of battalion and smaller units.

The study ordered by Webb was not completed until after Webb had resigned over unrelated differences with the new Secretary of Defense Frank Carlucci. The study produced 83 recommendations, of which 66 were approved for implementation by the Commandant of the Marine Corps, General Al Gray. Women would be assigned to many new jobs and units, including Hawk anti-aircraft missile battalions; barracks would be integrated to discourage lesbianism; the Marine Corps would seek expanded child-care and recreational facilities for women; and the Corps would work with the Navy to make female medical care more convenient. Gray did not approve several of the more controversial recommendations. He refused to allow women to crew C-130 transport aircraft and several small passenger jets, to deploy aboard amphibious ships, to undergo the same combat training as men, and to be assigned to the Corps' new security force battalions, which recently had taken on a counterterrorism mission.

Gray also rejected a recommendation that women be assigned as embassy security guards on the grounds that embassy guards are expected to be more than just fancy-dress doormen, but on that count he was overruled by Carlucci. Carlucci also later ordered women admitted to Marine security force battalions. While briefing DACOWITS on the results of the study, Gray made known his displeasure at being overruled as a result of the committee's meddling and disputed DACOWITS's claim that many women Marines wanted to be embassy guards. "I believe that was a carry-over from your agenda," he told DACOWITS. "I'm getting hustled along here. I'm having the opportunity to do what's best for my people taken away from me, and that gets my attention." At one point, he asserted his responsibility as the only government official charged solely with the complete responsibility for the good of the Marine Corps, saying, "I am the one who is totally responsible for their well-being. . . . I am the one who will make these kinds of decisions always," adding under his breath, "or you can get yourself another commandant."[14] The remark played in the press like a gauntlet slapped to the floor, but subsequent statements by Gray and by a spokesman for Carlucci denied that the two were at odds. A spokesman for Gray explained, "What the commandant really meant was that DACOWITS made a recommendation directly to the secretary without passing through him."[15]

The appointment of Frank Carlucci to replace Caspar Weinberger as Secretary of Defense was no improvement in the Pentagon's ability to defend itself against the feminist lobby. As Deputy Secretary of Defense in the early years of Weinberger's watch, Carlucci was largely responsible for shaping the Defense Department's official non-position on women in combat. Later, he was to confide in subordinates that he didn't share "Cap's hang-up about women in combat." Carlucci's wife, Marcia Carlucci, had been a member of DACOWITS from 1984 to 1986 and had shown nothing but support for the committee's agenda. Before that, she had helped get Miss Marybel Batjer, the youthful director of political affairs for the strongly feminist National Women's Political Caucus, into the job of special assistant to both the Secretary and the Deputy Secretary of Defense. Responsible for personally screening candidates for high-level offices in the Pentagon, Batjer was able to ensure that most offices were filled with people sympathetic to women in the military. The joke around the Pentagon was that a candidate had to be conservative enough to please the White House and liberal enough to please Marybel Batjer. If pleasing both were not possible, the White House was often the easier to be fooled. James Webb made it past Batjer because of Weinberger's patronage, but some of Webb's associates were not so fortunate.

As Secretary of Defense, Carlucci responded to DACOWITS's Far East visit by creating a new Task Force on Women in the Military headed by Dr. David J. Armor, a sociologist serving as Principal Deputy Assistant Secretary of Defense for Force Management and Personnel. Membership included, among others, Marybel Batjer, who had recently joined the staff of the National Security Council as deputy executive secretary, and Delbert Spurlock, the Assistant Secretary of the Army responsible for emasculating the WITA study. Jacquelyn Davis acted as an official observer. The task force was charged with examining three issues affecting women: career development, combat exclusions, and how women were regarded by their male counterparts. The task force contributed no new knowledge to the issues and developed all of its views within the confines of its Pentagon conference room. It presented its brief report to the House Armed Services Committee's military personnel subcommittee in January 1988.

Most of the task force's recommendations were modest renditions of demands made by DACOWITS. To aid the career development of servicewomen, the task force recommended that the Secretary of Defense direct the services to develop plans to draw more women into nontraditional career fields, which they had been trying to do for years with little success. To combat sexual harassment, the task force recommended that the services: improve sexual harassment training, establish a means outside the chain of command for reporting incidents of harassment, improve support facilities to "eliminate conditions that detract from Servicewomen becoming full and equal members of their units," and properly enforce the policy of providing servicewomen priority over dependent women for obstetrical and gynecological care.

The task force's only original contribution to policy concerned combat exclusions. The task force recommended that the Secretary of Defense instruct the services to adopt a new method of determining where women may or may not serve, based upon the principle of "equal risk." Noncombat units could be closed to women "provided that the type, degree, and duration of risk is equal to or greater than that experienced by associated combat units." To the Army, the principle of equal risk would mean "opening those [infantry or armored] brigade positions which, like forward support battalions, experience less risk than regular combat battalions." To the Navy, equal risk might mean opening more ships of the CLF, depending upon how the Navy decides to measure risk, said the task force. To the Air Force, any aircraft not incurring an equal risk with similar combat aircraft would be open to women. The task force expected that the Air Force's comparison of risk would keep some tactical reconnaissance aircraft, like the RF-4 Phantom, closed to women, but would open strategic reconnaissance aircraft like the SR-71 Blackbird, the U-2, and the TR-1. Some search and rescue aircraft might also be affected.

If applied to provide maximum opportunity to women, the doctrine of equal risk could have virtually the same effect as a bill sponsored in the 100th Congress by Senators William Proxmire of Wisconsin and William S. Cohen of Maine and by Congressman William L. Dickinson of Alabama. The Proxmire-Cohen bill would have permitted women to be assigned to all units, vessels, and aircraft that "have as their mission the direct support of combat units," without consideration for where they might be located or what threat they might face. The Air Force would have been forced to open all positions aboard tactical and strategic reconnaissance aircraft and transport aircraft, though such aircraft routinely operate over hostile territory. The Navy would have been forced to open all CLF ships. The Army would have been asked to open an estimated 140,000 positions in the main battle area.

The bill's sponsors insisted that the bill was a "moderate, combat support measure," not intended to "undermine" the combat exclusion laws but to provide a more efficient use of manpower and allow women greater opportunity for advancement. Members of their staffs, however, admitted that the bill, if passed, would have been a big step in the push for repeal of the combat exclusions. Others on Capitol Hill say the bill was intended not to become law but to please the feminist lobby by goading the Defense Department into extending of women's roles. After serving its purpose, the bill died in committee.

The real threat to the combat exclusions comes from the judicial branch of the federal government. With the Defense Department's policy of "equal risk" bringing women ever closer to combat, the courts might soon be asked to rule the combat exclusions laws unconstitutional on the grounds that the distinction between combat and noncombat is purely arbitrary. In *Rostker v. Goldberg,* the Supreme Court upheld the exemption of women from the draft by reasoning that the draft existed to provide the military with combat troops and because women were barred by law from combat, the draft exemption served a legitimate governmental purpose. But by not then addressing the issue of the constitutionality of the combat exclusion laws, the high court missed an opportunity to validate those laws when legal grounds for their constitutionality still existed.

Since *Rostker v. Goldberg,* the Reagan Defense Department has pulled all pillars of legal support out from under the combat exclusions by insisting that the exclusions rest solely upon the will of the American people, and recent opinion polls show a majority of Americans in favor of women in combat. Most Americans would qualify their endorsement of combat for women with the phrase "if they can do the job." They have not heard of WITA and know nothing of the political dangers facing anyone who says that many women cannot do the job. They have only the report of high-level Pentagon officials who are reliably effusive in their public praise of women in uniform. Such praise has watered the ground for growth of the repeal consensus, which thrives because the men closest to the issue, the men in the field and fleet, are prohibited from joining the debate.

NOTES ON CHAPTER VIII

1. Upon his appointment as governor of Algeria, then a French colony. Quoted by Philip Knightley, *The First Casualty* (New York: Harcourt Brace Jovanovich, 1975), p. 357.

2. Minutes to DACOWITS's Spring 1984 Meeting, p. 6.

3. Lawrence J. Korb, Statement to DACOWITS's Spring 1984 Meeting.

4. "Korb Says Women in Military 'Are Here to Stay,' " *Army Times*, 14 May 1984, p. 31.

5. Quoted by Senator William Proxmire in the Congressional Record, 21 March 1986.

6. Lawrence J. Korb, Statement to DACOWITS's Spring 1984 Meeting.

7. Caspar Weinberger, Statement to DACOWITS's Fall 1986 Meeting.

8. U.S. Air Force Special Studies Team, *An Analysis of the Effects of Varying Male and Female Force Levels* (Washington, D.C.: Department of the Air Force, 9 August 1985).

9. Sharon B. Young, "Need Told for Navy to Define Women's Sea Duty Clearly," *Navy Times*, 13 January 1986.

10. Tom Burgess, "DACOWITS Seeks Closer Look at Women's Role," *Air Force Times*, 6 May 1985, p. 30.

11. Sharon B. Young, "Navy Secretary Sees Chance of Women Having Greater Combat Support Roles," *Army Times*, 10 November 1986, p. 45.

12. Sharon B. Young, "Navy Fights Opening More Sea Billets to Women," *Navy Times*, 23 March 1987, p. 4.

13. Jacquelyn K. Davis, Letter to General Anthony Lukeman, 26 August 1987, subject: DACOWITS's 1987 WESTPAC Visit.

14. Mel Jones, "Gray's Tough Stand on His Responsibility Clarified," *Navy Times*, 9 May 1988, p. 4.

15. Jones.

CHAPTER IX

From Here to Maternity

*The whole of military activity must . . . relate directly or
indirectly to the engagement. The end for which a soldier is
recruited, clothed, armed, and trained, the whole object of his
sleeping, eating, drinking, and marching is simply that he
should fight at the right place and the right time.*

KARL VON CLAUSEWITZ

THE PARTY LINE IN WASHINGTON is that all is well with women in the
military, that with the exception of a few minor annoyances to be
dispelled by the magic wand of policy, sexual integration is proceeding smoothly without degrading military readiness. Women are "an
integral part" of the nation's defense, and they can do the job "as well
if not better" than their male comrades, say responsible officials,
some of whom seem quite willing to believe that women actually
make better soldiers than men do.

The proof, they say, is in the women's consistently faster rate of
promotion. Women are sometimes twice as likely as men to be
promoted. In the spring of 1987, the Army promoted 33 percent of
eligible women to the rank of E-7 but only 16 percent of eligible men.
DoD-wide, women are promoted with less time-in-service than men
to every grade from E-2 to O-7. Female officers are promoted to rear
admiral and brigadier general (O-7) fives years earlier than men, on
average. Enlisted women can expect promotion to senior NCO or

chief petty officer rank (E-7) two to four years earlier than enlisted men.

There are, however, several reasons for doubting the significance of promotion comparisons. Higher rates of attrition and lower rates of retention trim much of the deadwood from the women's ranks. In the past, those who survived until retirement were intensely dedicated women who forsook marriage and family for the sake of their careers. Today less dedicated women are favored by promotion systems that emphasize education, test scores, and personal appearance. Women tend to have higher levels of education, they perform well on written advancement examinations, and they often demonstrate greater poise, composure, and eloquence before promotion boards. Of course, promotions are centrally controlled and therefore not immune from manipulation for political or other purposes. The services do, in fact, exert considerable institutional pressure at all levels to safeguard the advancement of women.

The assertion that women in general are performing as well as or better than men is by no means proven. No doubt some women outperform some men, but the many good servicewomen who excel at their jobs do not compensate the services for the problems that women overall have caused them.

PHYSICAL LIMITATIONS

The general lack of physical strength among servicewomen bears directly upon their ability to perform assigned duties. Yet to many, the lack of physical strength among women seems hardly worth mentioning. The notion that technology has alleviated the need for physical strength is almost universally accepted. Say the words "modern warfare" and the minds of many Americans fill with images of control consoles and video displays. "There's an awful lot of button-pushing going on out there," says a reporter for *Time* magazine who thinks the physical demands of the military have been exaggerated.

There is, however, no real evidence that technology has in fact reduced the need for physical strength among military men and women. What evidence there is shows that many military jobs still require more physical strength than most women possess. Technology has not affected the way many simple, unavoidable wartime tasks are performed. It has not provided the Air Force with automatic litter-loaders to move wounded soldiers onto MEDEVAC aircraft when female loadmasters are unable to do so, nor has it relieved the Army of the task of sorting artillery rounds by hand. What technology has done is made service members able to do more, thereby making more for them to do. Many of the buttons that need pushing are attached to large pieces of equipment that must be hauled with haste back and forth across the battlefield.

Though estimations vary, there is without doubt a significant gap between the physical abilities of men and women. Tests of men and women entering the West Point class of 1980 found that, on average, the upperbody strength of women is 56 percent of the strength of men, their leg strength is 80 percent, and their gripping strength is 69 percent. Even when height is kept constant, women possess only 80 percent of the overall strength of men. When one considers differences in power (the combination of strength and speed) and in work performed within a span of time, both of which factor in the greater lung capacity and endurance of men, the disparity between the physical abilities of men and women appears more extreme. After eight weeks of intensive training, male plebes demonstrated 32 percent more power in the lower body and performed 48 percent more work at the leg press than female plebes. At the bench press, the men demonstrated 270 percent more power and performed an extraordinary 473 percent more work than the women.[1]

It is little wonder then that servicewomen should find so many workaday duties beyond their ability. Even in the modern Air Force, routine tasks are often too much for them. The GAO found that 62 of 97 female aircraft mechanics could not perform required tasks such as changing aircraft tires and brakes, removing batteries and crew seats, closing drag chute doors, breaking torque on bolts, and lifting heavy stands.[2] Female missile mechanics often lack the strength and physical confidence to harness and move warheads and to maneuver large pieces of machinery. Some have trouble carrying their own tool boxes.

In the late 1970s, the Air Force began screening recruits using the "X-Factor" strength indicator, but Army researchers found that the screening had degenerated in practice into a meaningless question-and-answer drill. Had the X-Factor actually kept women out of jobs for which they were unfit, it would have gone the way of the Army's MEPSCAT. Any attempt to relate job requirements to physical ability threatens the participation of women in the military. Their very presence in the ranks was made possible only by lowering or eliminating physical standards. When the services found that weight standards for recruits excluded 22 percent of potential female recruits but only 3 percent of potential male recruits, the standards were revised to resemble the insurance industry's standards, exluding 7.3 percent of women and 5.8 percent of men. A five-foot-six-inch female may now enlist in the Army weighing a hefty 165 lbs. Never mind that men lose weight much faster than women, or that the insurance industry's concern is with general health and not appearance or physical performance. All of the services have double standards for men and women on all the events of their regular physical fitness tests. Young male marines must perform at least 3 pull-ups to pass the test, but women marines must only hang from the bar with arms flexed for 16 seconds. In the Army, the youngest women are given an extra three minutes to complete a two-mile run. All of the services require men to perform more situps than women, despite the much-vaunted strength of the female midsection.

To justify the double standard, the American military abandoned the worldwide consensus as to the purpose of physical training for members of the military. All the world still thinks that soldiers should be harder, stronger, quicker, and more physically able than the rest of the populace. The U.S. military prefers weak but healthy people because they are cheaper in the long run. Physical training is meant to "ensure a minimum level of fitness, not to delineate any measure of job-related productivity," thus "the premise that men 'do more' because they must achieve higher physical fitness standards is not a valid one."[3]

Of course, on the job, men do actually do more to make up for the limitations of their female co-workers, though their extra work often passes unnoticed. As long as there are enough men around, commanders can pretend that women have not degraded a unit's ability to accomplish its mission. But as the number of women in the services has increased without an even spread of women throughout all units, the concentration of women in some support units has, in fact, begun to threaten mission accomplishment. Naval Air Station Adak in the Aleutian Islands of Alaska recently boasted a fire department that was 76 percent female. Fifty-one of the station's 67 firefighters were Navy enlisted women. The women were issued special, lighter fire-fighting equipment, and portions of the International Fire Service Association manuals were re-written to cover how the women should cope with physically demanding tasks. But because the women were still unable to perform such routine fire-fighting tasks as opening and closing fire hydrants, connecting large diameter hoses, advancing hose lines, and controlling nozzles, the department was forced to assign five women to an engine company which normally required only four men—a 25 percent increase in personnel to do the same job.

Recently the importance of physical strength and weight training to military members has been rediscovered by a handful of military fitness experts and concerned commanders. Army experts who were not personally involved in the WITA study have innocently compared a soldier's need for strength to an athlete's need, without considering the implications of the comparison for the Army's use of women. According to Major James Wright, chief of the Exercise Science Branch of the U.S. Army Fitness School:

> Upper-body strength is an important component of virtually every Army task. There are still hundreds of manual-type tasks which require strength. There will always be a lot of setting up and tearing down of equipment when units go to the field. In fact, several studies show that the lack of upper-body strength is actually a limiting factor for our overall military readiness.[4]

Navy Lieutenant Ed Marcinik, an exercise physiologist working with the Naval Health and Physical Readiness Program, agrees:

> There are general shipboard tasks that every sailor must perform, all requiring upper-body strength: extricating injured per-

sonnel, controlling fire hose nozzles, handling stores, and opening and securing watertight hatches, doors, and scuttles.[5]

Marcinik says that fully 84 percent of all shipboard duties involve
heavy lifting, carrying, or pulling. Four ratings (boatswain's mate,
gunner's mate, hull technician, and machinist's mate) are among the
most physically demanding jobs in the military. In recognition of the
need for physical strength among sailors, the Navy developed a
program of shipboard weight training called SPARTEN, or Scientific
Program of Aerobic and Resistance Training Exercise in the Navy.
One part of SPARTEN involved the installation of nautilus equipment on ships like the battleship *New Jersey.*

To military women, however, any new emphasis on physical
strength is anathema. If men in the military are encouraged to think
that being strong and quick is good, the professional reputation of
military women will surely suffer. Limiting the emphasis on physical
strength to all-male "combat" units will only encourage the belief
that women, as noncombatants, are second-class service members.
To protect and advance women as equals, the services are committed
to preaching the devaluation of physical prowess as a professional
virtue, which is why programs like SPARTEN are only marginally
effective. The services cannot improve the physical competence of
servicemen because to do so would adversely affect the status of
servicewomen.

Besides the impact of the lack of strength and speed on individual
and unit performance, the smaller size and different shape of women
has caused innumerable problems solved only by a boom in the
development and procurement of special clothing and equipment.
The defense inventory has burgeoned with end-items specially designed for use by both sexes or by women only, including smaller
everything from snowshoes to flightsuits: smaller wire-cutters,
longer wrenches, lighter firefighters' helmets, specially cut boots;
special helicopter seats because women complained of back pain
from sitting in standard seats; flakvests to accommodate female
breasts; gas-masks to fit softer, smaller, less bony faces; and a dispos-
able cardboard tube to enable female soldiers to urinate in the field

without dropping their trousers (developed but not adopted). In the interest of uniformity and standardization, the Army has tried to develop clothing that will fit both men and women with minimum variation in size, but the results have been unsightly compromises which fit neither sex well.

A more serious result of the differences of shape and size is the relaxation of anthropometric standards devised to fit the operator to the equipment. The services have always shown a willingness to relax standards for height, weight, and reach in order to admit women to special programs and training. None of the first women to undergo Navy flight training in 1975 satisfied the Navy's own stringent standards that excluded many men. In 1983, in the interest of pilot safety and aircraft performance, the Navy revised its anthropometric standards for Naval aviators to tighten requirements for sitting height, leg length, buttock-to-knee length, and functional reach, but when female aviators complained that only a quarter of them would qualify under the new standards, the Navy backed off.

Anthropometric differences also affect the design of new systems and equipment with potentially serious consequences. Trying to design ever more sophisticated military hardware for use by both six-foot-five males and five-foot-nothing females will inevitably lead to trading off safety and performance. There is no such thing as a one-size-fits-all high performance jet fighter. For the safety of the pilot and for the performance of the aircraft, cockpits are made to be tight fits. When designers introduce a 25 percent variable in the size of the pilot, something must give.

The need to accommodate smaller, weaker soldiers played a part in the Army's decision to replace the M1911 45 caliber Colt pistol with the 9 millimeter Beretta. The best buy the Army ever made, the .45 automatic was designed to stop a drug-crazed Moro warrior dead in his tracks. It served all of the services well in every war since World War I but lately fell victim to complaints that it was difficult to use effectively because it was unwieldy and heavy—so heavy that female military policemen were issued 38 caliber revolvers instead.

The Army insists that the .45's ineffectiveness and the need for standardization of caliber within NATO motivated the change and denies that the inability of women to use the .45 was even a consideration, but the arguments for standardization and effectiveness raise the question of why the Army is not also considering a replacement for the M-16 rifle. Since its adoption, the M-16 has been criticized by experienced soldiers as being mechanically unreliable, lacking in stopping power, ineffective at long ranges, and too fragile for combat use. The NATO standard rifle caliber is 7.65 mm, but the M-16 is a 5.56 mm rifle and United States is the only country in NATO to use it. Since rifles are far more important and more common on the battlefield than pistols, replacing the M-16 would make great sense, except that any 7.65 mm alternative to the M-16 would weigh many pounds more, posing a significant problem for female soldiers. Because in almost every instance the good of equal opportunity takes precedence over the good of the service, American soldiers are unlikely to get the weapon they need if it makes life more difficult for women.

MEDICAL DIFFERENCES

Lack of physical strength contributes to another problem with women in the military: they need greater medical attention. Women in all of the services are hospitalized two to three times as often as men, a difference corresponding to that found in the civilian community. In the 1970s, the percentage of Navy women requiring hospitalization fluctuated between 25 and 30 percent while hospitalization of Navy men declined from 13 percent in 1966 to 11 percent in 1975. When men and women are subjected to the same work requirements and living conditions, as during recruit and cadet training, women's hospitalization rates are significantly higher than men's rates for nearly all diagnoses: mental disorders, musculoskeletal afflictions, acute upper-respiratory infections, medical and surgical aftercare, rubella, infective and parasitic diseases, and digestive, diarrheal, and genitourinary disorders.[6]

In the services at large, differences in military occupation and off-duty behavior mean different rates of hospitalization for the various diagnoses. Men are generally more prone to injury (fractures, lacerations, and dislocations) because of their poorer driving records and greater involvement in hazardous work and athletics, though Navy women in the lower grades assigned nontraditional jobs have shown "considerably higher" rates of injury than similarly assigned men, probably because of their lack of physical confidence, mechanical experience, and upperbody strength.[7] Women generally are still more prone to mental illness, genitourinary disorders, and disease, with pregnancy-related conditions accounting for one third or more of all women hospitalized. Among mental disorders, men show higher rates of schizophrenia, alcoholism, and drug-related conditions, while women show higher rates of neuroses, eating disorders, and "transient situational disturbances."[8]

Though many military women deny or downplay the effects of pre-menstrual syndrome (PMS) on the behavior of women, medical experts estimate that 5 to 10 percent of all pre-menopausal women experience severe PMS-related symptoms, including incapacitating depression, suicidal thoughts, extreme mood swings, self-abuse, and violence. "These are women who suffer chronic, debilitating distress—women who are often unable to take care of themselves or their family," says Nancy Reame, associate professor of nursing at the University of Michigan at Ann Arbor.[9] Most women experience milder symptoms such as bloating, headaches, backaches, irritability, depression, breast tenderness, and food cravings. Roughly half of all women who suffer PMS characterize the condition as "mildly distressing." Only about 10 percent of pre-menopausal women experience no symptoms of PMS. The impact of PMS on unit effectiveness is compounded by the natural, involuntary tendency of women living in close quarters to synchronize their menstrual cycles.

Much of the debate about the medical cost-effectiveness of women versus men has focused on rates of "noneffectiveness" or "nonavailability," the amount of duty time service members miss while receiving medical attention. The medical nonavailability rate for women is consistently 2 to 2.5 times the rate for men. Much of the difference is attributable to pregnancy, but the women's rate exceeds the men's rate for all diagnoses. The women's nonavailability rate is 8.7 times the male rate for genitourinary disorders, 2.6 times the men's rate for morbidity (disease), 1.4 times the men's rate for mental illness, and 3.8 times the men's rate for spurious complaints. Women lose five times as much time as men for attempted suicide but are successful at suicide only half as many times as men.[10]

The significance of the greater medical needs of women has been very effectively suppressed by proponents of women in the military who point out, whenever the subject comes up, that though women lose more time for medical reasons, men lose more time for disciplinary reasons. The greater need of women for medical attention and the greater trouble men cause by undisciplined behavior are quite different problems, however, and the discussion should not end with a simple comparison of lost time.

The lack of discipline among men is itself the fault of a feminized force, a force that fails to instill discipline during basic training because of its be-nice-to-privates approach to attracting and managing troops. Still, a commander has much more control over a unit's disciplinary problems than its medical problems, and rates of nonavailability for indiscipline vary dramatically from unit to unit and from time to time. Since the comparison of nonavailability for all reasons was last made in 1980, rates of indiscipline among men have declined as the services have attracted better quality recruits. The Defense Department no longer knows whether men or women lose more time overall.

In contrast, the medical demands of women in the peacetime force have been relatively steady. Modifications of clothing and equipment have reduced the rate at which women seek medical attention only slightly. Sex education has done little to reduce rates of pregnancy. If the medical nonavailability rates of women change at all, they are likely to increase as more and more women are assigned nontraditional duties for which they have not the physical ability. Nonavailability will also increase if women are employed closer to the fighting in wartime. The services can expect an increase in mental illness and infectious disorders among women. Unsanitary conditions combined with inevitable shortages of such items as sanitary napkins will aggravate genitourinary infections. In Honduras, servicewomen were forced to use sponges and birth control pills when there was nothing else. In future wars, even those poor comforts may be luxuries.

That servicewomen place a considerable additional burden on the already overburdened military medical system is generally admitted, but the weight of the burden is unknown and not likely to become known for political reasons. In 1985, the Defense Department's Health Studies Task Force recommended that the department fund an independent study of the full impact of integration on the health care requirements of the services, at a cost of $780,000. The task force noted that a joint study by the Defense Department and the Veterans Administration would cost less but would be "suspect in the civilian community and among various women's groups" and might "provoke a political controversy."[11] No study, independent or in-house, has ever been done.

ATTRITION

One problem with women in the military that does receive some attention is the problem of attrition, defined as the failure to complete an enlistment contract. Attrition reduces service strength, increases personnel turbulence, and robs the service of its training investment. Women consistently attrit at higher rates than men. The difference is most dramatic between male and female high school graduates, the very people the services want most to keep. In 1981, nearly half of all Marine Corps female high school graduates failed to complete their enlistment contracts, more than double the rate for male high school graduates: 48 to 23.5 percent. In the Army, the attrition rate for female graduates was two-thirds higher than for male graduates: 40.3 to 24.8 percent. More recently, attrition among all servicewomen has been 36 percent higher than attrition among male servicemen: 34 to 25 percent.[12] The difference is least in the Navy, in which men see an unequal share of sea duty. As more women are required to go to sea involuntarily, attrition rates for Navy women will soar.

Defenders of women in the military have often suggested that the combat restrictions frustrate the ambitions of women and thus contribute to their higher rates of attrition, but all evidence shows otherwise. Attrition among women in nontraditional career fields is consistently higher than among women in traditional career fields, and studies indicate that women who attrit tend to hold more traditional views regarding the roles of men and women. A Marine Corps study indentified "traditional family and career orientation" as the most important factor among women who attrited.[13] Thus, those inclined toward leaving service are not likely to be persuaded to stay if offered opportunities for nontraditional work, and those who complain about limited opportunities are not likely to leave service because their ambitions are not fully satisfied. As the services push more women into nontraditional jobs, attrition among women will increase.

PREGNANCY

By far, the largest reason for attrition among women is pregnancy. The services estimate that 25 to 50 percent of women who fail to complete enlistment contracts do so because of pregnancy. Pregnancy and parenthood accounted for 23 percent of all women discharged in 1980. It is estimated that 7 to 17 percent of servicewomen become pregnant each year. As mentioned earlier, the Army found that one third of the women who became pregnant opted for voluntary discharges under the policy that leaves the decision to stay in or get out in the hands of the woman.

The services once handled pregnancy very differently. Executive Order No. 10240, signed by President Truman in 1951, authorized the services to involuntarily separate women, married or unmarried, who were pregnant, gave birth while in service, or had custody of dependent children under 18 years of age. For twenty years, the heads of the women's components zealously defended the right of the services to involuntarily separate pregnant women and mothers for the good of all concerned: the service, the women's components, the mother, and the child. A few activists like Jeanne Holm thought the policy discriminated against women because men were not similarly treated for fatherhood. They adopted the argument that the sevices should take no notice of pregnancy or motherhood because the "ultimate responsibility for the care and welfare of children rests with the parent, not, we submit, with the Air Force."[14] Most senior officers, however, took the view of Brigadier General Elizabeth P. Hoisington, director of the WAC, who held that different treatment was justified because mothers and fathers in service were, in legal terms, not *similarly situated:*

> no basis exists to consider equalizing Army policy for male and female members concerning parenthood through adoption or other means. A valid comparison cannot be made between the civilian wife of a male member and the military wife of a male member. The interests of the Army will best be served by women who are free to travel. The interests of the children will best be served by women who have no military obligation.[15]

Hoisington's successor, Brigadier General Mildred C. Bailey, repeated the argument in 1974:

> No matter what you say about equal opportunity you cannot deal with the situation of an expectant father and an expectant mother in the same way. Mothers have a role in child rearing that is different from fathers and we have to think about the effect this has on mission readiness and our ability to be available for worldwide assignment.[16]

In 1972, however, servicewomen were granted two new options which might have defused the issue: the option of requesting waivers to stay in service and the option of having an abortion. The first came as a result of the AVF's need to retain more women and the services' desire to avoid negative publicity and court challenges. Waivers were liberally granted by all services. While the Army granted waivers to 60 percent of the women who applied, the Air Force, Navy, and Marine Corps granted waivers to more than 90 percent. The second option came as a result of the Supreme Court's decision in *Roe v. Wade* striking down laws in all fifty states banning abortion and allowing servicewomen to have abortions at government expense, until Congress banned federally funded abortions in 1978.

Still, court challenges continued until a federal circuit court in 1976 settled the case of *Crawford v. Cushman* by ruling that the discharge of a pregnant marine was an unconstitutional violation of the 5th Amendment's guarantee of due process. The court termed pregnancy a "temporary disability" and noted that no other temporary disability resulted in automatic involuntary discharge. Rather than fight the ruling, the Defense Department ordered the services to stop involuntarily separating pregnant women and to allow voluntary separations.

The classification of pregnancy as a "temporary disability" had long been an objective of feminist litigation against civilian employers. The term secured for civilian women job-related medical benefits and prohibited civilian employers from penalizing pregnant employees for the inconvenience their condition caused.

In the military, however, the term protects women from involuntary discharge but serves no other purpose. The military already assumes full responsibility for the medical health of its members regardless of the cause or nature of their infirmity. The term "temporary disability" itself does not protect servicewomen from adverse personnel actions because, unlike civilian employees, service members can be court-martialed under Article 115 of the Uniform Code of Military Justice for any self-inflicted disability that interferes with their performance of duty—from shooting themselves in the foot to avoid combat, to lying on the beach long enough to become too sunburned to wear a uniform. If a soldier's own negligence or misconduct was the proximate cause of his injury, it does not matter whether the injury was intentional or unintentional. The soldier can be made to reimburse the government for his medical expenses.

Pregnancy, however, is the only temporary disability that service members can inflict upon themselves without fear of punishment. It is also the only temporary disability that earns a service member the right to decide for herself whether to stay in the service or get out, notwithstanding the desires of her commander or the needs of the service. The court's ruling that pregnancy is like any other temporary disability has been applied only to favor and protect women.

The problem with allowing the woman to decide whether she should stay in the service is that the only way the service comes out ahead is if the woman elects to have an abortion. Otherwise, either the woman contributes to the problem of attrition (and still receives military maternity care until six weeks after delivery) or she becomes a burden to her unit. Restrictions vary from service to service, but the typical pregnant service member is exempt from a variety of routine duties and requirements. She must not be made to stand at attention or parade rest for more than 15 minutes (no parades or ceremonies). She must not be exposed to harmful chemicals or vapors (no chemical warfare training, no painting, limited duties in the motorpool). She must not receive routine immunizations (no deployments overseas). She must not remain aboard ship in port past her 20th week and must not go to sea (no sea duty). She must not be assigned to remote installations where there are limited medical facilities. She must not be assigned duties in which nausea, easy fatigue, sudden lightheadedness, or loss of consciousness would be hazardous to her or anyone else (no flying, driving, diving, or operating large machinery). The Navy bars pregnant sailors from participating in swim tests, drown-proofing, field training, and weapons training. The Army exempts pregnant women from overnight duty and limits their work-week to 40 hours or less, with frequent rest periods.

The pregnant service member may, at her discretion or upon the advice of her doctor, participate in regular physical training but not physical testing. Feminists minimize the dangers of exercise to pregnant women, just as they minimize the extent to which pregnancy interferes with one's duty performance, but in practice most military doctors err on the side of safety and advise against participating in physical training if the mother is not already well-accustomed to exercise. Exertion from infrequent exercise can cause hyperthermia, which can lead to birth defects in the first two months of pregnancy and to premature labor after the fourth month. Naturally, most servicewomen are more than happy to follow doctors' orders.

Pregnant service members may choose to have their babies at the military hospital nearest their home and are allowed up to six weeks of paid leave not charged to their leave account. Difficult pregnancies may prompt a doctor to relieve a servicewoman of all duties for as long as necessary, sometimes six or seven months before birth, during which the woman is a complete loss to her unit, though her unit is not permitted to request a replacement because she is still on its roster.

Needless to say, pregnancy is not viewed by many as just another temporary disability, like a hernia or a broken leg. Most men and many women, particularly women officers, view it as a unique indulgence the military is obliged to allow its female members for no good reason. Many of the most dedicated men and women see motherhood and military service as conflicting obligations. Many military men still like to think that they endure the danger and hardships of service so that mothers and children can be safe at home. Whatever they think about equal opportunity, they still find the site of a pregnant woman heading a formation of troops unsettling. Few people, civilian or military, can escape the notion that pregnancy is inconsistent with the role of the warrior, that the killing spirit and motherly love are necessarily inimical to each other, and that where the two are combined, the one is weakened and the other perverted. The services themselves are extremely sensitive to this glaring inconsistency. When the Army unveiled its new camouflage maternity uniform, it insisted that the uniform is not a battle dress uniform, which it resembles so closely; it is a "maternity work uniform and will be referred to as such." The reason for the difference was not explained.

Pregnancy is perhaps the single greatest obstacle to the acceptance of women in the military among military men. Charles Moskos, professor of sociology at the University of Chicago, after interviewing Army women with their units in Honduras, concluded, "When there are no pregnant women, the incorporation of women into nontraditional roles is greatest." He added, "If there is an absolute precondition of the effective utilization of women in field duty, it must be exclusion of pregnant women."[17]

The services would be more than happy to exclude pregnant women altogether, but their hands are tied. The policy of tolerating pregnant women in uniform, forced upon the military from above, has put the services in an impossible position. The services are duty bound to reduce pregnancies to improve readiness but legally and politically bound to honor pregnant women as fully accepted service members in good standing. They dare not recommend abortion to pregnant women, nor can they actively encourage pregnant women to opt for voluntary discharge, nor can they apply official disincentives to discourage women from becoming pregnant. Their efforts to make life easier for pregnant women only make pregnancy less of a thing to avoid. The services view pregnancy as a serious problem, but many of the women who become pregnant apparently do not.

The little the services have done to reduce the incidence of pregnancy might have had the reverse effect. Recruits receive a few hours of sex education in basic training, after which they rarely receive more. The lack of additional training probably does more to reduce pregnancy than anything else, because the services have been, and probably always will be, woefully ineffective at discouraging sexual activity through education. Far from discouraging women from having sex, the services' non-judgmental, safety-first, girls-will-be-girls approach tends to encourage promiscuity, even to the point of advising female soldiers on how to properly have sex in the field environment. Following the scout's motto, a pamphlet entitled "Feminine Hygiene in the Field Setting," published and distributed at Fort Meade, Maryland, advises women to always be prepared:

> Sex does not just happen in the garrison setting. If you are on
> birth control pills, make sure that you bring enough packs along
> to last you for the exercise, and an extra pack in case something
> happens to the pack you're currently on.

It might have been more in the interest of the service to advise women that sex does not *just happen* anywhere and that they have no business making it happen while on maneuvers. Unfortunately, the good of the service has all but been abandoned in dealing with the problem of pregnancy.

MOTHERHOOD AND MARRIAGE

Problems for the service and the servicewoman do not end with delivery. Having elected to keep the child and remain in service, the woman must struggle to fulfill her duties as a mother and as a soldier, sailor, airman, or marine. She is required to certify in writing that provisions have been made for the care of her dependents during regular duty hours, extended duty hours, readiness exercises, unaccompanied tours, temporary duty, changes of station, and actual emergencies. If overseas, she must arrange for someone to escort her dependents during a possible evacuation of noncombatants. Should any of her arrangements fail, she is still required to report to duty. Failure to provide for the care of her children or to perform her military duty is grounds for receiving a bar to reenlistment or being involuntarily separated. Few women are separated for such failure, however, as commanders are reluctant to punish young mothers so severely and most have more important things to do than checking to see that everyone's child-care plan is working. The dependent care certificate is, in most cases, a bureaucratic formality. A recent Navy survey found that only half of all Navy mothers even had them.

All problems multiply if the mother is single, as an estimated 24,000 service mothers are. Eleven percent of all servicewomen are single-parents, and estimations are that more than a third of all pregnant servicewomen are unmarried.[18]

Just how many service fathers are unmarried is unknown because the Defense Department includes divorced servicemen paying child support in its count of "sole parents." There is, of course, a vast difference between the obligation to pay a few hundred dollars a month to support a child in someone else's custody and the obligation to care for a child in one's own custody, but by lumping the two together the Defense Department can tell the world, as it has since 1981, that "more than three-quarters of the military sole parents are males."[19]

The Defense Department knows better, however, and its efforts to exculpate women for the single-parent problem constitute a deliberate deceit. In 1980, the services defined single-parents differently. The Army and Marine Corps included those with custody and those paying child-support. The Navy and Air Force counted only service members with actual custody, producing the embarrassing truth that Navy women were eight times as likely and Air Force women were five times as likely as Navy and Air Force men to be single-parents.[20]

These statistics, along with the inflated figures of the Army and Marine Corps, were reported in the Defense Department's 1981 background review, with footnotes explaining the inconsistency. Since then, however, the Defense Department, having assumed the responsibility for keeping such statistics for the services, has included those who pay child-support in the count.

The Defense Department is also aware that the ratio of male single-parents to female single-parents shrinks as the number of women in service increases. Today, the Air Force, with women as not quite 14 percent of its personnel strength, estimates that half of its single-parents are men and half are women, making Air Force women more than six times more likely than Air Force men to be single-parents. Odds on the sex of single-parents may vary considerably among the services. A recent survey of an eleven-thousand-man (13 percent female) Marine headquarters battalion at Twentynine Palms, California, found that female Marines were 14 times more likely to be single-parents than male Marines.[21]

Yet, single-parenthood is not just an overwhelmingly female problem but a problem that would not exist if there were no women in the services. Prior to the expansion of women in the military in the 1970s, the services often separated service members who became single-parents by any circumstance. Only because the services were forced to protect servicewomen from factors aggravating female attrition did they adopt their present policy of tolerating some 50,000 service members who are single-parents. The peculiar policy of tolerating service members who become single-parents while not enlisting people who are already single-parents has invited numerous lawsuits challenging the ban on single-parent enlistments on the grounds that it illegally discriminates against women because the great majority of civilian single-parents are female. So far, the ban has withstood all assaults, but in response to the apparent inconsistency in single-parent policy and the continuing cry of discrimination, Congress in 1986 amended Title 10 to permit single-parents who had previously served in the regular armed forces to enlist in the reserves, so long as their single-parenthood was not the cause of their discharge from service.

By and large, single-parents in the military are a sorry lot. Duty calls at odd times and single-parents are often scrambling to arrange for somebody to take their child. All of the normal inconveniences of service life—overnight duty, field exercises, sudden deployments, early morning physical training, and late nights in the motor pool—cause scheduling problems for single-parents. Some pay others in their unit to pull duty for them when they can't find babysitters. Some bring their children to their unit, where the children loiter in the barracks while their mothers are on duty. Some leave their children alone at home, perhaps for a few hours after school or until the center opens up in the morning, but sometimes all day.

The problems of many married service mothers are much the same. Two thirds are married to servicemen and almost none have husbands who stay at home with the children. Deployments, emergencies, and evacuations are still a problem, but most married service mothers can at least afford to pay for routine child-care when it is available.

More and more, the military is making it available, rapidly expanding the number of child-care facilities to accommodate the growing legions of dependent children. In 1988, there were 581 military child-care centers on 412 installations, with another 100 centers planned for the next six years. Though current capacity is suitable for more than 20,000 children, the Defense Department estimates that 80,000 spaces are needed. The cost of caring for everyone's children has already eaten up funds for other projects. For 1987, Congress approved more than $20 million for nearly all child-care construction projects requested by the services, but denied funding for nearly all other facilities related to morale, welfare, and recreation—chapels, libraries, theaters, exchanges, commissaries, and recreation centers. For fiscal year 1989, the Defense Department estimated needing $80 million for operation and construction of child-care facilities. Fortunately for the services, the child-care boom is one military buildup Congress still enthusiasticly supports.

With or without children, marriages between service members are a problem. One third of all servicewomen are married to servicemen. In 1981, there were some 45,000 "dual-service" or "in-service" couples (90,000 service members). Today there are more than

56,000 dual-service couples. Some involve both officer and enlisted personnel, some involve members of different services, and more than half involve children. For all the talk about expanding opportunities for women to make more efficient use of manpower, the services are resigned to making very inefficient use of manpower to accommodate dual-service couples. Dual-service couples do not simply "come down on orders" to Korea or Turkey. Each assignment for a dual-service couple must be negotiated with special assignment managers who handle only "joint domicile" assignments. Elaborate computerized systems for making such assignments have not alleviated the need for sacrifice. Either the couple must sacrifice their time together to further their careers or sacrifice their careers to have more time together. Usually the couple is asked to decide whose career will take precedence and who will simply tag along to fill any available space in the area. Recent cost-cutting measures that keep military personnel in one place longer have exacerbated the problem. Where the Army once could boast of providing joint domicile assignments (within 50 miles) to 90 percent of dual-service couples, it has lately warned that such assignments "may get increasingly difficult to approve."[22] As more women enter service and the number of dual-service couples grows, joint-domicile assignments will become even harder to make.

Not surprisingly, the demands of family take a heavy toll among female officers and enlisted personnel. Reenlistment rates are consistently lower for women than for men in all of the services, particularly in the middle grades. The demands of family are regarded as the single greatest reason for lower retention among women after their first reenlistment. Service officials have no idea how to stop the drain except to build more child-care centers. "We must find ways to retain [women]," the vice commandant of the Coast Guard told DACOWITS. "If family rearing is a major factor, we must explore alternatives."[23] Alternatives to what, he did not say. A Marine Corps study made a similar recommendation that the Corps "help women develop short-term alternatives to marriage and pregnancy for overcoming loneliness."[24] It gave no examples.

FRATERNIZATION

The problems of pregnancy, single-parents, and dual-service couples were made possible largely by the erosion of the age-old ban on fraternization between the ranks. To be sure, the American military has been moving toward greater and greater egalitarianism for some time, but nothing has done more to cheapen rank and diminish respect for authority than cute little female lieutenants and privates. Military customs and regulations are no match for the forces that draw men and women together in pairs without regard for differences in pay grade. Cupid mocks Mars. Lust and love laugh in the face of martial pomp and the pretensions of power.

The services could hardly prevent nature from taking her course, but they might have had greater success enforcing and preserving the customs of service if servicewomen had not been so opposed to their efforts. The call for liberalization of social restrictions has characterized the military service of American women from World War II and to the present day. Many women who wander into a recruiting office know and care little about military tradition, and their initial training does nothing to correct their essentially civilian regard for the same. Many consider the customs of service quaint, silly, and boyish. Few understand the necessity for restrictions on social relationships that interfere with their love lives.

Instead of making servicewomen conform to the service, the services have conformed service policy to the presence of women and developed a more permissive definition of fraternization. Fraternization was traditionally understood to occur anytime persons of different rank set aside their rank to deal with each other as equals. Now the term *fraternization* is used only to describe certain officer-enlisted relationships forbidden by the Uniform Code of Military Justice (UCMJ). All other relationships between persons of different rank are permitted so long as one of the persons involved does not exercise supervisory authority over the other and the relationship does not result in favoritism or harm morale.

The Navy and Marine Corps still prohibit romantic relationships between officers and enlisted personnel. The Army and Air Force, however, liberalized officer and enlisted relations years ago. The Army announced its new fraternization policy in 1984, insisting that the old policy had simply been "clarified—not relaxed." The practical effect of the clarification, however, was to legitimize many relationships which were previously considered improper. Where once officers eschewed social involvement with all enlisted personnel, now they must only avoid social involvement with those directly under them. The finer points of propriety, such as whether or not a lieutenant should escort his enlisted girlfriend to an officers' dining-out, are left for the individual to decide. Holding an individual's decision against him is extremely difficult, because the burden of proof rests with the accuser and the negative effect of the decision upon the service must be "demonstrated and documented."[25]

Instead of clarifying the issue, the new policy only caused confusion. Its authors had failed to consider the complexity of the problem. Commanders complained that the new policy was too permissive and set no clear rule for what was proper and what was improper. Experienced soldiers might know where to draw the line, but less experienced soldiers, both officer and enlisted, would not. Commanders themselves were unsure what they should condone and what they should discourage. They were also uncertain of the grounds for taking action against someone perceived as having acted improperly. The Army's explanation of the policy included examples of inappropriate relationships that caused a "noticeable drop in morale," but what is noticeable to one commander might not be noticeable to another, and experienced commanders are likely to notice the effect of inappropriate behavior before the effect becomes documentable. The requirement for "clearly predictable" harm to morale was also highly subjective and sure to invite second-guessing by higher authorities in any contested case. Commanders were therefore wise to be cautious and to permit more than they would prefer to permit.

Increasingly, rank is seen as something one puts on before breakfast and takes off before dinner. Distinctions of class, culture, and calling, never well understood by Americans, are now not even acknowledged, and traditions that once seemed self-evidently sensible are surrendered without argument to a simple ideological imperative.

It speaks not well for American military professionals that in defense of a liberalized fraternization policy, the policymakers indulge in much unmanly maundering about the value of personal relationships, as if to argue that liberalization is actually good for the military and not simply an easy way to avoid coming to terms with a difficult problem:

> Personal relationships have always had a positive side. Close relationships are desired and required if we are to build cohesive units that can fight, survive, and win on the battlefield. Building this cohesion requires a professional sensitivity toward one another.[26]

The ancient Spartans took a similar view of the connection between personal relationships and unit cohesion, believing that homosexuality increased the bond between comrades-in-arms. The modern American military also benefits homosexuality in ways it will not admit.

HOMOSEXUALITY

Lesbianism has always been common in the military, but for many years, while women comprised a small fraction of their total strength, the services preferred to deny and ignore its existence completely. The truth, according to Helen Rogan, author of *Mixed Company,* was that after World War II, the women's components became havens for female homosexuals, who were naturally attracted to the opportunity for intimate association with other women and to the authoritarian structure of the services, in which personal relationships are based upon "dominance and submission."[27]

Despite the wholesome, feminine image of servicewomen presented to the public by the scandal-sensitive services, Rogan found that the style among lesbian members of the Women's Army Corps was exaggeratedly masculine. The stereotypical image of the homosexual dyke was well-founded in fact. "If you were going to be gay, you wanted to be like a guy, because they were the ones who could get things on," says one lesbian veteran in a documentary film quoted by Rogan. Women cut their hair in men's styles, donned men's clothing when off-duty, sat and walked the way men do, and even wore Old Spice aftershave. They partied together and sat around in the clubs drinking beer and were active in sports.

Within the women's components, lesbians created a secret society with their own informal chain of command that sometimes ignored traditional distinctions between ranks. Rogan quotes one woman whose homosexuality began when she was seduced by her company commander:

> As a baby troop, I noticed there was an in crowd, and all of them, all the important and nice-to-know people, were gay. It was desirable to be gay. The straight young enlisted person finds that out, and then she has to decide what to do. The assumption was that we didn't need men, not for our jobs.[28]

Senior WAC officers, most of whom had come up through the ranks, were more careful to avoid the appearance of lesbianism than enlisted personnel and junior officers. "Oh, sure, of course there were gays [among senior officers], but never publicly," one veteran told Rogan. Low-ranking lesbians respected the need of senior officers to be more discreet in their conduct, and senior officers, in turn, protected everyone's career and the reputation of the Corps by turning a blind eye toward homosexuality. The male heads of the Army left the women to themselves, and no place was safer than Fort McClellan, Alabama, the home of the WAC. There women lived their lives as they pleased. "We had no need to conform to an artificial standard [of heterosexuality]," one woman told Rogan. "Women were entrenched at Ft. McClellan, with *real power.*"[29] (Original emphasis.)

Ironically, the expanded use of women by the services in the 1970s was an unwelcome event to many lesbians already in service. The influx of large numbers of heterosexual women eroded the power of gays over straights, and the integration of the women's components into the services stripped lesbians of their insulation against the heterosexual world. Once male commanders were relieved of their *naïveté* regarding lesbianism by complaints from heterosexual women, the nation's newspapers began to sizzle with sordid stories of secret homosexual rings among American servicewomen. In 1980, the USS *Norton Sound* earned an unhappy reputation as "the Ship of Queens" when 24 of 61 women aboard were accused of homosexual activity. In February 1984, the Army charged 11 women stationed at Fort Leavenworth, Kansas, with homosexuality. In October 1986, 8 of 35 female military policemen assigned to the Military Academy at West Point were discharged for the same. In March 1988, the Defense Department revealed that women were three times more likely to be discharged for homosexuality than men. The disparity between the sexes in the number of investigations for homosexuality is even greater, with the rate of investigations involving women being four times the rate of investigations involving men.

Servicewomen accused of lesbianism have often denied the charge and argued that they were being persecuted for their masculine mannerism. Members of DACOWITS have opined that perhaps the services are not enforcing the ban on homosexuality with equal vigor among men and women. One member has suggested that "perhaps the women are just more visible and get caught more readily" because "they don't have the places to go for homosexual bars like the men do."[30]

All indications are, however, that homosexuality is many times more common among female service members than among male service members. Several female West Point graduates told Army researchers that they had been approached by lesbians in the service; no male graduates who were interviewed mentioned being approached by male homosexuals. Charles Moskos, professor of sociology at Northwestern University in Evanston, Illinois, found that lesbianism was a common cause of complaint among women deployed with U.S. forces in Honduras in 1985. "Accounts of lesbians would come up spontaneously in most extended interviews with female soldiers," he wrote.[31] Most recently, DACOWITS heard numerous complaints of lesbianism from Navy and Marine Corps women during a 1987 tour of installations in the Far East. Lesbianism was reportedly so rampant that one barracks was widely referred to as "Lessy Land." Naturally, DACOWITS blamed the Navy for allowing women to live in substandard quarters which contribute "to conditions in which extremist behavior (lesbianism) is fostered and, in some cases, supported by the chain of command."[32] (Of course, men are often quartered in squalid barracks without any apparent increase in the same kind of "extremist behavior.") Yet when the Marine Corps moved promptly against 8 female Marines at Camp Lejeune, North Carolina, accused of homosexuality, among other offenses, DACOWITS chairwoman Jacquelyn Davis complained that the committee had not intended to spark a "witch hunt" for lesbians.[33]

For once, the boast of the homosexual community that gays comprise 10 percent of the population sounds modest. Some lesbians have estimated their strength among servicewomen to be closer to 20 percent. In some jobs and assignments, it is possible that lesbians actually predominate. Drill sergeant duty has always been a favorite among lesbian NCOs because it bestows upon them great personal power over many young and impressionable female recruits, and lesbians have been attracted to small, remote installations and to duty aboard ships, where they can exert greater influence over other women and thereby receive greater protection and greater opportunity for license.

DACOWITS's charge that the chain of command sometimes supports or encourages lesbianism is not entirely without merit. Few men view lesbianism with as much revulsion as they view male homosexuality. Many have been fooled into believing that the dyke stereotype has no foundation in fact and are wary of appearing, even to themselves, like crazed homophobes. All too many officers have adopted a relativist moral attitude which inclines them toward tolerance, despite law and policy. Then, too, lesbians are often their best female soldiers. Lesbians thrive in the military not only because it provides them the society of other lesbians, but also because it allows and encourages them to act like men. Compared with heterosexual women, lesbians are generally more at home in the military. They are more martial in their personal bearing, more athletically inclined, more accepting of the lot of soldiers or sailors, and often more committed to their jobs and their careers. They never become pregnant and are rarely burdened with dependents.

For these reasons, commanders are reluctant to investigate allegations of lesbianism thoroughly, preferring to conduct their own informal investigations instead of involving criminal investigators, who are also reluctant to get involved, though homosexuality is officially within their purview. Many commanders are especially averse to reporting such allegations to their service's security clearance custodian, as required by regulation. A common procedure is to collect statements and evidence, confront the accused, and hope that she submits quietly to an administrative discharge. Most accused homosexuals are discharged under officially honorable conditions. Very few are prosecuted for the criminal offense of sodomy. Of 4,316 men and women discharged for homosexuality from 1984 to 1987, only two were discharged following courts-martial.[34]

PSYCHOLOGICAL DIFFERENCES

Underlying all of the problems with women in the military are significant psychological differences between men and women. At one time, all who were interested in the issue of women in the military were eager to analyze the ways in which men and women behave differently. Lately, however, the operating assumption has been that there are no significant differences in the behaviors of men and women, and official research efforts seem intent upon proving the assumption. Sociologists studying academy graduates marvel at the psychological similarities between men and women and minimize their differences. When exceptions are granted, they are usually presented to show that women are in some way superior to men.

Significant differences do exist, however, and few are to the women's advantage. One obvious difference is that the military is still far more popular among young men than among young women. "Women do not grow up with the notion that they're going to be a soldier," explains the Army's chief of personnel, "They need a lot of convincing."[35] The expansion of the 1970s quickly exhausted the small pool of high quality women who were eager to enter the military. Today, the supply of young women bent on military careers barely meets the demand. Army recruiters must approach three times as many women as men for each enlistment. The quality of female recruits is becoming increasingly difficult to maintain, and the services fear that if Congress forces them to recruit more women, they will have no choice but to lower standards further.

Already, quality is no longer an advantage of recruiting women over men, as the quality of male recruits has improved dramatically in the last eight years. Women are still more likely to have high school diplomas, but the number of men entering the Army with high school diplomas has risen from 54.3 percent in 1980 to 90.8 percent in 1986. Today, more than 90 percent of active-duty enlisted males in all of the services have high school diplomas. Test scores for men have also improved, so that men now score higher than women on five out of eight tests of the Armed Services Vocational Aptitude Battery (ASVAB). The ASVAB tests on which men score better than women are those most likely to indicate aptitude for the majority of jobs in the modern military: general science, arithmetic reasoning, auto/shop information, mathematical knowledge, and electronics. The tests on which women score better than men are those most closely related to traditionally female jobs: reading comprehension, numerical operations, and coding speed. Researchers have concluded that men are better suited for most military jobs and that women are best suited for those traditional jobs to which they are most attracted.[36] In view of these differences, the Defense Department's commitment to putting more women in nontraditional jobs makes little sense.

Men and women entering the services also differ in what they expect of their military careers. Charles Moskos found that few enlisted women saw themselves as future NCOs, certainly not in nontraditional jobs or assignments with extended field duty:

> Most of the enlisted women, in contrast with the men, saw NCO status as inconsistent with their life goals and present or future family plans.[37]

The Defense Department's 1981 background review found that while men evaluate military jobs in the same manner as they do civilian jobs, being willing to accept less satisfying occupations to increase promotion opportunities, women tend to be less career-minded:

> Findings indicate that women forgo promotion opportunities in favor of job settings less likely to interfere with commitments to husbands and children.[38]

Even when men and women in the military make the same choices they often do so for different reasons. Their motivations for entering the military are widely separate. Women are much more likely to list practical, selfish reasons for joining the services. Education, travel, and money rank high on their list. The background review found that women tended to think they could earn more money in the service than in the civilian world, while men tended to believe that they were giving up brighter economic opportunities on the outside by remaining in service. Women simply do not feel the same attraction and attachment to military service that men feel. They are much less interested in military history and world affairs. A 1986 poll by CBS News found that only 25 percent of American women knew which side the United States was supporting in Nicaragua, while 50 percent of the men did. The same disparity exists among members of the military.

Men tend to give others reasons for joining the military, such as patriotism or love of country, but these lofty ideals usually serve to hide other, less respectable reasons. Most are too embarrassed to confess that they derive a profound sense of personal importance from their role as protector. Navy Lieutenant Niel L. Golightly, a fighter pilot and Olmsted Scholar, is not embarrassed. He writes:

> [C]onsider the young man under fire and neck deep in the mud of a jungle foxhole, sustained in that purgatory by the vision of home—a warm, feminine place that represents all the good things that his battlefield is not. Somewhere in that soldier's world view, though he may not be able to articulate it, is the notion that he is here . . . so that all the higher ideals of home embodied in mother, sister, and girlfriend do not have to be here.[39]

Not too long ago, this was conventional wisdom, admitted un-abashedly by everyone from Harvard to Hollywood. In a scene from the movie *Operation Petticoat,* the crew of a submarine watches in awe as a group of nurses are brought aboard. The boat's executive officer says to a sailor, "If anybody asks you what you're fighting for, there's your answer." Today the same line might be intended to invite snickers at a caricature of sexism.

Many men are attracted to the military by its intensely masculine and deeply romantic character. The uniforms, the rank, the danger, the purposefulness, the opportunity to earn the respect of men and the admiration of women, all contribute to the military's enduring hold on the imagination of men and boys. Such things have inspired many men to greatness, but they too seem embarrassingly puerile in today's world. Progressive society prides itself with having evolved to a higher level where ancient impulses are deplored as childish *machismo* and where the most socially respectable motivations are, ironically, the most material and the most selfish. Young men today dare not confess their captivation with the romance of martial glory, even to themselves. Instead, when asked why they entered the mili-tary, they say patriotism. The more thoughtful among them have better answers, but they are equally evasive. Ask a young man entering a service academy today why he wishes to go there and he is likely to answer "to get a good education" or "to pursue a military career." Such answers sound good but tell us nothing about the man.

Women, however, are blissfully unbothered by the psychological complications of masculinity. They are not impressed with physical prowess, they do not relish competition, they are not intrigued by danger, they do not need to prove their manhood, and they see little reason to hide their weaknesses, psychological or physical. One researcher has suggested that women have higher rates of morbidity because they are not as reluctant as men to report feeling sick, perhaps because it is generally more acceptable for a woman to complain of sickness or injury and because the role of the patient is more compatible with the woman's passive, dependent role in soci-ety.[40]

The absence of *machismo* among military women is no advantage.

In war, physical prowess is important, dangers must be faced, and petty personal concerns cannot be allowed to interfere with greater events. The military quite naturally holds physical infirmity in contempt. It encourages the suppression of personal hurts and stigmatizes those who hurt too easily or too often as "gimps" and "snivellers." Good soldiers pride themselves on avoiding injury, ignoring illness, and enduring pain. They strive never to be found among the "sick, lame, and lazy."

Smart, ambitious female officers know this and do their best to assume masculine attitudes toward everything, as several studies have shown. Success depends upon becoming male as much as possible. They drive fast cars, they compete fiercely at sports, they disdain weakness, they reject association with other women, they devote themselves totally to their careers, and they adopt male attitudes toward sex, marriage, and family. Women of the 1980 West Point class showed less interest in marriage and family than their male classmates. They also tended to describe themselves as psychologically more masculine than they were before entering the academy. Older female officers tend to view marriage and family as incompatible with military service for women. Despite assurances from feminist ideologues that they can have both, these women often choose to remain single for the good of their careers.

Unfortunately for the services, most women do not manage or even attempt the conversion to masculinity. Not all are that dedicated, but even among the many dedicated military women the task of conversion is too much to ask. They would be kicking against the goads of Nature by adopting mannish ways, for many fundamental behavioral differences between men and women are firmly rooted in biology.

Many feminists still reject the possibility that sex differences are biologically based and therefore beyond the reach of social reform. Some cite the work of Howard A. Moss of the National Institute of Health, whose experiments showed that men and women respond differently to even newborn baby boys and girls, unwittingly influencing their future sex differentiation. Moss made no claim that all psychological sex differences are the result of the different ways adults treat babies, but his findings have been accepted as the last word on the subject by feminists who have lost patience with biologically based explanations. The reaction of a female Army colonel is typically dismissive: "Don't give me any of that hormones shit! I've had it up to here with hormones!"

The evidence is fairly conclusive, however, that hormones do play a significant role. A study by John Money and Anke A. Ehrhardt found that baby girls who had been exposed to androgen-like hormones in the early stages of growth in the womb developed "tomboy" characteristics such as an interest in vigorous outdoor activities and competitive sports. They were also slower to develop an interest in boys and dating, though still less aggressive than most boys of the same age.[41]

Similarities between boys and tomboys diminish as both sexes reach puberty. Tomboys develop into young women with the introduction of the female sex hormone estrogen, while boys receive an extra charge of masculinity in the form of the male sex hormone testosterone. As an artificial steroid, testosterone is sometimes used by athletes to improve their performance. It accelerates their metabolism, heightens their urge for exertion, and quickens their recovery. Before the use of steroids was outlawed in the Olympics, a U.S. Olympic athlete privately confessed, "I take one steroid that makes it possible for me to go through a brick wall. I take a second steroid that *demands* that I go through the brick wall." The "demand" steroid was testosterone.[42]

Testosterone's effects on behavior are plainly seen in the greater aggressiveness of men, "one of the best established, and most pervasive, of all psychological sex differences," say feminist scholars Eleanor Maccoby and Carol Jacklin of Stanford University. In *The Psychology of Sex Differences,* Maccoby and Jacklin write:

> (1) Males are more aggressive than females in all human societies for which evidence is available. (2) The sex differences are found early in life, at a time when there is no evidence that differential socialization pressures have been brought to bear by adults to "shape" aggression differently in the two sexes. (3) Similar sex differences are found in man and subhuman primates. (4) Aggression is related to levels of sex hormones, and can be changed by experimental administration of these hormones.[43]

Traditional socialization, therefore, merely confirms what has been ordained already by biology. It ensures that a child's physical development and psychological development proceed in the same direction, and it teaches boys and girls to make sense of themselves, their bodies, and their relations with the opposite sex.

A favorite feminist theory holds that proper, non-sexist socialization can, over time, correct biology, producing women as psychologically aggressive and as physically capable as men. There is, however, no evidence that the biological contribution to sex differences can be completely overcome without the assistance of modern drugs.

Some feminists argue that modern warriors need not be as aggressive as warriors of the past, or that the lack of aggressiveness offers definite advantages to the modern military. Women make better soldiers, they say, because they are well-behaved, less dangerous to themselves and others, and better suited for many routine tasks that men find tedious. Two Army studies indicate that women are better at routine, repetitive tasks. One, during World War II, found that women performed much better than men when assigned the monotonous task of monitoring a radar screen for an anti-aircraft battery in Nova Scotia. The other, in 1984, found that female officers were quicker than men to decide on a course of action when presented with familiar situations, but slower than men to make up their minds in unfamiliar situations.

If war were always tedious and routine, women would be better suited for it. But war is not always tedious and routine, though its participants might find periods of both, before and after moments of emergency and upheaval. For those crucial moments, women are ill-suited. Even in peacetime, many military jobs require quickness and daring. Female intelligence personnel assigned to shadow Soviet Military Liaison Mission (SMLM) vehicles have proven too timid to keep up the chase through crowded German towns and on the open autobahn, where speeds in excess of 130 m.p.h. are common. The implications of this example for female fighter pilots are obvious, but Defense officials will not admit that women lack the killer instinct. Proof of their deficiency must await their first actual dogfights with real, all-male enemies.

A final problem with women in the military, one which has nothing to do with comparative abilities of men and women, is the impact of the presence of women on the behavior of men. It is not just a problem of morale. The morale of men has hardly been a concern during the integration process. When integration of the academies caused bitter resentment among male cadets and midshipmen, integrators dismissed low morale as sexist irrationality. When Navy surveys showed junior enlisted men aboard integrated ships approving the presence of women, however, integrators heralded higher morale as women's contribution to readiness.

The different responses among men to integration are an indication of the complexity of the problem. On the one hand, the best educated and most intellectual men with a keener appreciation of military ethics and tradition overwhelmingly opposed the presence of women. On the other hand, the less educated, less intellectual, and less career-minded men enjoyed their presence. At the same time, charges of sexual harassment are aimed most often at junior enlisted men, while senior enlisted men and senior officers are more prone to fraternization and usually most outspoken in defense of women. Clearly the integrators are mistaken in believing that opposition to women comes from older men simply because they are old-fashioned and the lowest ranks simply because they are uneducated. Things are not that simple.

The roots of group behavior among men run deep into our being. All-male groups have existed in virtually every known society. Most anthropologists agree that all-male groups produce a peculiar kind of non-erotic psychological bond that men crave and cannot find elsewhere. In some societies, bonds between male friends are stronger and more sacred than bonds between husbands and wives. In his book *Men and Marriage,* bestselling author George Gilder writes:

> The closest tie in virtually all societies, primate and human, is between women and children. But the next most common and strong connection may well be the all-male bond. The translation of the rudimentary impulse of love into intense ties between specific men and women appears to have been em-

phasized and sanctified later, in the course of creating civilized societies.[44]

Typically, says Gilder, the all-male group is strongly hierarchical, placing heavy emphasis on leadership, loyalty, and excitement. Members are admitted and ranked according to their demonstrated ability to contribute to the group's common purpose. Competition is the key to entry and advancement. It is also a source of excitement. Leaders command the loyalty and respect of inferiors because they best personify the values of the group.

The military is also strongly hierarchical. It begs for leadership, demands loyalty, and lives for excitement. It is this way, first, because it was created by men, and, second, because such characteristics make it effective at making war. The military depends upon men acting as a team at the very moment when every man is under great temptation to seek his own comfort and save his own life. The personal bonds that men form with each other, as leaders, as followers, as comrades-in-arms, often enable ordinary men to perform acts of extreme self-sacrifice when ideals such as duty, country, or cause no longer compel. The all-male condition reinforces all of the military's highest organizational values.

The presence of women inhibits male bonding, corrupts allegiance to the hierarchy, and diminishes the desire of men to compete for anything but the attentions of women. Pushing women into the military academies made a mockery of the academies' essential nature and most honored values. Integration of Army basic training by the Carter administration undercut the motivation of male recruits. Drill sergeants noticed that the remaining all-male companies regularly exceeded training standards for tests of motivation and endurance, such as the twelve-mile road march, while integrated companies rarely exceeded standards for such events. When the difference, dubbed a "stretch factor," was brought to the attention of the Army's chief of staff in 1982, basic training was resegregated.[45]

The impact of the presence of women on all-male units is a major reason why most military leaders still silently oppose integration of combat units. In the public debate over integration, however, politics have forced the military to concede all ground on the issue. The services themselves are the primary source of assertions that the presence of women has nothing but a positive effect on the behavior of men—assertions made possible by a social phenomenon that has received nearly no attention from either side of the debate.

The services are painfully aware that individual men and women form romantic and sexual relationships that defy regulation, but they have not yet noticed the effect of *charm* on the daily work relations of all men and women. The facts are plain: men like women. Beauty and femininity increase this liking, but generally all women qualify for it in some degree. Because men like women, men have difficulty treating women as they treat other men. They cannot be indifferent to sex. They are rarely as firm, as harsh, or as critical with women. Some men may retaliate against women out of resentment or hatred, but the problem most military men face is trying not to be too kind.

Charm does not affect all men equally. Men who are senior in age and rank tend to be most susceptible because their superior-subordinate relationship with women closely resembles traditional sex roles. Women find the maturity and authority of their male seniors attractive, and men are charmed by the youth and submissiveness of younger women. Because of this affinity between the two groups, the services have made special efforts to warn commanding officers of the dangers of fraternizing with women in their command.

Even if charm does not lead to fraternization, it does affect a woman's treatment and prestige. Charles Moskos reported that male supervisors of the women he interviewed in Honduras were "defensive" about their women and reluctant to criticize their performance.[46] ROTC cadets have complained that women "get babied too much by the drill sergeants."[47] Comely and confident women who perform well will almost always win exaggerated praise. Some are more successful at their jobs because they can easily elicit the cooperation of charmed men. It is not a matter of flirting to get their way, or of using sex as a bribe; few women do either. It is simply a matter of letting men act as men rather than as sexless bureaucrats. "Anyone who doesn't think he's a man first and a soldier second just isn't paying attention," says one old soldier, explaining his practice of sending his pleasant and attractive female sergeant to brief senior officers.

Unfortunately for the services, there are too many senior officers who aren't paying attention, too many who believe that our deepest thoughts can be easily manipulated, that the way men have always been is not the way they are now or will be soon. These men pretend that sex can be easily ignored. They insist that professionalism means putting aside one's manhood as a relic of prehistory and that the difficulties caused by having women in the military are merely "management problems."

NOTES ON CHAPTER IX

1. Department of Physical Education, *Project Summertime* (West Point, N.Y.: U.S. Military Academy, 1976), pp. 25–30. Differences between men and women were even greater before training, as the physical performance of men actually declined during the eight weeks of training in which little emphasis was placed on strength and power.

2. Martin Binkin and Shirley Bach, *Women and the Military* (Washington, D.C.: The Brookings Institution, 1977), p. 80.

3. Colonel R.W. Lind, Office of Assistant Secretary of Defense for Force Management & Personnel, Letter to Penny Pullen, State Representative, Illinois State Assembly, 6 December 1985.

4. Jay Blucher, "Mass Appeal," *Army Times,* 6 July 1987, p. 68.

5. Blucher, p. 68.

6. See memo from Colonel Ronald A. Redman, U.S. Air Force, to Dr. Mayer, subject: "The Health of Women in the Services," 14 May 1985; Anne Hoiberg, "Sex and Occupational Differences in Hospitalization Rates Among Navy Enlisted Personnel," *Journal of Occupational Medicine,* October 1980, p. 686; and Anne Hoiberg, "Health Care Needs of Women in the Navy," *Military Medicine,* February 1979, p. 109.

7. See "Sex Differentials of Time Lost Due to Hospitalization, Male and Female Active Duty Army Personnel: Worldwide, CY 1976-1981," *Supplement to Health of the Army,* December 1983, pp. 60–61; and Hoiberg, "Sex and Oc-

cupational Differences in Hospitalization Rates Among Navy Enlisted Personnel," p. 689.

8. Redman.

9. Quoted by Joyce Price, "Supply of Brain's Pain Killer Tied to Pre-menstrual Blues," *The Washington Times,* 29 June 1987, p. A3.

10. Redman.

11. Ronald A. Redman, "The Feasibility of a Cohort Study on the Health Needs of Women in the Services," Health Studies Task Force, Office of the Assistant Secretary of Defense (Health Affairs), 15 May 1985, pp. 6–7.

12. Office of the Assistant Secretary of Defense, *Military Women in the Department of Defense* (Washington, D.C.: Department of Defense, July 1987), p. 63.

13. Marjorie H. Royle, *Factors Affecting Attrition Among Marine Corps Women* (San Diego, Calif.: Naval Personnel Research and Development Center, 1985), p. vii.

14. Jeanne Holm, *Women in the Military: An Unfinished Revolution* (Novato, Calif.: Presidio Press, 1982), p. 293.

15. Letter from the Chief of Promotion, Separation, and Transition Division, Deputy Chief of Staff for Personnel, Department of the Army, to Department of the Air Force, 23 April 1970, quoted by Holm, p. 294.

16. Quoted by Holm, p. 300.

17. "Female GIs in the Field: Report from Honduras" (Evanston, Ill.: Northwestern University, 1985), p. 17.

18. Charlie Schill, "Navy's Unwed Pregnancy Rate 37%," *Navy Times,* 28 November 1988, p. 2.

19. Office of the Assistant Secretary of Defense, *Background Review: Women in the Military* (Washington, D.C.: Department of Defense, 1981), p. 7.

20. *Background Review: Women in the Military,* p. 81.

21. Lt. Col. Steven M. Hinds, "Single Parents and the Marine Corps," *Marine Corps Gazette,* January 1989, p. 64.

22. Message from Commander, U.S. Army Intelligence and Security Command, to subordinate units, subject: "Married Army Couples," 20 November 1986.

23. Minutes, DACOWITS Spring Meeting, 1984, p. C-7.

24. Royle, p. vii.

25. Letter form the Adjutant General, U.S. Army, to all commands, subject: "Fraternization and Regulatory Policy Regarding Relationships Between Members of Different Ranks," 21 November 1986.

26. Letter from the Adjutant General.

27. Helen Rogan, *Mixed Company: Women in the Modern Army* (New York: G. P. Putnam's Sons, 1981), p. 154.

28. Rogan, p. 155.

29. Rogan, p. 156.

30. Quoted by Grant Willis, "More Women Than Men Discharged as Homosexuals," *Navy Times*, 29 February 1988, p. 3.

31. Moskos, p. 11.

32. Jacquelyn K. Davis, DACOWITS chairwoman, Memo to General Anthony Lukeman, USMC, subject: "1987 WESTPAC Visit of the DACOWITS," 26 August 1987.

33. Grant Willis, " 'Witch-Hunt' for Lesbians Never Intended," *Army Times*, 28 March 1988.

34. Willis, "More Women Than Men Discharged as Homosexuals."

35. Quoted by Larry Carney, "Ono Hails Quality of Army's Newest," *Army Times*, 15 June 1987, p. 8.

36. Martin Binkin and Mark J. Eitelberg, "Women and Minorities in the All-Volunteer Force," in *The All-Volunteer Force After a Decade: Retrospect and Prospect*, ed. William Bowman, et. al., (Washington, D.C.: Pergamon-Brassey's, 1986), pp. 96–97. There was no difference on one test segment, word power. The Defense Department has recently added emphasis to the mathematic segments of the test battery and de-emphasized the importance of certain clerical segments.

37. Moskos, p. 5.

38. *Background Review: Women in the Military*, p. 149.

39. Niel L. Golightly, "No Right to Fight," U.S. Naval Institute *Proceedings*, December 1987, p. 48.

40. Hoiberg, "Sex and Occupational Differences in Hospitalization Rates Among Navy Enlisted Personnel," p. 689.

41. John Money and Anke A. Ehrhardt, *Man and Woman, Boy and Girl: The Differentiation and Dimorphism of Gender Identity from Conception to Maturity* (Baltimore, Md.: Johns Hopkins University Press, 1972).

42. Scott Pengelly and James C. Benfield, "Handicapping the Battle of the Sexes," *The Washington Post*, 11 September 1988, p. C3.

43. Eleanor Maccoby and Carol Jacklin, *The Psychology of Sex Differences* (Stanford, Calif.: Stanford University Press, 1974), pp. 242-243.

44. George Gilder, *Men and Marriage* (Gretna, La.: Pelican Books Publishing Co., 1986), p. 33.

45. Allen Carrier, "Defense EO Chief Decries End of Army Coed Basic," *Army Times,* 12 July 1982, p. 28.

46. Moskos, p. 10.

47. Quoted by Theodore C. Mataxis, "How Realistic Are Female Test Scores?" *Army Times,* 21 March 1977, p. 15.

CHAPTER X

The Fog of Peace

*Marriage, to women as to men, must be a luxury, not a
necessity; an incident of life, not all of it. And the only
possible way to accomplish this great change is to accord to
women equal power in the making, shaping and controlling of
the circumstances of life.*

SUSAN B. ANTHONY[1]

THERE IS CONFUSION in the camp and division in the ranks. Having
won battle after battle, many feminists have begun to think they
might have lost the war. Their tactical success has failed to yield a
strategic victory, and the victors are now wondering what it was they
were fighting for and what their victories mean.

The source of their unsettledness is feminism itself. In her recent
book *Women and War,* Jean Bethke Elshtain, feminist author and
professor of political science at the University of Massachusetts at
Amherst, writes:

> From its inception, feminism has not quite known whether to
> fight men or to join them; whether to lament sex differences and
> deny their importance or to acknowledge and even valorize such
> differences; whether to condemn all wars outright or to extol
> women's contributions to war efforts. At times, feminists have
> done all of these things, with scant regard for consistency.[2]

Certainly some military feminists have been willing to argue anything to get what they wanted. DACOWITS argues alternatively that women are needed to make the AVF work and that the view of women as "fillers" to make the AVF work harms women's morale. Antonia Handler Chayes, as undersecretary of the Air Force, told the House Armed Services Committee in November 1979, "The Air Force would be pleased to exceed its goal [for women]. Many of the most critical shortages—engineers, scientists, pilots—can be filled by qualified women." One month later, she told a conference on the AVF, "The fact is, we don't find large numbers of women to fill the technical areas, neither enlisted nor officers. It's very hard to find women engineers."[3]

Often feminists cannot agree among themselves on the way to achieve their goals. Since 1974, feminists have argued for an ever narrower definition of combat that would open as many jobs to women as possible within legal constraints, but in 1984 feminists at the Air Force Academy recommended expanding the definition of combat to cover jobs in which women are already serving, so that male cadets could not complain that women do not belong at the Academy because they do not serve in combat. Sharon Lord, Deputy Assistant Secretary of Defense for Equal Opportunity under President Reagan, decried the resegregation of Army basic training in 1982, saying, "If soldiers are going to be asked to support and trust one another, it is important to believe that they have completed strenuous training."[4] Two years later, Air Force Academy feminists recommended resegregating cadet intramural sports to keep male cadets from noticing the physical limitations of female cadets.

Certainly deceit and disagreement can be found among the followers of any movement, but a further indication of serious trouble beneath the feminist flag is the deep division that exists between female officers and female enlisted personnel. While female officers clamor to get into jobs previously closed to them, enlisted women are quite satisfied with those traditional jobs they already hold. The services have expended considerable effort to channel women into nontraditional jobs and have acheived some success. A third of all servicewomen are working in traditionally male jobs, while only 3 percent of women in the civilian work force have taken such jobs.

Still, enlisted women in nontraditional jobs suffer greater job dissatisfaction and higher rates of attrition. Many enlisted women enter nontraditional jobs as a second choice and migrate to traditionally female jobs at their first opportunity.

"The plain fact," wrote Charles Moskos, after his visit to Honduras, "is that the two female groups [officer and enlisted] had different career agendas and therefore different attitudes toward their positions in the Army." He continued:

> Female officers often expressed resentment, sometimes anger, at emerging career constraints within the military. Female enlisted saw their time in the Army as a stepping stone from an unsatisfactory pre-military existence to a more hopeful post-military life. Female officers tended to deemphasize physiological and emotional differences between men and women while female enlisted were much more likely to acknowledge distinctions between the sexes.[5]

Enlisted women almost always referred to themselves as "girls" though female officers rarely did. Female officers were much more concerned about presenting a good view of women in the military than were female enlisteds, who readily complained about conditions in the field, the lack of privacy, and approaches from lesbians. Enlisted women favored a special chain of communication for reporting female complaints, but female officers opposed the idea as an impediment to complete assimilation. The only complaints more often heard from female officers than from female enlisteds concerned sexual harassment. Enlisted women defined sexual harassment narrowly as unwanted sexual advances. Female officers defined sexual harassment broadly as anything that offended their feminist sensibilities, including sexist language, traditional sex roles, and the combat restrictions. Enlisted women tended to think that individual women were responsible for defending themselves against sexual harassment without involving the chain of command, while female officers saw the suppression of sexual harassment as a command responsibility.

Female officers and enlisted women are most at odds on the issue of combat. Half of the enlisted women Moskos interviewed thought that women should not be allowed in combat, while the other half thought that women should be allowed in combat, but only if they volunteered. Among officers, however, half said that women should be allowed to volunteer for combat, and half said that women should be ordered into combat involuntarily, just as men are. None of the enlisted women said they would volunteer for combat if it was open to them, but several of the officers said they would.

Comparisons of the observations of other researchers confirm Moskos's findings and vividly show that the views of female officers and those of female enlisteds are not just different but fundamentally antagonistic. Michael Rustad quotes enlisted women complaining about the harshness of Army life: "I don't feel we should have to work more than eight-hour days. I think the military should treat us as persons and not as instruments," says one. Another says, "I cannot understand why military persons have to be so tough and callous."[6] These women would be horrified by the coarse bravado of lunchtime conversation among female officers at West Point, reported by Helen Rogan. "Women can easily do Ranger school," says a female officer. "As for that business about men and women sharing foxholes, if you are next to a male in a foxhole in a combat situation and you need to urinate or change your Tampax, you'll just *go ahead and do it!*" says a second officer. (Original emphasis.) "Why, I'd just bleed right through!" says a third, to the laughter of the group.[7]

At times, it seems, feminists want all people to be more like women. At other times, they want themselves to be more like men. The cause of this schizophrenia is a fundamental conflict inherent in feminist ideology. It is the conflict between feminist egalitarianism and—a seeming oxymoron—feminist sexism.

Feminism owes nearly all of its success to the Western world's unqualified enthusiasm for an ill-defined doctrine of equality. Once the leaders of the American and French revolutions thoroughly discredited the belief that God arranged societies according to His own inscrutable design, giving some men authority over others and all men authority over women, nothing remained to keep the proposition that all men are created equal from being extended, in the minds of some, to include women.

For early feminists, however, the problem with the doctrine of equality was that, to most men and women, the sexes were not in fact equal. Daily life presented abundant evidence to both sexes that significant differences existed between them, necessitating unequal, though not necessarily unjust, treatment. To overcome the obstacle of reality, feminists began arguing that men and women are equal for many specific purposes. As early as 1869, when Susan Brownell Anthony first used the slogan "Equal Pay for Equal Work," feminists were advancing the idea that sex should not matter as long as individual women are capable of fulfilling a handful of specific requirements directly related to a given job. Considerations that might still have motivated different treatment for men and women, such as an employer's personal preference or religious beliefs or broader sociological concerns, were deemed irrelevant and unjust and were finally outlawed a hundred years later with the passage of the Equal Pay Act of 1963 and the Civil Rights Act of 1964.

Though neither act applied directly to the military, the reasoning behind both was used later to speed integration of the services. Proponents of integration moved the argument away from concerns about the general nature of military service to an examination of specific requirements for individual jobs. This tactic was deftly exposed by William J. Gregor in an essay entitled "Women, Combat, and the Draft: Placing Details in Context." Gregor, an Army officer on the faculty at the U.S. Military Academy, argued that feminists purposefully ignored the complex reality of both combat and most combat organizations in order to reduce military service to a matter of performing a limited number of identifiable, measurable, job-related tasks. Their assumption was, in his words, "If you place in a position a person capable of performing the tasks assigned to a position and train the person in those critical tasks, those tasks will be performed and the unit will be effective."[8] Tests like REFWAC, MAXWAC, and the Female Artillery Study all focused on the completion of limited, easily measurable individual or unit tasks. Completion of the tasks led automatically to the conclusion that women did not adversely affect the ability of a unit to accomplish its mission.

This approach yields feminists two advantages. First, it permits them to eliminate many concerns of war-wise military men without ever addressing them. Any old soldier who tries to drag into the argument his gut-feelings about the effects of integration on morale is required to substantiate his concern with empirical evidence. When he produces none, his concern is dismissed as unfounded. The second advantage is that it permits the integrationists to pick and choose among jobs requirements for those that favor women. Academics rose to supreme importance at the academies because the grade point averages of women compare favorably with those of men. High school diplomas are preferred as a qualification for enlistment because women are more likely than men to have them. Requirements which tend to favor men are attacked as unrelated to job performance. Boxing, observed Judith Stiehm, is "an activity in which [Air Force officers] would never participate in combat" and therefore should be eliminated from the Air Force Academy's curriculum. Likewise, the practice of shaving the heads of male recruits should be abandoned in favor of unspecified "new ways to encourage group bonding" that do not exclude women.

The tactic of limiting obnoxious requirements can only go so far, however. Proponents of women in the military still must confront the reality that some differences between the sexes do matter much more in the military than in most other sectors of society. But rather than concede that the military role of women may be justifiably limited, many feminists adopt the argument that all sex differences, physical and mental, are solely the result of environmental influences. In the controversy of Nature versus Nurture, they side solidly with the environmentalists, who argue that the way we are nurtured or raised determines who and what we are, the assumption being that the nurturing process can be altered to minimize sex differences. These feminists theorize that the participation of women in activities previously closed to them will cause women to develop greater physical strength and aggressiveness. They reject all evidence that sex differences are rooted in biology, for to admit that nature has any say in the differentiation of the sexes is to confess that there are biological laws beyond the reach of social reform.

Yet, for all their talk of equality and insistence on the mutability of the sexes, many feminists still evince a strong belief in the moral superiority of women over men. They did not originate the idea. No doubt long before Aristophanes' *Lysistrata,* peace-loving women have been a reproach to warlike men. Feminism received a boost in the 19th Century from the belief, common in many Protestant Christian churches, that women were more favorably disposed toward religion, love, and peace and therefore superior to men. Today, many leading feminists have denounced Christianity as a male religion, but their fanatical sense of sisterhood and tendency to view all problems as matters of women versus the world have preserved and encouraged a chauvinistic belief in their own superiority.

In the view of these "sexist" feminists, the purpose of freeing women to participate in the governing of society is not so that women might enjoy the thrill of killing, but so that society will be less violent and more peace-loving with women in charge. Pacifism has been a constant characteristic of the feminist movement. The American feminist movement of the 1960s was intensely anti-war, and the present bevy of women's peace and disarmament groups are all ideologically feminist. Many feminist intellectuals are quite willing to blame men for all forms and acts of violence. Mary Jo Salter wonders in *The Atlantic Monthly* whether "we might not have invented war" had the world been populated solely by women.[9] Ellen Goodman, feminist columnist for *The Boston Globe,* still hopes that women will yet save men from destroying the world:

> Over the past year, in one poll after another, women have staked out a clear position—against Reaganomics, against nuclear arms—and gradually men have drifted over to share those beliefs.[10]

Some, like Betty Friedan in her book *The Second Stage,* still continue to press for an ever greater role for women in politics and in the military not for equality's sake, but as a way of weakening the forces of aggression in the world.

For pacifistic feminists, egalitarian feminism poses grave philosophical problems. Absolute sexual egalitarianism denies that either sex is inherently superior to the other, morally or otherwise, and thereby robs feminists of their self-satisfying righteousness, their comforting sense of common identity and innate worth as women. Likewise, the environmentalist view of sex differences puts feminists in the embarrassing position of having to credit a society they hate for their own virtues. If society alone is responsible for making men and women what they are, then the nonviolence of women is the product of patriarchy. If women are not inherently nonviolent and nonviolence is not peculiar to them, then pacisfistic feminism ceases to have anything but an accidental association with women.

It should not surprise anyone, then, that many feminists have actively opposed efforts to militarize American women. Some have organized anti-recruiting campaigns to counter the efforts of the services to recruit women. Others have openly attacked proponents of women in the military in print and in person. In 1976, at DACOWITS's twenty-fifth anniversary meeting, the only opposition to the call for repeal of the combat exclusion laws came from three women representing the American Civil Liberties Union who found DACOWITS's argument that women were needed to make the AVF work repellent:

> Military studies refer to the utilization of women (one might ask by whom). And articles in both the civilian and military press refer to women as filling the gaps recruiters can't plug with men.[11]

The trio equated utilization with exploitation and argued that women should not give up "feminist ideals of nurturing, caring, and life-giving concerns" so that they might be used by the military. Women should, instead, work "to have their fellow soldiers think of all humans as human beings first rather than animals to be casually slaughtered."

Nevertheless, environmental, egalitarian feminism goes a long way toward convincing people that women can be warriors too. Neither pacifism nor the supposed moral superiority of women hold great appeal with the American public. Integration of the military would never have happened if the officials responsible for it had believed that its purpose was to make the American military less military. Many prominent feminists seem quite willing to walk all over feminism's traditional pacifism to advance the cause of military women. Dr. Nora Scott Kinzer, employed by the Carter Pentagon, told Mary Jo Salter, "we are brought up with a myth that women are nicer than men, that they are the keepers of the hearth and the mothers. . . . "[12] When asked by the House Armed Services Committee in 1979 about the aversion to violence and killing among women, Antonia Handler Chayes, Carter's undersecretary of the Air Force, replied:

> I do not see that there is any sex or gender difference in the degree of pacifism or willingness to go to war . . . . I think that is a cultural concept that really does not necessarily accord with the truth now . . . . I think that women throughout history, even in mythology, have taken up arms, and very effectively. Look at the Amazons.[13]

In the last decade, military feminists have looked frequently at the Amazons, often in hopes of finding some evidence that they actually existed. After ten years of research for her book *The War Against the Amazons,* Abby Weltan Kleinbaum, professor of social science at the City University of New York, concluded that they did not. To some, her book was an unwelcome revelation:

> At least one woman told me that when she read in my introduction that the particular Amazon nation described in the well-known stories told by Greek and Latin authors probably never existed, she felt like crying.[14]

Most other feminists seem unable to understand that the ancient Greeks and Romans entertained themselves with stories of Amazons for much the same reason that people today enjoy stories about vicious aliens from outer space. It was the very barbarity of a society ruled by women that excited their imagination, not the actual or possible existence of such a society.

Other myths have served to advance the cause of military women, the most popular of which surrounds Israeli women. The popular image of the tough but womanly Israeli *sabra* who bravely deals death to the enemies of her embattled nation is almost entirely a creation of Hollywood, reinforced today by pictures in the press of Uzi-toting Israeli women in olive drab. The truth is so much less glamorous that feminists who know better never mention the Israelis in any debate. If Israel is discussed at all among feminists, it is as an example of failure—a country founded originally by men and women with radically egalitarian ideals that was forced by a hostile environment to adopt more traditional ways. Concern for what went wrong inspired the book *Israeli Women: The Reality Behind the Myth* by feminist author Lesley Hazelton. Hazelton identified and dispelled three common fallacies about Israeli women. First, the early Zionist settlers were no more sexually liberated than anyone else at the time. Second, the Israeli army during the War for Independence did not make great use of women in combat. Third, Israeli women today are far less feminist than most Western women.[15]

There were attempts to achieve sexual equality among the radically socialist Jews who migrated from Europe to Palestine around the time of World War I, but the reality of the barren, hostile land was too much for their dreams to bear. By the 1940s, Jewish society in Palestine had sorted itself out along more traditional lines. Following the large influx of Jewish refugees after World War II, egalitarian ideals were revived briefly. During the War for Independence, the Jewish defense organization, the *Hagana,* employed women extensively for reasons of both necessity and ideology. In 1948, a handful of women did see combat with the *Hagana's* fighting arm, the *Polmach,* but their presence resulted in both sides suffering higher casualties. Israeli men risked their lives and missions to protect their women, and Arab troops fought more fiercely to avoid the humiliation of being defeated by women. The women were withdrawn after three weeks. Hazelton quotes Yigal Allon, a leading *Polmach* commander:

> The girls stormed at any proposed discrimination, arguing that it ran counter to the spirit of the new society being built in Palestine. . . . In the end, the wiser counsel prevailed: the girls were still trained for combat, but placed in units of their own. Whenever possible, they were trained for defensive warfare only.[16]

For the rest of the war, the role of women was strictly subordinate and supportive. "When things got too hot the women would clean and reload the rifles for the men, so they could increase their rate of fire," wrote Hazelton. Most served as radio operators, nurses, quartermasters, or couriers. They were particularly useful for smuggling arms, ammunition explosives, and other contraband past chivalrous British guards who would not search women. Women who played a larger role were circumstantial exceptions to the rule.

Today, the Israelis use women far more conservatively than most NATO nations. Conscription is universal, but with exemptions for marriage, motherhood, religion, health, and unsuitability, barely half of all eligible eighteen-year-old women are required to serve. (Female recruits joke that the Hebrew initials of the Israeli Defense Force, THL, stand for three Hebrew words meaning "We should have gotten married.")

Only the IDF's training units use women in nontraditional roles as instructors of weapons and tactics and temporary leaders of men. In these roles they are supposed to be particularly successful, partly because of the sexist belief, accepted among many Israelis, that if a woman can do it, so can any man. The use of women as trainers is seen as a way of keeping women out of operational forces while still making use of the available manpower and truly freeing more men to fight.

Elsewhere in the IDF, the jobs open to women are few. Members of the women's component, the *Chen,* serve mostly as secretaries, clerks, teletypists, nurses, teachers, and army social workers. *Chen* women are barred from many jobs involving physical strain, adverse environmental conditions, or combat. They do not serve as pilots, nor on ships, nor where there are no shower facilities. They do not pump gas and they do not drive trucks. As a *Chen* colonel explained to Hazelton, "And even if a girl could drive a truck, where would she drive it in wartime? To the front. And we don't send girls to the front in wartime."[17] Israeli law requires that women be evacuated from the front in the event of hostilities. The experience of women captured in 1948 and of men captured by the Syrians more recently has confirmed fears that women would suffer unspeakable tortures if captured today.

Chen women do not have equal status with male soldiers. They are payed less and serve only two years instead of three for men. Training for both officers and enlisted personnel is segregated by sex. *Chen* training emphasizes traditionally feminine skills and touches lightly on basic soldiering skills for morale purposes. Weapons training is cursory and does not include their combat use. *Chen* women are taught to assemble and disassemble weapons, to clean and to operate them, but they do not practice marksmanship. After basic training, the only time most *Chen* women carry weapons is on parade, a photo opportunity for journalists interested in perpetuating a myth.

Only in the *Nahal*, a special corps charged with protecting frontier settlements, do women routinely carry weapons and train to use them, but according to Lionel Tiger and Joseph Shepler, authors of *Women in the Kibbutz*, "even in the *Nahal*, the attitude to female military activity is relatively unserious, and the military functions of women are sharply curtailed."[18] Standing orders are for women to take to the bunkers in the event of attack. *Nahal* women are armed with older, inferior weapons, and target practice is often the occasion of lighthearted ridicule of the women's marksmanship. No one, least of all the women themselves, takes their participation in the military seriously. Whereas a man's rank and specialty in the army greatly affects his status in the kibbutz, what a woman does in the army makes scarcely any difference at all, unless she happens to have a special skill much needed in the kibbutz.

Elsewhere also, the social status of *Chen* women depends not upon what they do, but upon the men they work with. Parachute riggers, whose work is menial, enjoy enhanced prestige because of their close association with male paratroops, the army's elite. On the other hand, the work of an intelligence analyst, though more mentally challenging, is regarded with much less esteem by the brightest *Chen* women.

The duality of the sexes is everywhere apparent in Israeli military service, a fact much bemoaned by Israeli feminists, who, according to Hazelton, see military service as reinforcing traditional sex roles and the subordination of women. Jobs like rigger and typist that are open to women are not open to men. The fact that "*Chen*," an abbreviation of *Cheil Nashim* or "women's army," is also a Hebrew word meaning "grace" or "charm" is not entirely accidental. The *Chen* takes great care to preserve the feminine charm of its women. "We never disregard the fact that the girls here are going to be married and become mothers," a *Chen* commander told Tiger and

Shepler, "We don't want to impair their feminine personality in any way."[19]

The Israeli military's respect for sexual duality is a reflection of the importance of that duality in Israeli society. Israeli art quite often uses medieval imagery to romanticize Israeli women as damsels in distress and Israeli fighter pilots and paratroops as their knightly champions. A reversal of those images is unconscionable for both practical and aesthetic reasons. One senior *Chen* officer told Hazelton:

> A woman's just not built for fighting, physically or mentally. Her aspirations lie in another direction altogether—marrying and having children. . . . I don't think women should fight, not because they're soft, but because their purpose in life is to tend to the next generation.[20]

Another told her:

> You don't even need to go into the whole question of mental and physical ability. The simple fact is that in wartime the whole country is organized for men to be out fighting. How can I call a married woman with children into reserve service when her husband's already been called up?[21]

To most Israelis, a woman's primary civic responsibility is to be a wife and mother. Her brief stint of military service is solely to free men to fight. As for the idea of women in combat, Hazelton reports that 90 percent of Israeli women oppose the idea. Those who favor it are not in the *Chen*.

In the desperate search for precedent, some feminists turn to the Lucy Brewers of revisionist history. Others admire the exploits of women pressed into military service by wartime totalitarian states, though our knowledge of these women comes solely from state propaganda and none of these states now employ many women in the military or any in combat. Still others see hope in the deadly daring of suicidal female terrorists and the rising rate of homicides committed by women.

Still, the world does not see angry bands of women rising up in arms against their male oppressors, and even feminists who would relish such a sight admit that women, whether feminist or not, are, in the words of Judith Stiehm, "de facto pacifists." Says Stiehm, "Women have almost no credibility with regard to the use of force; they are believed to have no capacity for forceful insistence or retaliation."[22] If women were to surprise the world by assuming fully the male role of warrior and protector, says Steihm, "it will be a change so radical that one must turn to fiction rather than history to find a parallel."[23]

Feminists are rapidly writing the fiction they need to further their cause, creating the illusion that military women deal well with danger and privation in a field environment. Many women are overly impressed with their ability to endure what men consider minor inconveniences. Consider the following report filed by a feminist sociologist employed by the Air Force to pontificate professionally on the subject of women in the military at the Air University:

> The living and working conditions for everyone during this entire period were very primitive and dangerous. At no time was this made clearer than on the day when an Army airborne unit just 20 miles south of us suffered 120 injuries and 4 fatalities. Hostile environment conditions, which played a large part in this incident, also plagued our unit, and even though we experienced no fatalities and only a limited number of injuries ourselves, the knowledge of what had happened to a unit so close by had a sobering effect upon our morale for days.[24]

What caused the four deaths and hundred odd injuries? Frostbite? Wild boars? In fact, they were all caused by high winds and peculiar topography, a special danger only to paratroopers participating in a mass tactical parachute drop by the 82nd Airborne Division. The author of this fiction was assigned to a safe and stationary radar site with tents, showers, hot meals, and portable latrines, yet she leads the reader to believe that her unit faced the same dangers as the unfortunate paratroopers.

Other researchers with less intent to deceive have nevertheless contributed to the fiction that women perform well "in the field." The women in Honduras interviewed by Charles Moskos for his report entitled "Female GIs in the Field," enjoyed the comforts of televisions, stereos, hot showers twice a day, electrical lighting, a local post exchange, and frequent trips into town. To a dogfaced infantryman, these are all the comforts of home. None of the women in the military today have endured the discomforts that infantrymen bear regularly. Despite proud boasts that women can easily "do Ranger school," no woman presently in service has done anything like it. Not one of them has ever walked day and night through freezing rain, up and down the Tennessee Valley Divide with a 70-pound ruck on her back and a 23-pound machinegun in her arms. Not one of them has gone nine days without sleep, with a single cold meal a day and nothing over her head but a canvas cap.

Such are the discomforts of not combat but training. Combat—the business of barbarians, Byron's "brain-spattering windpipe-slitting art"—is many times worse. Of his time as a Marine platoon commander in Vietnam, James Webb wrote:

> We would go months without bathing, except when we could stand naked among each other next to a village well or in a stream or in the muddy water of a bomb crater. It was nothing to begin walking at midnight, laden with packs and weapons and ammunition and supplies, seventy pounds or more of gear, and still be walking when the sun broke over mud-slick paddies that had sucked our boots all night. We carried our own gear and when we took casualties we carried the weapons of those who had been hit.
>
> When we stopped moving we started digging, furiously throwing out the heavy soil until we had made chest-deep fighting holes. . . . We slept in makeshift hooches made out of ponchos, or simply wrapped up in a poncho, sometimes so exhausted that we did not feel the rain fall on our own faces. Most of us caught hookworm, dysentery, malaria, or yaws, and some of us had all of them.
>
> We became vicious and aggressive and debased, and reveled in it, because combat is all of those things and we were surviving. I once woke up in the middle of the night to the sounds of one of my machinegunners stabbing an already-dead enemy soldier, emptying his fear and frustrations into the corpse's chest. . . . [25]

Webb's experiences were not unique, for soldiers in all wars have known similar hardships, equally gruesome. A Korean War veteran recalls the battle for Pork Chop Hill:

> As I called for my final protective line fires, I looked up from the trenches, the enemy seemed to blanket the whole hillside. Men were screaming and shouting. . . . The fight was mass confusion and exhausting. We were like vicious animals in the hand-to-hand fighting that followed. . . .
>
> As daylight broke that morning, we could see the hill was covered with bodies, some of which had been there several days from previous battles. Our first task was to clean out the trenches by throwing the dismembered hands and limbs, caused from grenade and artillery explosions, over the tops of the parapets. . . .
>
> Later that morning the hot summer sun, with no wind, began to bear down upon the bare hilltop and the deathly scent of ripened bodies, several days old, created such an unendurable nausea that aircraft had to be called upon to spray the area.[26]

Such experiences should hardly need retelling. In the late 20th century, macabre depictions of war's horrors in art and literature have become so commonplace that they no longer shock. Yet every day combat seems less and less horrible to many in Washington and elsewhere who think of military service as, in Webb's words, "something akin to a commute to the Pentagon." A reflexive opposition to war, especially nuclear war, remains, but the horror of old-fashioned, hand-to-throat combat, war's favorite form, is hidden in a fog of forgetful peace, allowing the rhetoric of sexual equality to turn the brain-spattering art into a career opportunity.

This changing view of war has feminism confused and divided. Thoughtful feminists have not missed the irony that a movement dedicated to womanly nonviolence and life-giving concerns has been largely, if not solely, responsible for trivializing war. Yet few feminists have risen up to denounce the work of the integrationists, though many have quietly lamented the changing face of feminism. The half-heartedness of their objection to the new feminism evinces a growing ambivalence toward "the militarization of women's lives." Many feminists are caught between an automatic revulsion at anything military and the recognition that, like it or not, the military is doing what pacifistic feminism is not. It is changing American society. "The armed forces have done as much, if not more, to advance the social and economic role of women in our society than practically any other factor or organization I can think of," says Sue Berryman, a researcher for the Rand Corporation.[27] Her perspective, shared by many, is that "the country's verbal and legal war over whether women should be trained and used in combat can ultimately be seen as a war over women's rights and obligations not only in the military but also in the larger society."

It is the *power* of the military to direct society that calls all feminists together in pursuit of a greater role for military women. Power is a favorite word among feminists of all persuasions and one that they are not at all embarrassed to use. Carolyn Becraft, who for years headed the Women's Equity Action League's Military Project, told a panel on the military at the 18th Annual Conference on Women and the Law, "The issue of women in the military is really an issue of power—power, policy, and women in policy positions."[28] DACOWITS never ceases to demand that women be placed in policy-making positions. When the Marine Corps established two panels to investigate complaints from marine women, a marine spokeswoman boasted that the panels would include "enough women to have real influence." A study group at the Air Force Academy recommended that cadets receive classes on "power relationships" and on the transition of women from "powerless to the power broker" positions. Lois DeFleur, for so long the Academy's adjunct feminist, once complained that "it is clear to everyone at the Academy that the power is in the hands of males and the current positions of females confirm this."[29] She recommended putting women in the "power positions" of commandant and superintendent.

Power is what the military has to offer all feminists—not just power for individual women over others in the military, but power for all women over all of society. Writing for *Parameters,* the journal of the Army War College, Judith Stiehm explains:

> Women, who are rarely collectively violent, may not realize that their lack of violence represents a political limitation. . . .

Women have been deliberately and often legally excluded from
society's legitimate, organized, planned, rewarded, technologi-
cal force—the force applicable by the police and the military.[30]

Stiehm presents a sound, practical argument against women in
combat but nevertheless endorses their involvement in combat because "the implications of exempting women from combat thus seem
to include the exclusion of women from full citizenship." Stiehm sees
"full citizenship" as an end and power as a means to an end, but she
is unclear as to the value of full citizenship, except insofar as it
empowers women to wield more power in society's political arena.

Other women, those who benefit directly from the advancement of
all women in the military, are clearer about their objectives. Helen
Rogan witnessed a brash display of personal power by senior military
women at the second biennial reunion of the Women's Army Corps.
She tells of General Elizabeth P. Hoisington telling the crowd, "On
the program it says 'Mistress of Ceremonies.' I'm no mistress of
ceremonies, I'm master of ceremonies." Another female general,
Mary E. Clarke, told them, "We had that little bit of rain out there at
the review because it was so hot out there, and we *decided* to have
rain." (Original emphasis.) A former director of the WAC said, "I
was sitting next to General Hoisington on the stand, and when it
started to rain she told it to stop, and it did." Says Rogan, "It was the
first time I had seen powerful women joke so openly about their
power."[31]

Such boastfulness would have been considered extremely bad
form coming from military men. Pretensions of personal power are
incompatible with the ideal of selfless service. In any civilized military, the force exerted by superiors over subordinates is not power; it
is authority. Men who exercise authority acknowledge that they
themselves are subordinate to others. Men who wield power answer
to no one. In the armed forces of a democratic republic, the only
power that should matter is firepower.

NOTES ON CHAPTER X

1. Speech on Social Purity, Spring 1875.

2. Jean Bethke Elshtain, *Women and War* (New York: Basic Books, 1987), p. 231.

3. Panel discussion, in *Registration and the Draft,* Martin Anderson, ed. (Standford, Calif.: Hoover Institution, 1982), p. 42. Michael Levin reported this inconsistency in *Feminism and Freedom* (New Brunswick, N.J.: Transaction Books, 1987).

4. Allen Carrier, "Defense EO Chief Decries End of Army Coed Basic," *Army Times,* 12 July 1982, p. 28.

5. Charles C. Moskos, "Female GIs in the Field: Report from Honduras," unpublished report, 1985, p. 17.

6. Michael L. Rustad, *Women in Khaki* (New York: Praeger Publishers, 1982), p. 219.

7. Helen Rogan, *Mixed Company: Women in the Modern Army* (New York: G. P. Putnam's Sons, 1981), p. 186.

8. William J. Gregor, "Women, Combat, and the Draft: Placing Details in Context," in *Defense Manpower Planning: Issues for the 1980s,* eds. William J. Taylor, et. al. (New York: Pergamon Press, 1981), p. 39.

9. Mary Jo Salter, "Annie, Don't Get Your Gun," *The Atlantic Monthly,* June 1980, p. 83.

10. Ellen Goodman, "Women for Peace, From Way Back," *The Washington Post,* 22 May 1982, p. A19.

11. Kathleen Guest-Smith and Ellen Wilkinson, "Why Women in the Military," Statement presented to the Defense Advisory Committee on Women in the Services, 14 November 1976, p. 3.

12. Salter, p. 84.

13. Hearings before the Military Personnel Subcommittee of the House Armed Services Committee, Subject: Women in the Military, 13–16 November 1979 and 11 February 1980, pp. 55-56.

14. *Minerva: Quarterly Report on Women and the Military,* Spring 1985, p. 95.

15. Lesley Hazelton, *Israeli Women: The Reality Behind the Myth* (New York: Simon and Schuster, 1977).

16. Hazelton, p. 20.

17. Hazelton, p. 139.

18. Lionel Tiger and Joseph Shepler, *Women in the Kibbutz* (New York: Harcourt Brace Jovanovich, 1975), p. 189.

19. Tiger, p. 204.

20. Hazelton, p. 139.

21. Hazelton, p. 141.

22. Judith H. Stiehm, "Women and the Combat Exception," *Parameters: Journal of the U.S. Army War College,* June 1980. p. 57.

23. Judith H. Stiehm, *Bring Me Men and Women: Mandated Change at the U.S. Air Force Academy* (Berkeley, Calif.: University of California Press, 1981), p. 2.

24. M.C. Devilbiss, "Gender Integration and Unit Deployment: A Study of G.I. Jo," *Armed Forces and Society,* Summer 1985, p. 525.

25. James Webb, "Women Can't Fight," *The Washingtonian,* November 1979, p. 144.

26. Brig. Gen. Andrew J. Gatsis, Testimony before the Military Personnel Subcommittee of the House Armed Services Committee, 13–16 November 1980, p. 279.

27. "Women's Work," *Parade Magazine,* 5 January 1986, p. 17.

28. *Minerva,* Fall 1987, p. 33.

29. Lois B. DeFleur with Frank Woods, Dick Harris, David Gillman, and William Marshak, *Four Years of Sex Integration at the United States Air Force Academy: Problems and Issues* (Colorado Springs, Colo.: U.S. Air Force Academy, August 1985).

30. Stiehm, "Women and the Combat Exception," p. 57.

31. Rogan, p. 164.

CHAPTER XI

Today's Charmed Forces

It will avail us little if the members of our defeated force are all equal. History will treat us for what we were: a social curiosity that failed.

> PROFESSOR RICHARD A. GABRIEL,
> ST. ANSELM'S COLLEGE[1]

EACH YEAR, concern grows that the All-Volunteer Force may not be capable of continually meeting the nation's defense needs. Critics charge that the AVF has burdened the services with chronic, debilitating concerns for recruitment and retention; that it has displaced military values of duty, service, and sacrifice with essentially selfish values of the marketplace; that it is already too expensive to man, that it will become even more expensive in future years, and that it still might not provide the manpower the services will need. Those responsible for making the AVF work insist that it is working and will continue to work as long as Congress is willing to put up the money for regular pay raises, improved benefits, and increased enlistment and retention bonuses. Some members of Congress, however, are beginning to believe that the leader of the free world should not expect to meet its global defense commitments with a volunteer force. In fact, Senator John Glenn of Ohio has cautioned the services against praising the AVF too loudly, in case a return to the draft becomes necessary.

216

The AVF can do better, but not as a sexually integrated organization. Integration has only aggravated the AVF's problems, many of which could have been avoided if the architects of the AVF had better understood the natures of men and of military service. This point was made in 1980 by Charles Moskos:

> The main fault stems from the economists' assumption that the armed forces are just another part of the labor market, and from an unwillingness to grasp the essential distinctions between military service and civilian occupations. It is this faulty theoretical underpinning, not the end of conscription, that has brought the American military to its present plight.[2]

One essential distinction the economists missed was the importance of the military's masculine character in attracting men. In all societies, it is necessary for young males to do things that establish their identity as men. In our own society, the proof of manhood often takes frivolous and destructive forms: restless young men devote themselves fanatically to sports, rock music, or crime. In healthier societies, the proof is more constructive. Young men can be persuaded to endure years of dirt, danger, and drudgery in occupations whose only attraction is their manly character. Military service has always been considered the most manly of roles and therefore has always been able to attract recruits, despite its abundance of detractions.

These constant truths were lost upon the members of the Gates Commission, as well as upon the members of the Defense Department's Central All-Volunteer Task Force, who tossed away the AVF's trump card when it opted for the political expedient of expanding the use of women to reduce the need for men. In the early years of the AVF, the American feminist movement was very successful at destroying sex roles, denigrating masculinity, and integrating civilian occupations. The military could have capitalized on the movement's success by offering military service as a refuge for men who still wanted to be traditional men. Young men would have rallied to the colors had the services asked only for a few good men. The service that made such a request increased its share of the high quality male manpower pool and got all the men it needed; the services that advertised an integrated force saw their shares of the same pool decline and their billets go unfilled.[3]

Today the situation is much the same. Feminists continue to protest that sexism is still firmly entrenched in our society. Young American males know enough to profess socially acceptable opinions, but at heart, they are no more feminist than young men were twenty years ago, only more confused about what it means to be a man.

The AVF might still exploit the need for young American men to prove themselves, and easily make up the number of women now in service, if it aggressively portrayed itself as a place for men only. By highlighting its integrated aspects and aggressively pursuing young women, however, the AVF is actually working to eliminate any remaining attractions that the military might hold for young men. Recruiting commercials with cute coeds bragging about being "airborne" are guaranteed to turn away men more effectively than they attract women. Men simply do not aspire to be women or to emulate women, and whatever women are, men will seek to be anything other.

This, too, is admitted by many feminists. Judith Stiehm warns:

> If women were to enter combat, men would lose a crucial identity which is uniquely theirs, a role which has been male-defining as child-bearing has been female-defining. Yet 'warrior' is not an inherently attractive role, and one wonders if a male would accept it if it no longer defined him as a man.[4]

Stiehm quotes famed aviatrix Amelia Earhart making the same point—that if women were to fill all military roles, men might "rather vacate the arena altogether than share it with women."[5] The greatest threat to future military recruiting is not the shrinking male manpower pool, but the shrinking respect among young American men for the sexually integrated military.

To overcome this loss of respect, the services must offer extraordinary benefits, all of which appeal to a potential recruit's interest in what he or she can get out of the service rather than what belonging to the service might mean in a larger sense. To retain trained personnel, the services must expand benefits further to keep up with growing needs. A dramatic increase in married enlisted members in the last decade has boosted the demand for family housing, medical care, recreational facilities, youth activities, dependent schooling, spousal employment, and child-care. Besides the expense of this service-sponsored socialism, the paternal military must bear a load of parasites who stay on because they want or need someone to take care of them. Many officers and senior enlisted men believe the services tolerate too many people who are out of place in the military. "We're too much of a social organization already," a female Army lieutenant told Helen Rogan. "We rehabilitate by curing drunks and teaching people to read. The Army should be for the strong and not the weak."[6]

The addiction of many servicemembers to the benefits of service might very well prove disastrous if ever those benefits are taken away. If reductions in defense expenditures forced the services to reduce benefits, the morale of the military would crumble. Wartime discomforts would extract a heavier toll among the many who have joined the services for no better reason than personal gain, but, then, it must be remembered, the present volunteer military is strictly a peacetime force. Any extended conflict is expected to require a return to the draft.

If the AVF's focus on self-interest is inimical to traditional military virtues of service and sacrifice, as many critics claim, it is nevertheless quite consistent with the philosophy motivating the demands of military women. American servicewomen are a privileged lot. They can complain constantly about their careers and not be accused of careerism. They can treat war lightly and not be thought fools. For these women—whose sin is selfishness, whose philosophy is egoism—serving in the military is something owed to them. They denounce the Pentagon's Military Women's Corridor as "implicitly anti-feminist" because its exhibits contain offensive phrases like "allowed to serve," "permitted to serve," and "to release men for combat."[7] They base their complaint on "a woman's right to serve her country," as if one could selfishly claim a right to perform a selfless act.

The services have yet to realize that their endorsement of feminism is a repudiation of many ideals upon which the military depends. A civilized military is necessarily hierarchical, anti-egalitarian, and altruistic. It places some in authority over others, it distributes privileges and responsibilities unequally, and it demands that all serve not themselves but a higher common good. Feminism, on the other hand, is rights-oriented, egalitarian, and egoistic. It elevates the rights of individuals above the exercise of authority, it condemns inequality as presumedly unjust, it places a premium on personal independence, and it encourages individuals to claim their rights without regard for the good of the whole.

Feminism and the military are at odds in other ways, too. The military practices killing people; feminism is essentially pacifistic. The military is strongly identified with masculinity; feminism is contemptuous of *machismo*. Feminists blame the services for "the encouragement of a 'macho' male image" which they say contributes to the problem of sexual harassment.[8] They insist that masculinity is an accidental characteristic of military service, not essential to the military way of doing things. According to a West Point study group on the integration of women:

> There is nothing inherent in what the Army does that must be done in a masculine way; therefore, women must be offered the opportunity to be feminine and nothing should be done to deny women opportunities to be feminine.[9]

Yet the experience of women in the military has shown that those who conform most to the male image are most successful leading men, and those who insist upon retaining their femininity receive the least respect. "People just don't give you commands [of units] when you're pregnant," complains a female West Point graduate. "They want you in the staff someplace."[10]

The feminist response has been to insist that the attributes of a leader are neither masculine nor feminine, that attributes traditionally considered masculine or feminine can be found in both sexes, and that the military should look elsewhere for an androgynous model of leadership not based upon the ubiquitous male model. Some feminists, indeed, hold androgyny to be the ideal for both sexes. They seek to make the words *masculine* and *feminine* meaningless, except in reference to genitalia. Most feminists, however, cling to a bias in favor of traditionally feminine characteristics. They talk about neutered ideals but intend truly to make everything more feminine.

Attempts by the services to reconcile the masculine military and a feminist philosophy have produced strange results. Servicewomen have become somewhat more macho, but the military has been thoroughly feminized. The modern military considers war a slim possibility. Combat is trivialized as incidental to military service, to be superseded by more pressing peacetime concerns for equal opportunity. After all, only a small minority of service personnel hold combat jobs, say the integrators. The dictum "every Marine, a rifleman" is no longer meaningful. The Army's Basic Combat Training has been reduced to Basic Training, with many of the more rigorous drills taken out. Among officers, only those who attend a handful of special schools have experienced anything remotely resembling combat. Posters entitled "One Army" show a single combat soldier crowded into the background by nineteen smiling support persons, many of them women. The words "fighting man" have been deleted from the Code of Conduct, so as not to offend feminist sensibilities. What began and ended with "I am an American fighting man" now begins and ends simply with "I am an American." Personal identity, so important to the isolated prisoner of war for whom the code was written, is now supposed to exclude both sex and profession. The reformers have whittled away the core and left the hollowed bark.

The American military itself seems sometimes embarrassed by the brutal business of war. The services go to great lengths to convince members that they are "caring" organizations:

> We want soldiers, of all ranks, feeling they belong to a "family". . . . Building the "family" requires a professional sensitivity toward and caring for one another. . . . We want these professional, caring relationships because they are necessary to build the vertical bonds which tie leader to led.[12]

The Army's recently published definition of the "warrior spirit" says nothing about combativeness, aggressiveness, an eagerness to fight, a willingness to die, or the courage to kill. Elsewhere, soldiers are told that military values mirror "the ethic of our people which denies any assertive national power doctrine and projects a love and mercy to all."[13] The military exists to protect the "supremacy of the individual" and therefore needs leaders "who embrace a value system that places the individual soldier and citizen at the center of society."[14]

This excessive regard for the rights of individuals has forced discipline out of fashion. "Discipline is the soul of the Army. It makes small numbers formidable; procures success to the weak, and esteem to all," wrote George Washington, in a letter of instruction to the officers under him. Most militaries of the world still place heavy emphasis on discipline, but the American military has replaced it with something kinder: leadership. Leadership is to American military officers what holiness is to the saints. They write about it, they talk about it, they argue about it, they study it, they preach it, and they try to practice it. They can never quite agree on all that it is, but they are sure that it is the preeminent virtue of the military person and the key to organizational success.

To be sure, some form of leadership has always played a visible role in military history, but the modern, feminized force is becoming increasingly dependent upon leadership as the primary means to accomplish its ends. More than just a matter of gaining the confidence and trust of the led, leadership, as taught by the military today, is the ability to influence the attitudes and opinions of others to move them to do what the leader wants them to do. It is the science of behavior modification and the art of manipulating people. Whereas in earlier times it was assumed that servicemen did as they were told, no questions asked, it is now believed that the best way to ensure obedience is for leaders at the lowest levels to win the good favor of their men and women so that they will want to obey. This approach has three serious shortcomings: it is not suitable for all circumstances; it expects too much from low-level leaders who are often young and inexperienced; and it makes a leader's concern for the welfare of the led appear insincere. In times past, commanders cared for their men out of comradeship and shared manhood and, in the West, out of Christian charity, all of which transcend rank. Now their reason for caring is that it builds "vertical bonds" to be used like strings on a marionette. Nevertheless, because the services fail to instill and maintain proper discipline, manipulation is often the only tool available to them.

The services use manipulation to serve a variety of causes from AIDS awareness to energy conservation, but it is most frequently employed to propagate feminist ideology. To secure support for integration, the services work to convince service-members of the justness of sexual equality. Official publications of the services are filled with propaganda promoting a favorable view of servicewomen. Commanders are required to publicly endorse and enforce equal opportunity in the military. Units are assigned equal opportunity officers to watch over the climate of relations between the sexes and report violations of policy, much in the way the Soviet military has Communist Party officers assigned to units to keep commanders politically straight. Personnel are required to attend equal opportunity training, during which EO officers preach the sanctity of sexual equality and the folly and immorality of belief in traditional sex roles. The definition of sexual harassment has expanded to include the open expression of opposition to women in the military. Officers and senior enlisteds are kept in check by their performance reports; a "ding" in the block that reads "Supports Equal Opportunity" can have career-ending consequences.

It should surprise no one, then, that when a group of Army officers were asked by interviewers from West Point about women in the Army, many of the men responded that they did not wish even to discuss the subject. In the American military today, support for the policy of sexual equality is as much a matter of conscience as of action. The services require both behavioral compliance and intellectual conformity. It is not enough to do as one is told; one must also think as one is told. If one thinks otherwise, one had better keep those thoughts to oneself.

The military is becoming increasingly intolerant of deviations from the policy of sexual equality. In September 1986, Secretary Weinberger banned participation by military members in "groups which espouse or attempt to create overt discrimination based on race, creed, color, sex, religion or national origin." Participation in such groups is "utterly incompatible with military service," said the message.[15] The message specifically mentioned white supremacist and neo-Nazi groups, but by including sex in the series of invalid excuses for discrimination, Weinberger unwittingly outlawed membership in political organizations like Eagle Forum that oppose the ERA and religious sects that preach the subordination of women. The wording of the ban is indicative of the Defense Department's growing insensitivity to conservative social views, many of which are religiously based. Every effort is made not to offend the most radical feminist in the ranks, but conservative Christians, Jews, and Moslems will see their views dismissed during EO training as archaic, unenlightened, socially unacceptable, inconsistent with official orthodoxy, and self-evidently wrong.

Having pledged itself to defending and advancing both radical egalitarianism and "the supremacy of the individual," the American military is turning its back on the very ideals it has defended for over 200 years. It is also unwittingly undermining its own legitimacy, for if equality is the ultimate measure of justice, then where is the justification for rank and privilege? If the individual is indeed supreme, then why should one give of oneself for the good of the service or lay down one's life in defense of others? As it enters the 21st Century, the American military is increasingly unable to answer these questions. It proffers only empty talk about "professionalism" and gropes for answers in the New Age nonsense of Marilyn Ferguson's *The Aquarian Conspiracy,* officially recommended reading for U.S. Army officers.[16] The danger is that New Age ethics will be insufficiently grounded to hold officers and enlisted men to the high road when situational pressures mount. The example of senior military leaders living the lie of integration in the face of political pressure will only encourage the general retreat of honor and integrity.

The American military has been used—used by a political faction with no concern for national defense—for no other purpose than to advance feminism. So long as women remain restricted in any way in the military, so long as the military remains mostly male, the hounding of the services will never cease. To expect feminists to settle for less is to gravely mistake both their will and their intent. "Hopefully

[sic] in the near future we won't talk about good women pilots: we'll talk about good pilots," an Air Force general once told DACOWITS. The truth is that DACOWITS exists to keep the services always talking about good women pilots.[17] Feminists can be expected to oppose a return to the draft until the combat exclusion laws are struck down by the courts. When the legal basis for excluding women from the draft no longer exists, feminists are likely to support the draft as a means of forcing more American women into nontraditional life-styles.

An armed force half female may seem unthinkable, but our civic religion of equality demands it and the military's official non-position on women in combat allows it. The American public is being lulled into the mistaken belief that women can, indeed, perform as well as men in all military jobs. Certainly nothing said publicly today by any admiral or general would contradict that belief. One hopes that before we arrive at full sexual equality in the military, before the next war, brave men in uniform will stand up and speak out. Thus far, however, the march of folly has proceeded at a measured pace, and few have shown the selflessness, understanding, courage, or concern to fall on their sword to stop the disastrous triumph of ideology over reality.

NOTES ON CHAPTER XI

1. Richard A. Gabriel, "Women in Combat? Two Views," *Army,* March 1980, p. 44.

2. Charles Moskos, "How to Save the All-Volunteer Force," *The Public Interest,* Fall 1980, pp. 79–80.

3. Office of the Assistant Secretary of Defense, *Background Review: Women in the Military* (Washington, D.C.: Department of Defense, October 1981), p. 21.

4. Judith H. Stiehm, "Women and the Combat Exception," *Parameters,* June 1980, p. 56.

5. Judith H. Stiehm, *Bring Me Men and Women: Mandated Change at the U.S. Air Force Academy* (Berkeley, Calif.: University of California Press, 1981), p. 9.

6. Helen Rogan, *Mixed Company: Women in the Modern Army* (New York: G. P. Putnam's Sons, 1981), p. 256.

7. *Minerva: Quarterly Report on Women and the Military,* Winter 1984, p. 94.

8. Jacquelyn K. Davis, Memo to General Anthony Lukeman, 26 August 1987, subject: "1987 WESTPAC visit of the DACOWITS," p. 2.

9. Department of Behavioral Sciences and Leadership, *Project Athena: Report on the Admission of Women to the U.S. Military Academy* (West Point, N.Y.: U.S. Military Academy, 1 June 1979), Vol. III, p. 191.

10. Science Research Laboratory, *Early Career Preparation, Experiences, and Commitment of Female and Male West Point Graduates* (West Point, N.Y.: U.S. Military Academy, undated), p. 1-52.

11. Claudia Nichols, "An Officer and a Gentlewoman," *The Times Magazine,* supplement to *Army Times,* 3 June 1985, p. 10.

12. Letter from the Adjutant General of the Army, subject: "Fraternization and Regulatory Policy Regarding Relationships Between Members of Different Ranks," 21 November 1986.

13. John O. Marsh Jr., Secretary of the Army, "Soldierly Values: Vital Ingredients For a Ready Force," *Army,* October 1986, p. 15.

14. John O. Marsh Jr., Secretary of the Army, "On Values," *Soldiers,* November 1986, p. 2.

15. Caspar Weinberger, Secretary of Defense, SECDEF message to all Defense activities, subject: Policy on Activities of Military Personnel, 8 September 1986.

16. *Commanders Call,* May-June 1985, p. 26. The May-June 1985 issue was devoted to professional values and ethics. Ferguson's *The Aquarian Conspiracy: Personal and Social Transformation in the 1980's* is described as follows: "Ferguson believes a network exists which enlists the minds, hearts, and resources of some of America's most advanced thinkers. She calls this network the Aquarian Conspiracy. The basic theme of this book deals with how the conspiracy will affect the transformation of social consciousness in our time—a mental turnabout in individuals and organizations—focusing on societal and individual values, thinking, and practices in the future." The same issue of *Commanders Call* also recommends Robert A. Heinlein's *Starship Troopers.*

17. Gen. Jerome F. O'Malley, Vice Chief of Staff of the Air Force, Statement to DACOWITS's Spring meeting, 24-28 April 1983, p. E-4.

Index